Gary Lineker's GOLDEN BOOTS

The World Cup's Greatest Strikers 1930–1998

Gary Lineker and Stan Hey

Hodder & Stoughton

Copyright © The Worldmark Production Company Limited 1998

First published in Great Britain in 1998
by Hodder & Stoughton
A division of Hodder Headline PLC

The right of Gary Lineker and Stan Hey to be identified as the
Authors of the work has been asserted by them in accordance with
the Copyright, Designs and Patents Act 1988.

10 9 8 7 6 5 4 3 2 1

A CIP catalogue record for this title is available
from the British Library.

ISBN: 0 340 70846 8

Designed by Roger Walker

Printed and bound in Great Britain by
Butler & Tanner Ltd, Frome and London

Hodder & Stoughton
A division of Hodder Headline PLC
338 Euston Road
London NW1 3BH

Contents

Allez France! The omens look good for the biggest
World Cup ever this summer.

Introduction

At the 1986 World Cup in Mexico I was fortunate enough to win the Golden Boot for being the tournament's top goalscorer. When I was asked if I would like to find the other twenty Golden Boots from fifteen World Cup competitions, I jumped at the chance. It would mean travelling to fourteen different countries around the world – from Japan, where Toto Schillaci (1990) now plays, to Argentina, Chile and Brazil, which I'd never visited. It was all very exciting, and I hadn't realized just how many air miles I'd clock up!

Some of the top scorers were easier to find than others. There are those like Just Fontaine (1958), Eusebio (1966), Gerd Müller (1970) and Mario Kempes (1978) who remain famous names in football, but for some players, despite their few weeks of international fame, life hasn't been quite so rewarding. Gregorz Lato of Poland (1974) was never allowed to exploit his success, while Ademir of Brazil (1950), Sandor Kocsis of Hungary (1954) and Garrincha of Brazil (1962) all died too young in tragic circumstances. Paolo Rossi (1982), the Italian striker who emerged from the darkness of a two-year suspension to win his country the World Cup, has largely turned his back on football, but he gave me a rare interview about his dramatic redemption.

Unsurprisingly, the further back in history I went, the more difficult it was to find winners still alive; but I managed to find friends or colleagues to bear witness to the great skills of Leonidas da Silva of Brazil (1938), Oldrich Nejedly of Czechoslovakia (1934) and Guillermo Stabile of Argentina (1930). Indeed, it was a privilege to talk to Lucien Laurent of France, who scored the very first World Cup goal in 1930, and to Francisco Varallo of Argentina, the only survivor of the first World Cup final, sixty-eight years ago.

But it wasn't always a journey through the distant past. The very modern talents of Hristo Stoichkov of Bulgaria (1994) and Oleg Salenko of Russia (1994) had to share the Golden Boot at the last World Cup, which left Hristo a bit grumpy, as he told me during a ride on his power boat off Barcelona! Leonel Sanchez of Chile (1962), revealed how the winner of that tournament's Golden Boot was decided, not to mention his own involvement in the infamous Battle of Santiago against Italy. The 1998 World Cup President, Michel Platini, told me how he still feels France were robbed of World Cup glory in 1982; and Argentina's President, Carlos Menem, revealed the dangerous circumstances in which he watched his country's World Cup victory in 1978.

Meetings with other famous football names such as Zico, Bobby Charlton, Ferenc Puskas, Sandro Mazzola and Jürgen Klinsmann proved informative and generated lively discussion. Everyone I interviewed offered an opinion on which team would win this year's World Cup, of course, and which player would win the Golden Boot. I'm looking forward to seeing who's right. I hope you enjoy the pursuit of the Golden Boots as much as I did.

I would have liked to mention by name all those who helped in the production of this book, but sadly space does not allow this. There are so many people to thank, from those who arranged seemingly impossible meetings in the far-flung places of the world, to those who worked all night to put it all together, that the list would have filled half the book; and it would, of course, be invidious to leave anyone out. I hope, therefore, that everyone who helped will accept my heartfelt thanks and that they will enjoy the end result.

Argentina

This is a journey which began and ended in France – I started out there because I wanted to interview a notable figure in football history, Lucien Laurent, the man who scored the first goal in the very first World Cup in 1930. By chance, I was also able to visit the grave of Jules Rimet, which is just down the road from where Lucien now lives. Rimet, who was President of FIFA in the 1920s, was the founding father of the tournament, and it was his drive and vision which brought it into being. I completed my journey around the World Cup by returning to France, because the 1998 competition is to be held there, under the guiding hand of one of France's greatest players, Michel Platini. France is therefore the stage upon which the next Golden Boot winner will be enthroned, joining the list of distinguished football names featured in this book.

I hadn't fully realized, until I made this journey and talked with, or about, the other Golden Boot winners, just what unique company I had joined when I finished as top scorer in Mexico in 1986. It is, if you like, a brotherhood – a random collection of players from all corners of the footballing community, bound together by the simple historical fact that they became the leading scorers in one of the fifteen World Cup tournaments held so far, from 1930 to 1994.

To get some idea of what that first competition must have been like, I talked to Lucien Laurent whose distinctive moment in World Cup history arrived when he put France into the lead in the opening game against Mexico on 13 July 1930. Lucien is ninety years old now, but he still has clear memories of the tournament to which he travelled as a twenty-two-year-old amateur player, all of fifty-eight years ago. Though he took up drinking wine only when he was eighty – an odd lapse for a Frenchman – Lucien broke open a few choice bottles of red as we had dinner at a restaurant near his home and, sitting outdoors on a warm summer night, we toasted the past.

'France had no preparation for that World Cup,' he told me. 'We just received a letter a week in advance telling us to report to Marseille, so we could be measured

The original Jules Rimet trophy was awarded to Brazil in perpetuity in 1970 when they won it for the third time. It was stolen and, so rumour has it, melted down. This is a replica.

The ninety-year-old ex-footballer is on the left! Lucien Laurent, who scored the first goal in the 1930 World Cup in Uruguay and (*inset*) with his French team-mates on their fifteen-day boat journey to South America.

for our blazers and kit. There were sixteen players in the French squad, and we travelled with two other European teams, Romania and Belgium. The boat journey to Uruguay lasted fifteen days. We would get up in the morning at about 7.30, have breakfast, and then jog around the deck for exercise. We found a space inside the boat where we could kick a ball around. At night we just played cards or listened to music. The teams all talked to each other, so there was no unfriendliness, but we didn't see that much of each other. None of us knew what it was going to be like, but when we stopped at Rio de Janeiro to pick up the Brazilian team, we received a wonderful welcome, so we had a clue then that it would be exciting.'

Suitably fortified by Lucien's wine, I set off for Montevideo, the capital city of Uruguay where, in the latter half of July 1930, the first-ever World Cup tournament took place. My plane took a lot less time than Lucien's boat, but in a trip around the harbour of Montevideo, I could imagine what it must have felt like for those European footballers as they arrived in a strange country for an unknown experience.

How it must have looked approaching Montevideo. Sea-sickness is already setting in.

There's a sunken ship lying stern-up in the water, and it just happens to come from England. It's an apt symbol for our country's failure to take part in the 1930 World Cup because a row with FIFA had led us to withdraw from football's ruling organization. The Federation of International Football Associations had first discussed a World Cup at Antwerp in 1920, and its most staunch supporter was Jules Rimet, the President of the French Football Federation, whose name was ultimately given to the gold statuette awarded to the winners.

Up to that point, the main source of international football competition was the Olympic Games for strictly amateur players. But the growth of professionalism in the game inevitably meant that there would have to be an opportunity for these players to display their skills on the world stage. By 1928, FIFA had progressed to taking a successful vote in favour of holding a World Cup, and a second vote had nominated Uruguay to host it. It may seem bizarre now to have given such a prestigious new tournament to a tiny country such as Uruguay in the middle of their winter, but there were two decisive factors in Uruguay's favour.

Firstly, their team had been the Olympic football champions in 1924 and 1928, with both Games staged in Europe, so in theory they were the world's best team. Secondly, Uruguay was celebrating the centenary of its independence in 1930, so the event had an additional historical significance. The fact that the Uruguayans offered to pay all the competitors' travelling expenses and to build a new stadium especially for the tournament, helped to clinch the votes of FIFA's members. Money probably talked as much then as it does now, only quieter.

Lucien Laurent and his fellow footballers arrived in Montevideo on 8 July just five days before the tournament was due to begin, giving the European players in particular precious little time to find their land legs. Lucien recalls his team's less than perfect preparations.

'We trained every morning for five or six days, but only on an amateur scale. We had a small pitch about the size of a basketball court, to play on, and there weren't

The low-key opening ceremony for the first World Cup finals at the Centenario Stadium, Montevideo, 18 July 1930. No Diana Ross, no tenors...

GARY LINEKER'S GOLDEN BOOTS

even any goalposts! So training was rather limited. When we played against Mexico we simply decided to put all our hearts into the match – we certainly needed to.'

There were no photographers and no sports journalists present to record Lucien's historic goal, so we'll have to take his own modest account of it as gospel.

'I remember that we had lost our goalkeeper with a broken jaw early in the game. There were no substitutes in those days. We were playing in the W-M formation. Our centre-forward, André Maschinot, passed it out to the right-winger, Ernest Liberati, and when he crossed the ball, I got to it first and scored the goal. It was a good goal, but we didn't make all the fuss the players make nowadays, we didn't throw ourselves around on the ground!'

France won that inaugural game 4–1, but it was to be their only victory of the tournament. They were beaten 1–0 in their next game, just two days later, by Argentina, a match marred by an injury to Lucien Laurent, and by a small-scale pitch invasion of Argentinian fans after the referee had blown for time six minutes early. Laurent also missed France's last game, when they lost 1–0 to Chile, after which it was back on the boat for the return journey. Only Yugoslavia of the European teams had made it out of the pool stages to get through to the semi-finals.

In fact it was a pretty poor show all round by the established European football nations, because the majority didn't even bother to take part. All four of the British Football Associations had left FIFA in 1926 after a dispute over broken time payments for players in the amateur game, so as well as England, Scotland, Wales and Northern Ireland weren't eligible either. Then the four countries who had bid against Uruguay to be hosts – Italy, Holland, Spain and Sweden – had pulled out once the tournament had been awarded to the South Americans. Meanwhile, Germany, Austria and Hungary hadn't fancied the travel and the prospect of a month and a half away from home. Only direct pressure by Jules Rimet himself forced France to go, while King Carol of Romania actually picked the national team himself after he had arranged for the players to be given time off from their jobs without penalty. Belgium probably felt obliged to go once France had agreed. Yugoslavia, who only decided to go at the last minute, did best of the four European entrants, but still lost 6–1 to Argentina in the semi-finals.

This messy business had left an awkward entry of thirteen teams. Besides the four from Europe, South American teams turned out in force – Uruguay the hosts, Argentina, Peru, Brazil, Paraguay, Bolivia, Chile and Mexico with the United States also sending a team. This included several ex-British professionals who'd moved to America, hence such names in their line-up as Wood, Moorhouse, Gallacher, Auld and McGhee. The French team nicknamed them 'the shot-putters' because of their size.

The strongest South American sides were Uruguay and Argentina, who had met in the 1928 Olympic final in Amsterdam. Both had prepared very hard for the tournament, and evidence of how seriously they took it was shown even before it started when the Uruguayans booted their first-choice goalkeeper, Mazzali, out of

Members of the United States 1930 World Cup squad, including many former English and Scottish professionals, pose at their training ground. Is it just me, or does the one lying down look like Gazza?

the squad for not getting back to the team hotel inside the time of the arranged curfew. Uruguay duly won both their group games, against Peru and Romania, without conceding a goal. Their half-back line was known as *la costilla metallica*, which my Spanish tells me is literally 'the metal rib', but probably suggests an 'iron door' running through the centre of the team. Argentina, their neighbours from across the River Plate, were always likely to be the main threat and so it proved, as the Argentinians cruised through to the final by scoring sixteen goals in just four games. Yet the man who had been doing most of the damage for them with seven goals, Guillermo Stabile, had come into the team only in their second match when the captain, Manuel 'Nolo' Ferreira, had to take time off for a university exam. Stabile's three goals in the 6–3 win over Mexico brought him a permanent place in the Argentine team, and set him on the path to becoming the first Golden Boot winner.

Guillermo Stabile, the first Golden Boot winner, in action for Argentina.

Stabile was one of the younger players in the Argentinian squad, having been born in 1905. He played for the Huracan club, and later moved to Italy to play for Genoa and Napoli, and then for Red Star Paris, before a broken leg ended his career. After that he became the national coach for Argentina and kept the job for twenty years, despite the fact that Argentina's World Cup record was pretty dismal at that stage. Stabile died in 1966, the year that England beat Argentina in the quarter-finals of the World Cup at Wembley.

Nevertheless, I was able to find a witness to Stabile's Golden Boot achievement in the last surviving player from that 1930 World Cup final, the Argentinian forward Francisco Varallo. He still lives in La Plata, a town about thirty-five miles south-east of Buenos Aires, in the small house which he bought for himself and his parents using the signing-on fee he received from Boca Juniors in 1931, although angry fans from his previous club used to throw stones to keep him away from it.

Francisco is eighty-eight years old now, but he is by no means a forgotten man. On the wall outside his apartment is a plaque which announces 'Here lives a great sportsman of Argentine football'. Despite his years, Francisco Varallo is a spritely, alert and cheerful chap, who just loves talking about football. His memory is good, too, as I discovered when we began to talk about that first World Cup, sixty-eight years ago.

'There was a lot of expectation and excitement in both Uruguay and Argentina. I was playing for a club called Gimnasia at the time, and its President sent over two ships loaded with supporters every time Argentina played a game. There were even more for the final itself. There was already a great rivalry between us and Uruguay because we'd played so often against each other. So the Uruguayan crowds were always against us – even when we played France, they shouted for them not us. Some of the Argentinian players were a bit frightened by the atmosphere, but I was so young it didn't bother me.'

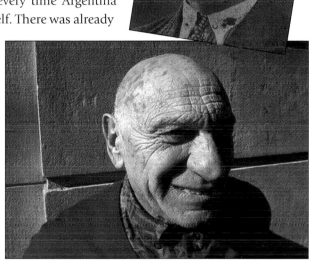

Varallo scored two goals in Argentina's 6–3 win over Mexico, with Stabile scoring three, the first hat-trick of the World Cup finals. One of Varallo's goals was scored with a shot so fierce that the ball became entangled high up in the net.

'I remember the newspapers in Buenos Aires writing about that goal. Scoring was a very emotional experience for me, and I used to go mad, shouting about it for an hour afterwards. It wasn't as bad as what they do today – hanging on the net, or taking their shirts off.'

Stabile's striking partner Francisco Varallo back then, and now outside his house at La Plata.

With France and Mexico beaten, and Stabile and Varallo established as the goalscorers, Argentina next played Chile in their last pool game and won 3–1. Stabile scored another two goals, but the match itself was a bit of a punch-up, with police having to come on to the pitch to break up the fighting.

I asked Francisco what his team-mate was like both as a person and a player.

'Stabile was a natural-born scorer. They used to call him "El Filtrador" – the filter – because he was good at getting goals close in, on the rebound, or from a short pass or a cross. All his goals would come from inside the box. He was very serious as a player, always wanted to win. But he was quite a private person.'

With Argentina beating the United States 6–1 in the semi-final – a game Varallo missed due to injury – and Uruguay thrashing Yugoslavia by the same score, the new Centenario Stadium, which wasn't completed until after the tournament started, was to be the setting for the first World Cup final between these two bitter rivals from opposite sides of the River Plate.

Uruguay's strong defensive line included players such as José Andrade, Lorenzo Fernandez, Alvaro Gestido and their captain and right-back, José Nasazzi. Pablo Dorado, Pedro Cea and Santos Iriarte were the main threats in attack. Argentina

> ### GARY'S GOLDEN NUGGETS
> Hector Castro, who scored two goals for Uruguay in the 1930 finals, was able to play football despite being born with part of one arm missing.

had the by now much-feared Stabile, Varallo and Carlito Peucelle in attack, and the defence was built around hard-man centre-half Luisito Monti. A crowd of 90,000 gathered to witness the match, and here is Francisco Varallo's account of how it went.

'Because I'd been injured against Chile I tested my fitness on the morning of the game, and I seemed to be okay. So the match started and pretty soon Uruguay took the lead when Pablo Dorado scored after twelve minutes. But then Carlito Peucelle equalized and after thirty-five minutes Stabile scored to put us ahead. It should

have been my goal, that one. I gave the ball to Ferreira, and he crossed, and as I went in, Stabile pushed me out of the way and scored. Because he is no longer alive, people might question what I'm saying, but all I can say is that I was furious about it because I should have scored that second goal! He was being selfish, I suppose.'

The Uruguayans in fact protested that this goal was offside anyway, but it's an interesting insight into Stabile's goalscoring mentality that he was prepared to push a team-mate out of the way in order to get the goal. I don't think I ever did it, but I might have thought about it, because the first thing that all strikers are taught is to be selfish. Anyway, at half-time Argentina led 2–1 and Varallo still felt confident that they would win.

'In the second half, I remember Nolo Ferreira crossed a ball to me, I got it from the left wing, and I bombed it against the edge of the bar. But five minutes later, I couldn't play any more. I was injured again, so I had to play out on the wing. My knee had played up again. There were no substitutes in those days, so I was a

Guillermo Stabile, arm raised after scoring Argentina's second goal which gave them a 2–1 lead at half-time. Uruguay came back strongly to win 4–2.

passenger. That's when they came back into the game. Indeed the second half was a disaster for us, as they scored three goals, from Cea, Iriarte and Castro. They probably would have scored eight if the game had kept going. Monti had been nervous throughout the tournament, I think he was a bit frightened by the Uruguayans. What was also strange was that we played with two balls – the Argentinian one in the first half and the Uruguayan one in the second. Their ball was bigger, ours was lighter. I think that must have made a difference. I probably shouldn't have played that day, and maybe Monti and two or three others shouldn't have played either. I saw Monti's face when they told him he was playing and he looked like he didn't want it. So we lost the World Cup. I didn't think that was going to happen in the first half, but the second half they won fair and square. I felt very sad afterwards, watching the Uruguayans kissing their shirts. It was probably the biggest sadness in my life.'

Jules Rimet hands over the trophy bearing his name to Uruguay's FA Chairman, Paul Jude. Not exactly wild celebrations, are they?

Millions of Argentinian fans had crowded the streets of Buenos Aires to hear reports of the match read out from a newspaper's telegraph machine, and they later gathered at the docks when the team returned in defeat.

For the Uruguayans, though, there was only triumph. A tiny nation of no more than two million people had produced a team to win the first World Cup, which Jules Rimet himself first presented to the victorious captain, José Nasazzi. Juan Alberto Schiaffino, who later scored one of the goals that won Uruguay a second World Cup in Brazil in 1950, was only five years old at the time of the first victory, but he can still remember that special day.

One of Uruguay's greatest forwards, Juan Alberto Schiaffino, a World Cup winner in 1950, tells me how he heard Uruguay's 1930 victory on the radio as a five year old.

'I was living in the old part of Montevideo, near the sea, with my mother and father and brothers, and I remember the street as if it were today, Calle Isla de Flores (Flowers Island Street). It was small and narrow and a tram used to pass by every so often. We were too poor to have a radio, but someone had put one on a podium, a tall table in the street, and everybody who lived in the street was listening to the match. The Centenario Stadium was a sell-out. Those who couldn't go listened. Every time Uruguay scored, everybody screamed and cheered, but in the first half, the Argentinian couple who lived above our house were waving their country's flag. As we scored the goals in the second half, everyone screamed and shouted. Then everybody celebrated the victory, dancing in the street, and when I went home I remember my father shouting "Uruguay has won, won, won!" He was very happy!'

Walking around the Centenario Stadium now, sixty-eight years after that memorable match on Wednesday, 30 July 1930, I could still sense a great feeling of history about the place. Montevideo is very much a Spanish-style city, not dissimilar to Barcelona only quieter, with the sea close at hand, and one or two nice beaches for the summer. The stadium is bigger than it was then, and is showing its age a bit.

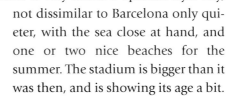

The Centenario Stadium in Montevideo was built specially for the 1930 World Cup and still looks an eye-catcher to me, sixty-eight years later.

The pitch is a bit ropy, but the exterior of the main stand has some smashing murals, and the whole thing is set in an open park where there are monuments to the two Uruguayan teams who won World Cups.

Although Francisco Varallo played on for Argentina, and became one of the top goalscorers for his club, Boca Juniors, it's quite staggering to realize that it took until 1978 for Argentina to win a World Cup. They lost 3–2 to Sweden in the first round of the 1934 finals in Italy and went straight home. Like Uruguay, they didn't go to the World Cup in France in 1938. Uruguay were still a bit sore about the poor show by European teams in 1930, and were also worried about their players being poached by the big Italian clubs, while Argentina were miffed at not being chosen as hosts in 1938. England, typically, were still at odds with FIFA, and because the English had done so much to encourage the growth of football in both Uruguay and Argentina, you have to wonder if petulance was one of the other features they had passed on to the South Americans.

A more substantial English influence is shown in the names of two of Argentina's most famous clubs, River Plate and Newell's Old Boys. Sailors, railway engineers and touring English Football League sides like Southampton, Nottingham Forest and Swindon Town, were all responsible for bringing the game to Argentina in the early part of the twentieth century. Later, the mass immigration of Italian families helped the culture of football to take root, but that also became Argentina's biggest problem, as many of their best players were lured away to play in Italy where the money was better. Indeed, they refused to send a full-strength team to Italy in 1934 because they were afraid that wholesale poaching would take place – three Argentinians actually played in the Italian side that year.

After the Second World War, Argentina refused to play in Brazil in 1950, didn't even enter for the 1954 World Cup in Switzerland, and when they *did* play in Sweden in 1958 and in Chile in 1962, they were knocked out in the early group stages of both competitions. West Germany (3–1) and Czechoslovakia (6–1) beat them in 1958, while England beat them

Argy-bargy – Sir Alf Ramsey stops England's George Cohen swapping shirts with an Argentinian player after the controversial quarter-final at Wembley in the 1966 World Cup.

3–1 in 1962, to pip them for second place in Group 4 of that tournament. Most English fans of a certain age will remember England's 1–0 win over Argentina in the quarter-final at Wembley in 1966, not just for Geoff Hurst's brilliant headed goal, but for the bad-tempered display by the Argentinian captain Antonio Rattin, which culminated in his sending-off. Alf Ramsey refused to let his England players swap shirts with the Argentinians after the match, although later Bobby Charlton and Rattin struck up a lasting friendship.

Argentina didn't even qualify for the 1970 World Cup, which is probably just as well, because if they'd come up against the brilliant Brazilians, they'd have lost badly which may well have provoked a small war between the two countries. Argentina did slightly better in West Germany in 1974, when they reached the second stage, but defeats by Holland (4–0) and Brazil (2–1) put them out. Nevertheless a dashing young forward with flowing hair who came into the Argentinian team during that tournament was to be the key factor in their victory on home soil in 1978. His name was Mario Kempes.

Born in July 1952, Kempes started his footballing career with Instituto Cordoba, before signing for Rosario Central.

'I always knew that I liked football,' Kempes told me. 'At school, though I enjoyed the lessons, I preferred the breaks because then we would play football. When you're around twelve or thirteen in the provinces, which was where I was born, you play a lot of "baby football" and that's when the people who saw me play said I had the potential to be a good player. But at thirteen, there are lots of kids who go off to do other things and never really get anywhere. I was always able to score goals, and not because I wanted to, but because it just seemed to happen. My childhood heroes were Boca Juniors players who weren't necessarily goalscorers – Paolo Valentin, who was Brazilian, and Rojas "The Tank", who *was* a great goalscorer. But my all-time hero was Pelé.'

Like a good many Argentinian players before and since, Kempes eventually moved to Europe in 1976, signing for the Spanish club Valencia, for whom he scored twenty-four goals in his first season. He was recalled to Argentina for the World Cup squad's intense preparations, under the watchful eyes of the country's military who had seized power in a coup in March 1976, and who expected nothing but victory for the nation they now ruled. When I talked to Kempes in the Rosario Stadium which he graced in 1978, I first asked him to describe the huge sense of expectation that bore down on the Argentinian squad.

'People were expecting great things from us. The country was in a difficult position – politically, the military regime was in power and people were repressed. What we, the wearers of the national shirt, wanted to do was bring them a little happiness. The only place we could do that was on the pitch, because the rest of the time we were surrounded by soldiers, just in case something happened. We went to see the Generals, Videla and Galtieri, at one stage. They were at the Pink House (Government Palace), but the audience was for only ten minutes. We didn't have any real contact with the military except of course if one of them arrived at the training ground by helicopter. We were here to compete in a sporting event and tried to have nothing to do with politics. The coach, Cesar Menotti, tried to protect us from all that as much as he could. But you couldn't help feeling the support of the fans on home turf. This can cause you to do things that are really mad, that is to say to try and score goals too early and then everything goes wrong.

> **GARY'S GOLDEN NUGGETS**
>
> Boca Juniors, one of Argentina's leading clubs, was founded by an Irishman, Patrick MacCarthy, although immigrant Italians soon turned it into the focal point of their community. When it came to choosing their colours, they decided to pick those of the flag on the next ship to dock in the harbour – it was Swedish, which is why Boca play in blue-and-yellow shirts.

'But Menotti mapped out a game plan for us, and we went out feeling very calm because we knew we had the full support of the coach, and we knew that we had a great team. We had two choices – either we did what the public wanted, or we did what we had planned with Menotti. If you attack and leave the defence open, it is very easy to lose the game. We also had some strong opponents – Hungary, Italy and France in the first stage. So we felt all the pressure but we didn't take it on to the pitch with us because we knew what we had to do. We didn't just close our eyes and charge.'

It must have been pretty difficult for the players of the Argentinian team to keep their nerve when their entry on to the pitch before every game was the cue for a mass cascade of tickertape and confetti from the stands all around the ground. The image of all that shredded paper, almost obliterating the television screen, is probably the strongest of all the ones that I can remember from watching that particular World Cup, as a seventeen-year-old apprentice with Leicester City. I might have got the odd toilet roll thrown at me, but say what you like about the Argentinians, they certainly knew how to recycle their newspapers! And even for someone like Kempes, an experienced international, the overwhelming display of all that passion was intimidating.

'I'd played in Buenos Aires before obviously, not in the new River Plate Stadium but in the old one, so I knew what the atmosphere might be like, but not on a World Cup level. It was truly impressive. For the first five minutes after coming out we'd be thinking, "What's going on here?" But gradually that began to go away. You have to get rid of your nerves and start concentrating on the game. You can save the memory of that first appearance from the tunnel, but then you have to get into the game one hundred per cent.'

Argentina's first game in Group 1 against Hungary was understandably tense, given the fevered atmosphere, which was heightened by Hungary's early lead. But a prompt equalizer from Kempes' striking partner, Leopoldo Luque, calmed the fluttering Argentinian hearts, before Bertoni scored the winner in the second half. It certainly helped the Argentinian side that two Hungarians were sent off, albeit late on, but they must have known from that first match that each game would be an emotional as well as physical battle.

'We went step by step, game by game,' Kempes recalls of that early stage of the tournament. 'We didn't think about getting to the final without having to play the first round, but we were conscious of being able to reach the final. When you get there, it's like a coin that you throw up in the air, it can land on heads or tails. We wanted to go as far as possible, and the more games we played, the greater our confidence became. So much so, that when we lost to Italy and had to come to Rosario to play in the next stage, we didn't really regret it.'

Argentina had beaten France 2–1 in their second Group 1 match (Luque and Passarella scoring) while the Italians had also beaten France and Hungary, so they had both qualified for the second stage by the time they met. There is a cynical theory that the Argentinians happily 'lost' the match with Italy – to a superbly worked Roberto Bettega goal, set up by Paolo Rossi – so that they could finish second in the group and go into what looked the weaker of the two second-stage groupings, with Poland, an unimpressive Brazil and Peru. Italy, as Group 1 winners, now went in with a still buoyant Holland, holders West Germany and Austria. The top team from each group would contest the final. All Kempes will say is that, 'With hindsight, and looking at the individual players and teams, it was a good thing for us to have been beaten by Italy because they were left to play in Buenos Aires against Holland, Austria and West Germany. That group was a lot stronger than ours, in spite of Brazil being in with us. We felt we could beat Poland, while with Brazil we couldn't be sure. We played Peru last, knowing what we had to achieve.'

The switch to Rosario, home of his original club, certainly helped Mario Kempes, who hadn't scored in the three previous games.

'The crowd were very supportive, even though I hadn't been back to Rosario for almost two years. The people were great to me, in the stadium, on the streets, and we felt that warmth from them all the time. For me it was doubly satisfying because to come back to the place that got me my move to Europe and to start scoring goals allowed me to give back some of that affection.'

Kempes ended his goal drought by scoring both goals against Poland in a 2–0 win. Brazil meanwhile were beating Peru easily, 3–0. When the two South American giants met in the second round of matches, however, it turned out to be a tense goalless draw. This left them both on three points, with one match each left.

'The two goals made me a lot stronger,' Kempes says, 'and a lot more confident. As a striker I wasn't happy being without goals, even though I was making them.'

Then, somewhat infamously, the decisive final matches were played at different times, in contrast to FIFA's policy in later tournaments. Brazil easily beat Poland 3–1 to head Group B on five points, with six goals scored and just one conceded. Argentina, with just two goals scored and none conceded, played later that night, knowing that they had to beat Peru by four clear goals to reach the World Cup final.

'The confidence we had by this stage was such that we felt we could score eight if necessary. There was a lot of talk about the Peru game afterwards, about how Peru lay down, but I remember clearly that they hit the woodwork twice early in the game, so the whole thing could have been different. Argentina wouldn't have got to the final if they had gone in. But our confidence was running so high that we had the Peruvians in their own six-yard box for almost the whole game. And once we had scored the four goals required, we just kept going. We didn't relent or start playing South American football. On the contrary, we tried to score more goals.'

Mario Kempes, the 1978 Golden Boot winner with six goals, successfully avoids a tackle from Ruud Krol during the final in the River Plate Stadium.

Argentina ended up 6–0 winners that wild night in Rosario, with Kempes notching another two, to put them into the final against the 1974 runners-up Holland. The rumour mill started immediately, and still turns to this day.

'Yes, there were lots of rumours,' Kempes admits. 'The Peruvian coach was recently in Argentina and he was still being asked about it. Honestly, I don't know if Peru lay down. We were there to play football. Just like politics, if we got involved in them, we couldn't do what we were here to do. I don't think money was involved, because if they had scored with the efforts that hit the woodwork, it would have been very difficult for us; we'd have had to score five or six goals. You couldn't say that their forwards were aiming for the crossbar, it was just a coincidence. I don't know who it was who thought up the idea that Argentina had paid the Peruvian side, it could have been the Brazilians, or Peru themselves. But anyway, we didn't play because of any money changing hands but because we wanted to win. So I don't think that two or three rumour mongers can bring a whole country into disrepute, or discredit all the hard work that we put into that World Cup. What's more, the people talking like that are not Argentinians, they're people working here from abroad who don't like Menotti or the 1978 World Cup squad. They're not just tainting Menotti and the players but everyone in Argentina, which is an insult to the country.'

Having secured their long-desired place in the final, Argentina, bombarded by a blinding cascade of tickertape from the fans and watched by a phalanx of the ruling military, knew they had to win. But with the gaze of a world-wide television audience upon them, the match had to be conspicuously fair. A tense, fragmented but dramatic game was a more than adequate test of the Argentinian team's credentials. They were taken to extra time by a defiant Holland, with Dirk Nanninga's

Daniel Bertoni (4), about to score Argentina's third goal against Holland.

header after eighty-two minutes equalizing Kempes' goal from the first half. Holland might easily have won in the dying minutes when Rob Rensenbrink, also with five goals in the tournament so far, hit the Argentine post with a close-range shot. His miss was to prove fateful for both Kempes and Argentinian, for in the first period of extra time, Kempes scored his sixth goal of the tournament, scrambling the ball past Jongbloed in the Dutch goal after Ossie Ardiles had split their defence with yet another of his inspired runs. Daniel Bertoni got the third from a pass by Kempes in the second period of extra time, and as the River Plate Stadium went wild with ecstasy, Argentina went up to collect the World Cup, under the approving gaze of the generals in the VIP box.

Whatever doubts remain about Argentina's tortuous route to the final, there was no doubt that Kempes himself had registered a great achievement, his three pairs of goals lifting Argentina at just the right time. Indeed it was the first occasion in World Cup history that the top scorer, the Golden Boot winner, had also been from the team which won the tournament. Kempes was truly a player of both personal and national destiny. His thoughts on the art of the great striker are these: 'Opportunism is the key. Never giving up if the ball is in the box. Having the speed to beat the defender helps. They say that goalscorers are selfish. I don't think I was, but then watching as much football as I do, you can see that the goalscorer is indeed selfish, and has to be so.'

Carlos Bilardo, who managed the 1986 World Cup-winning Argentina side, had direct experience of Kempes while he was a club manager, and his views provide an apt summary of Super Mario's talent.

'I always used to put a man on him constantly because once he turned on the halfway line, he was unstoppable. With the goal in his sights, he was unbeatable, very strong and tall. He shot at goal from way out and took chances like an opportunist. He also used his body very well. In that World Cup he was vital to the team, and he proved he was an important player. If you look at him now, he's still all there, still strong.'

The man who actually lifted the World Cup trophy on Sunday, 25 June 1978, was Daniel Passarella, the Argentinians' hard man and captain. A powerful, at times ruthless, central defender, Passarella is now the national coach, and I spoke to him about Kempes and 1978 before one of Argentina's vital qualifying games for the 1998 World Cup, against Peru in Buenos Aires. (I also got roped into doing a bit of match commentary with Victor Hugo, the Jonathon Pearce of Argentinian broadcasting, with his thirty-second exclamation of 'Goooooo-aaaaaa-l!!!') I asked Passarella first about the level of expectation that the home supporters had for their team.

'People were divided prior to the World Cup itself, as seems to be traditional here. There wasn't a great deal of confidence in the ability of the players, and the coach, Menotti, was supported by half the public and criticized by the rest. The only ones who believed we were capable of winning the World Cup were the players themselves. We had been involved in a four-year period of preparation, training very hard and making many sacrifices, and all we wanted to do was win the World Cup. We felt that the home crowd would be an advantage, it always is, but you have to have a good team as

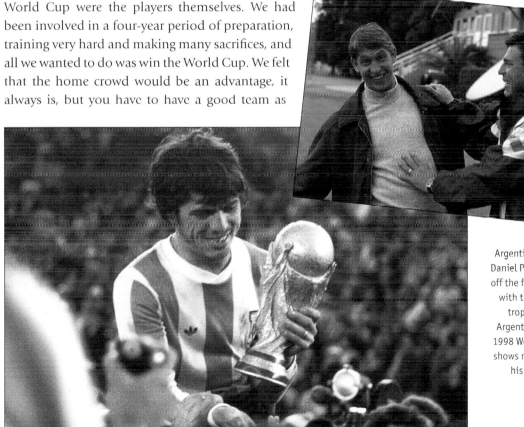

Argentina's 1978 captain, Daniel Passarella, is chaired off the field in Buenos Aires with the FIFA World Cup trophy. (*Inset*) Now Argentina's coach for the 1998 World Cup, Passarella shows me he's lost none of his marking skills!

well. Take Mexico in 1970, or Chile in 1962 – when they hosted the World Cup, they didn't win because their teams weren't good enough.'

Passarella then gave some insight into how the team helped turn Kempes into the match-winner he was always expected to be, a role that had looked beyond him in the first three matches.

'Mario was essential to the side, he was the man who made that Argentinian team in 1978. He didn't have a particularly happy first round. It wasn't that he was playing badly, he was always in the game, he just wasn't decisive in the way he was in the final round of matches. I think that we all helped him out a lot to keep his spirits up. He was the only player who had been playing abroad, and he was the star of the team, so to speak. All of that responsibility and the experience he had, which he was expected to pass on to us, became a burden to him. So we helped him a lot. I remember he had grown a moustache for the first-round games, and we told him he had stopped scoring because of the moustache. We told him to shave it off and after he did, in the very next game against Poland in Rosario, he scored two goals!'

Now footballers can be a superstitious breed, but this is the first time I've heard of a moustache making all the dif-

The Argentinian media can be every bit as demanding as our own, as I discovered when they ambushed me at the national squad's training camp.

ference between winning and losing a World Cup! No doubt some John Motson type can do an in-depth study into the success ratio of teams who have a majority of players with some form of facial hair. Thankfully, the clean-shaven Passarella also has a more rational explanation for Kempes' sudden improvement in form.

'I think he finally got there because he felt the Rosario crowd was right behind him. In fact none of us was really too badly affected by having to leave Buenos Aires, because to the mind of an Argentinian footballer it's not particularly nice to have to play in the River Plate Stadium. It's a very big stadium and I think that all of us at that time would have preferred to play in a smaller, more intimate stadium. Many players say this, and in the qualifying rounds of a competition all of these factors are important. In Mario's case, we were going to his footballing home. I think that's how he found himself again. The crowd was crying out for him to score even before the match, they were expecting him to score, so when he did, it was as if he had paid his debt to the crowd, and so he felt free of that obligation. He began to free up the team, hanging back and putting in crosses from miles out, and making it look easy. Mario was a goalscorer who started from the back and swept everything before him, but in that World Cup, he not only scored goals, he also made them, and that's what distinguishes the great players such as Maradona, Di Stefano and Pelé.'

That was captain Passarella's view of Kempes as an inspiration and as a goalscorer, but I wondered if the tough defender in Passarella also had an opinion of the striker's qualities from the technical point of view of someone who was sent out to stop Kempes, not admire him.

'I played against him a few times when he was at Rosario Central and I was at River Plate. I was a central defender, paired with Roberto Perfumo, who had also played at World Cup level. Perfumo played on the right side, I was on the left. Argentina always played four men at the back, and we were the middle two. Roberto said to me, "You go and mark Kempes and keep him out, and I'll double up when he comes closer." But I thought Mario would actually play on Perfumo, which is exactly what he did. There was one incident I particularly remember. Mario was about thirty yards from goal and Roberto, who was a really strong defender, was challenging and Mario had him on his shoulder for over twenty yards, and Perfumo just couldn't stop him getting in on goal and scoring. Mario was a very tricky man to mark because he would hang back and then just appear from nowhere. But then a great goalscorer has to be like a thief. When a burglar comes to steal from your home, he doesn't tell you he's coming, and goalscorers have to be like that.'

Passarella was certainly never a player you could take liberties with on the pitch, and he's just as forbidding off it. But I wanted to get his perspective on the rumours about that 6–0 Peru game in 1978. So I lit the blue touch paper, and stepped back. In fact, the retreat wasn't necessary; Passarella has long since perfected a defence against charges of malpractice.

Big hair day – the Argentinian team line up before the 1978 World Cup final. Can you spot future 'Totting-ham' favourite Ossie Ardiles, fourth from left?

'There was nothing wrong with that game against Peru. If you study the video, you'll see that they have two chances in the first five minutes. Munhante hits the bar, Oblitas just misses. Imagine how nervous we'd have been if those had gone in. Besides, a few months earlier we'd played them in Lima, and we were 3–0 up inside twenty minutes. And remember now that Peru were already out. They were a demoralized team, they had already started their holidays in Argentina! But I also think there were footballing differences between the two sides – Argentina had Tarantini, Ardiles, Kempes, me, Filiol, Bertoni, all players who have made a mark, who have succeeded in Europe. We were just the better team.'

I was on much less provocative ground when I asked Passarella to recall his emotions when he lifted the trophy celebrating Argentina's first World Cup win, forty-eight years after they'd lost to Uruguay in that first final.

'I didn't really realize what was happening. It was like an orgasm, a very long orgasm! And I couldn't really think straight then. I can now, but at the time, nothing. All I can remember is that my parents were there, and I couldn't believe it, because out of twenty-five million Argentinians I was the one lifting the World Cup. It was all very quick. For football players, life goes by very quickly, until you stop playing. Not everybody in the world can do what they want to do, with a passion. But we have had the chance. And when you do what you love to do, you have a good time, but it passes very quickly. It seems like yesterday that I started playing football. So on that day, I didn't really think about anything. I suppose I was just thinking about my dad, who was in the stadium watching.'

For Mario Kempes, life hasn't been quite so fulfilling since he stopped playing. He came back to Argentina after completing nine years of playing in Spain, and a further six in Austria. Unable to secure a coaching job in his home country, he has spent time in Malaysia, and most recently Albania, although the political upheaval there makes it unlikely he will return. He says that there are possibilities of coaching work in Central America, if all else fails.

'We triumphed when we played football and everyone chose what they thought best. Some went off to Europe, others stayed here, and it went better for some than for others. But really there are very few of us who are having a hard time. Every time we get together, we try to help each other out. There are players who don't want to coach, and we keep in contact to see who wants to go where. There aren't any problems, it's just that if you're given an opportunity to coach, they're going to expect you to have had some practical experience, but if you're not given the chance to coach, you'll never get that experience. That's why when they ask me why I went to Indonesia and Albania, I say because the opportunities I've had there were not given to me here in Argentina. And because I like travelling, it's not a problem for me to go. Yes, of course I would love to be the coach of the national side, it would be the greatest job I could get, but first must come work with a club team.'

Of course, Argentina didn't stop winning in 1978. A fifteen-year-old boy called Diego Maradona was left out when the final 1978 squad of twenty-five was cut to twenty-two. He made an inauspicious World Cup debut in Spain in 1982, when he was first stifled by a mass of Belgians, then marked out of it by a one-man Italian crowd called Gentile, before being sent off for a thigh-high tackle on Joao Batista of Brazil. But the boy genius fulfilled all his promise in Mexico in 1986, a tournament which is discussed in a later chapter.

Suffice to say for now that I think he was a great footballer. But trying to get an interview with him while I was in Argentina proved to be a frustrating farce, as agreed appointments were missed, or late-night calls to my hotel room proved to be false leads. I did catch sight of him at a press conference, but a huge scrum of media folk washed him away. So I didn't get to squeeze the Hand of God very tightly, as I'd hoped. In fact, it was easier to get close to him on the pitch in 1986! Even the interventions of the Argentinian President, Carlos Menem, proved fruitless. Maradona is his own man, for better or worse, as his petulant displays in the 1990 World Cup finals in Italy demonstrated. The drugs scandal which overwhelmed him in USA '94,

Afternoon tea with Argentina's football mad President, Carlos Menem. He fancies his boys' chances in France this year.

was a sad epitaph to his international career, but when all the bad things are stripped away, you are still left with a phenomenally gifted player.

My Argentinian trip ended with an audience at the official residence of the football-mad President Menem. In future, whenever Ron Atkinson uses the phrase 'they got out of jail', it will have a new meaning for me because Menem had an unusual view of his country's 1978 World Cup victory, to say the least.

'I was in prison at the time. I was arrested by the military dictatorship in 1976, and had to follow the World Cup from my cell on radio and television. We only had the TV for the final. It was black and white, but we had great pleasure watching the game, in spite of being behind bars. Kempes was, and is, an exceptional human being. I've even played in the odd friendly game with him and other players from that great squad. The Argentinians were very happy about winning, in spite of the political situation. It was our first World Cup win, and football in Argentina was boosted, with more and more children and young people taking up the sport. We are passionate about football, which was brought here by the English. It affects every level of society and is part of the lifestyle of the Argentinian people. In 1986, I was a provincial governor, and I was invited by a TV station to commentate on some of the games. So I watched that championship from a television studio. Of course, my dream now would be for Argentina to win in France. I think they'll have a great championship and win the final, and we may even produce the top scorer as well!'

Glenn Hoddle and England – please take note!

Italy

It is tempting to think of Italian football as purely a modern event. Their game seems to be so prominent, not only because we see so much of the fabulously wealthy and technically gifted *Serie A* on television, but also because of the increasing number of top-class Italian players who now grace the English and Scottish Premier Leagues. But Italian football is no Giancarlo come lately. It has a history that rivals the plot of a Verdi opera – triumph, political chicanery, tragedy, farce and disgrace. Italian football has roots and traditions which are as deep as England's, even deeper if we're talking about the World Cup.

For Italy was the first European country to win the Jules Rimet trophy back in 1934, a victory they repeated four years later when the tournament was held in France. When they won in Spain in 1982, Italy became the first Europeans to have claimed the World Cup three times, rivalling Brazil's South American grip on the trophy and for once beating the Germans to a landmark. Germany didn't complete their treble until 1990, after their wins in 1954 and 1974. England, with only one win in 1966, have some ground to make up, but not as much as France, Spain, Hungary and Holland, nations with great footballing traditions but no world crown to boast of. Italy and Germany are the two major European achievers of World Cup football, just as Brazil and Argentina are South America's most successful representatives.

Italy's power base was established in the early part of this century by Vittorio Pozzo, a remarkable man with a bush of hair and horn-rimmed spectacles. He was one of the founders of the Torino Football Club. Because of this early experience, he was asked to take charge of the 1912 Italian Olympic football team in Stockholm, and after the war he became the country's principal football coach. Operating with some of the tactical formations he had seen when he'd watched football as a student in England, Pozzo established a reign that lasted, with a few interruptions here and there, from 1912 all the way to 1948. Of the 95 international games for which he was in charge, Italy won 63 and lost only 15, scoring 233 goals, conceding 127.

In Italy, I managed to find one of the oldest surviving Italian players, to give me eyewitness testimony of those early days of ascendancy. Aldo Olivieri was the goalkeeper for their 1938 World Cup win in France. Olivieri's family owns a beachside café in the Mediterranean resort of Viareggio, and while we talked he demonstrated some of the goals he remembered by using the glasses, salt and pepper pots, and an ashtray. Are you watching, Andy Gray?

Though he's now in his late eighties, Aldo Olivieri had a pretty good memory of Pozzo, the World Cup tournaments, and what it was like to play under the gaze

of the Fascist dictator Benito Mussolini in the 1930s. Mussolini had made Italy's success at football one of his top priorities in an attempt to show the benefits of his system of government. Italy winning the World Cup in 1934 on home soil, therefore, became as much a political victory as a footballing one. Before the final in Rome against Czechoslovakia, the Italian team obediently gave the Fascist salute. Mussolini, who had attended all of their games, hosted a reception for the team after their hard-fought 2–1 victory in extra time. On their way

to the final, Italy had beaten the United States (7–1), Spain (1–0 in a replay) and Austria (1–0) – not exactly the results of a master race, but obviously good enough on the day. The reports of the time describe them as a tough, physical side, which had been strengthened by importing several Argentinian players of Italian descent, *oriundi*, a policy which was to continue right through to the 1960s.

The 1934 World Cup – and the Italian team dutifully salute Mussolini before the final against Czechoslovakia. (*Inset*) Italian troops make sure the match commentator is suitably biased...

Aldo Olivieri was playing in goal for the *Serie B* team Lucchese before the 1934 finals, and missed seeing a few games because of injury, but he recalls, 'The celebrations after Italy's victory were quite low key, not like nowadays. But then the Fascist regime was pretty strict about public demonstrations. The politics didn't affect the players too much because Pozzo was in charge, and he protected them from it. He was a good bloke, Pozzo, very clever, fluent in several languages. He didn't have any great tactical secret, he just picked the team using the best players. We did a lot of training, but he basically left the players free to organize themselves. I worked with him for five years.'

The Czechs might easily have won the first World Cup finals to be played on European soil, as they took the lead against Italy with just twenty minutes to go with a goal by Antonin Puc, and had chances to extend their lead. We'll be hearing more about their adventures when the goalscoring feats of Oldrich Nejedly, the top scorer in that tournament, are discussed later on. But eight minutes from time, a bizarre swerving shot by one of the imported Italians, Raimondo Orsi, took the game into extra time, where Schiavio, an amateur player, scored the winning goal for the jubilant hosts.

Felice Borel, who played for Italy in the replayed second-round game against Spain but not in the final itself, said that, 'We won thanks to Orsi and our goalkeeper Giampiero Combi. In extra time the teams became very tired, and didn't mark properly, and Schiavio was left on his own on the right wing, and ran through to score the winner.'

By the time of the 1938 World Cup held in France, Olivieri, who had started his sporting career as a bicycle racer, and didn't take up football until he was eighteen, was Italy's first choice goalkeeper. His team, Lucchese, had been promoted to

Serie A which meant that he couldn't play in the controversial 1936 Berlin Olympics, which Italy had won. Several players from that successful team were quickly recruited to the professional ranks and made their way into Pozzo's new team – only Giuseppe Meazza, who was one of Italy's great goalscorers, and Giovanni Ferrari survived from the 1934 team.

So Italy were certainly among the favourites, but might well have gone out in their first game against Norway in Marseille.

'It was our most difficult game in the whole competition,' Olivieri says, miming a save across the café table to indicate his contributions. Italy took an early lead through Ferrari, but the Norwegian centre-forward Brunyldsen and the left-winger Brustad attacked the Italian defence, hitting the woodwork three times between them. In the second half Brustad equalized, and it was only thanks to several fine saves by Olivieri that Italy survived into extra time.

'We could easily have lost. But right towards the end of extra time, I caught a high ball and threw it out to Meazza, who took it up the field. Then he crossed for Silvio Piola to score. If one of those Norwegian chances had gone in, we'd have been on our way home. There was some hostility towards us anyway, because of Mussolini, so we were booed off the pitch, and had to leave on the bus quickly without changing out of our kit!'

Italy were more convincing in the next match, where they beat the hosts France 3–1 in front of a 58,000 crowd at the Stade de Colombes in Paris, with two goals coming from Piola. Olivieri maintains that this performance won over the French fans as well which, if it's true, says something about the sportsmanship of the home supporters.

The Italians then beat the formidable Brazilians 2–1 in the semi-final, with the South Americans leaving out their best goalscorer, Leonidas da Silva, and several other first-choice players, apparently being confident that they could beat Italy without them. They were wrong – goals by Colaussi and Meazza beat one by Romeu to put the Italians into the final.

'The Brazilians were so sure of winning,' Aldo remembers. 'They came down to Marseille by plane, and when Pozzo asked their travel manager if we could use it if we won the semi-final, he was told "no" because Brazil would need it to take them back to Paris for the final.' So while Brazil were sent flying down to Rio, Italy took the Blue Train back up to Paris to take on the free-scoring Hungarians, who'd put six goals past the Dutch East Indies in the first round, two past Switzerland in the second and five past Sweden in the semi-final.

Aldo remembers that the Italian team arrived too early at the stadium, having changed into their kit at the hotel. Pozzo made the bus-driver turn around and take the team on a short coach tour of Paris before the game! In my career, I've known managers who would have made the players *run* all the way to the stadium, but Pozzo was obviously a more sensitive individual. In any case, Italy's relaxed approach seemed justified as they eased past Hungary with a fluent display, Colaussi and Piola scoring two goals each in a 4–2 win.

> ### GARY'S GOLDEN NUGGETS
> Two of Italy's great forwards from the 1930s remain near the top of their international scoring records to this day: Meazza has thirty-three goals, while Piola scored thirty.

The captains meet – Meazza (left) for Italy and Sarosi for Hungary – as the 1938 World Cup final in Paris gets under way. Italy won 4–2.

'We played very well against Hungary, who were a good team,' Olivieri says, his face showing a warm glow of remembrance. 'It was a very good game, really good from a technical point of view. But we felt comfortable playing against them. I remember one of Colaussi's goals where he dummied to pass the ball to Piola in the centre, and then went on and scored himself.' Aldo demonstrated this goal to me using his table-top 'chalk-board' – the salt-cellar passed to the pepper-pot and then the ashtray went clean through to score!

The Italian team returned to Rome as heroes, welcomed at the Palazzo Venezia by Mussolini, who awarded them all bronze medals, rather than gold – but then he must have been saving up for his war effort. Aldo remembers Mussolini 'making a powerful impression on us – he would make you tremble if he looked at you and you caught his eye. But he said "Bravo" to me, because he thought I had saved Italy in that first game against Norway.'

The Second World War – already under starter's orders as the tournament took place, with Hitler having merged Austria into greater Germany and Mussolini having seized Ethiopia – soon condemned the fraternity of world football to irrelevance. But with two World Cup wins and an Olympic title inside four years, Italy had shown that they would be a major force once the warmongers and the Fascists had lost their own little game; or that's how it must have seemed, at any rate.

But Italy's attempts to pick up the threads of their 1930s' success were dealt a mortal blow in 1949 when the plane carrying their most powerful club team, Torino, crashed into a mountain, Superga, wiping out a whole generation of Italian international footballers. *Il Gran Torino*, as they were called, had just taken the *Scudetto*, the Italian championship, five years on the run, and eight of their team were in the Italian national side, a fair measure of the footballing as well as the human cost of the Superga crash. It was, in a way, a terrible foreshadowing of the Munich disaster of 1958 which killed so many talented Manchester United players. But at Munich, at least there were survivors – at Superga, there were none. The accident is still remembered every year with a candlelit procession and a religious service around the monument which bears the names of the dead at the crash site.

Not surprisingly, Italy groped around in the dark at the 1950 World Cup in Brazil. They were knocked out of their three-team group by a 3–2 defeat at the hands of Sweden. This marked the beginning of a long fallow period for Italian World Cup football. Sandro Mazzola airs his views on the reasons for this later on. Mazzola, currently on the Inter Milan board, was one of Italy's great internationals and goalscorers. His father Valentino, the Italian national captain, was killed at Superga.

But first, let's flash forward to 1982 and Italy's long-awaited third World Cup triumph, a victory earned for them by the goals of the returned exile, Paolo Rossi, and by the stubborn determination of their coach, Enzo Bearzot. Rossi's story, as I hinted at the start, does indeed sound like the *libretto* for a grand opera – a promising young career is threatened by injury, but the player is determined and defies all rejections to win a place in the national team, only to find himself banned from the game for his alleged involvement in a match-betting scandal; but once the suspension is lifted, a wise old man, Enzo Bearzot, who has always believed in Rossi's integrity and ability, picks him for his World Cup team, despite national protest; the disapproval grows as Rossi fails to score in three matches, but then magically, he is transformed into a world-class striker and scores six goals in three matches to help Italy lift the World Cup. Sounds farfetched even for an opera plot, doesn't it? But it's all true.

I travelled to Vicenza in north-eastern Italy, where Rossi manages his successful real-estate business, to talk to Italy's hero of 1982. Rossi's switchback career began with a small peak of achievement – being signed by the mighty Juventus at the tender age of sixteen, which I imagine is every Italian boy's dream. But even as he learnt the game in the youth squad – *il primavera* – Rossi suffered the first of many setbacks. At seventeen he had cartilages removed from both knees after suffering pain. For a youngster whose whole game was based on speed, both on the wing and in the penalty area, this could have been a disastrous handicap. He was soon loaned out to Como. Then Juventus sold a half-share in him to Vicenza in *Serie B*.

'I felt a terrible failure,' Rossi says. 'Only my father believed in me. I was already afraid that with the injuries I'd had I would have to give up the game. That's why I didn't abandon my accountancy studies when I was at Juventus. But at Vicenza I was lucky to find a coach, Gian Battista Fabri, who helped me understand what an opportunity I had. He gave me a place in the first team, and decided that I should play, not as a winger or inside-forward, but as a central striker. I'd always scored goals, right from when I started playing football at the age of ten, and my hero was Pelé, who was nothing if not a goalscorer!'

Rossi's first season at Vicenza, 1976–7, brought him twenty-one goals, and promotion back to *Serie A* for his team. But Juventus, who still part-owned him, continued to ignore his talent and bought a striker from Cagliari, Pietro Paolo Virdis, instead. Rossi scored his first *Serie A* hat-trick in a 4–3 win over Roma in November 1977, and the following month he was given his first cap by national manager Enzo Bearzot in a friendly against Belgium. As he continued to score goals at a furious rate – twenty-four in that season back in the highest division – he was in obvious contention for Italy's squad for the 1978 World Cup in Argentina; nevertheless, most pundits expected Bearzot to opt for the more experienced Francesco Graziani. Italy, remember, had finished ahead of England on goal difference in their qualifying group, which is just one more reason why our qualification for 1998 ahead of them was enjoyable!

> **GARY'S GOLDEN NUGGETS**
>
> Italy's 1970 World Cup semi-final against West Germany was voted the 'Best-ever World Cup Game' by a poll of fifty of the world's greatest footballers for the French sports magazine *L'Equipe*. Their defeat in the final by Brazil was voted second best, and their win over Brazil in 1982 was voted third! Not bad, eh?

World Cup '78 in Argentina: Paolo Rossi (second left) equalizes for Italy after France had taken the lead through Lacombe in the first minute.

After a good performance in a warm-up game, it was Rossi, not Graziani, who was pitched in as the partner for the splendid Roberto Bettega.

'Bettega was a great player,' Rossi says, 'but I felt that in that tournament in Argentina we lacked the will to win. We were certainly a strong team with great players but, in the end, I don't think we had the conviction to win that World Cup.'

This somewhat downplays Italy's early impact on the tournament, as they won all of their three Group 1 matches. France, who had scored in the opening minute of the match through Lacombe, were overcome 2–1, with Rossi getting his first World Cup goal; then Rossi and Bettega scored a goal apiece, Benetti getting the third, as Hungary were beaten 3–1; in the last group game, Italy beat the hosts Argentina, with Rossi and Bettega combining in a sweeping move for Bettega's winning goal. Of course both teams were already through by then, and as we heard from Mario Kempes, there was more than a suspicion that Argentina were happy to finish below Italy in the group so that they could avoid Holland and West Germany in the next phase.

Italy play Brazil for third place in '78, with Nelinho (right) one of Brazil's scorers in a 2–1 win. Italy's Roberto Bettega doesn't look too bothered.

Sure enough, the two other European rivals proved too strong for Italy, with Holland beating them 2–1 and Germany holding them to a goalless draw. But a 1–0 win over Austria, courtesy of Rossi's third goal of the competition, placed them second in the group behind Holland, who went on to lose to Argentina in the final.

The hosts had left Brazil in second place, so the play-off for third place, a mostly fatuous game between two tired and disconsolate teams, became an ironic repeat of that glorious 1970 World Cup final between Italy and Brazil. Brazil won it 2–1. Nevertheless, Italy's form augured well for the 1980s, and a return to international consistency.

Rossi returned to Italy as the country's new star turn. Juventus's half-share in him had been bought out by his ambitious Vicenza club for £1.75 million just before the World Cup. He was fêted at an official reception for the team in Rome, he won sponsorship deals with two big companies, one soft drinks the other sportswear, and he was nominated for many awards by Italy's assorted sports clubs. Almost inevitably, fatigue and injury caught up with him the following season, and he was loaned out by Vicenza to Perugia. Within a year, a betting and bribes scandal flared up over a game between Perugia and Avellino. Though it pains him to this day to talk about it, Rossi managed to talk me through the horror of what happened over the next two years.

'It's a very complicated story, and yet at the same time quite simple. I was accused, unfairly, of being involved in a match-betting scandal, over a 2–2 draw we played with Avellino. People said that the players had fixed the game, and the Italian Football Federation held a judicial inquiry, at which I and others from the Perugia team were accused of fixing the result. It's ironic because I scored both Perugia's goals in the match. So I was involved in this episode indirectly, not directly. But the judge chose to believe the rumours rather than the players, or me, and I was banned from football for three years, although it was reduced to two on appeal. It was completely crazy. Sometimes, unfortunately, this sort of thing crops up in football and yet once it had happened, I never thought about giving up, even though it was all quite traumatic.

'Even if you have a clear conscience, to be accused of something you haven't done is a terrible thing. It was more difficult because I was in the public eye. So, I worked in a sportswear company for a couple of years, but kept up with my training, here in Vicenza. Before the end of the ban Juventus stepped in to buy me for £600,000 and I was able to train for a year in Turin. They were two difficult years for me, without playing a proper match, but I overcame that because I still wanted to play football. I consoled myself with the thought that, in life, positive events are followed by negative ones, and vice versa.'

Rossi's ban was lifted in April 1982, just over two months short of the 1982 World Cup in Spain. It seemed almost impossible that he could be considered for the squad, not just because of the stigma of his ban, but also because of his lack of match fitness.

'I hoped to go to the World Cup and play, but I knew there was a big question mark hanging over me. After two years out, I couldn't know exactly what my fitness level was.'

Fortunately for Rossi, Enzo Bearzot had kept faith with him, and simply defied press and public opinion by giving Rossi the chance of making the squad. Bearzot, with his wonderful prize-fighter's face and a permanently lit pipe, has a real presence about him and is sharp as a tack. He was quite adamant, when I asked him, that recalling Rossi after the ban was no big deal as far as he was concerned.

'It wasn't a difficult decision because I knew that if Rossi wasn't in Spain with us, I wouldn't have had an opportunist inside the penalty-box. In that area he was

> **GARY'S GOLDEN NUGGETS**
>
> Another little brain-teaser: which Italian forward didn't start a World Cup final, and didn't finish it either, but still managed to score a goal?
>
> **Answer:** Alessandro Altobelli, who came on for Graziani in Spain in 1982, then came off for Causio in the same match.

Paolo Rossi gives me the low-down from high-up over Vicenza.

really good, really fast, always ready to run away by using feints, they were his best qualities. In attack it is necessary to have a fast striker, he doesn't have to be tall, but he must be quick in order to exploit the counterattack. So I waited for Rossi. He had played only two matches at the tail-end of the season, but once a professional has paid his debt to justice, I think he's got the right to play again.'

Rossi ploughed through two months of intensive training, trying to pick up match fitness as Bearzot made encouraging noises about him.

'He was a great manager and, more importantly, a great person too. From a person like him, I would have accepted whatever decision he made. What was important for me was that he never abandoned me. To have the support of someone like that really made all the difference to me, particularly when things weren't going well. When he selected me for the 1982 squad, the Italian press and everyone seemed against me. It was a big risk on his part, because I was not in ideal shape to play football, but he must have known that eventually I would overcome this and get back to full fitness.'

Bearzot has such a poker-player's face that when he tells you he wasn't worried about Rossi, you have to believe him. It was a colossal gamble on his part, and after Italy's three Group 1 matches, it looked as though Bearzot had lost, because Rossi was goalless and Italy had scraped just three draws, but he lays out his case with calm authority.

Would you argue with this man? Italy's 1982 World Cup-winning manager, Enzo Bearzot, makes a point in forceful style.

'It was only a question of waiting. I remember the first match against Poland (0–0); I thought Rossi had a good game as often happens with a player who has missed his football for a long time. But in the second match, against Peru (1–1), I accept that he was a failure. He missed two or three chances, and that began a critical period for him. He was so bad that I had to substitute him after forty-six minutes, but I told him to prepare himself for the next game. If I'd let him carry on, the press would have destroyed him. But the journalists didn't know anything about us because we were as closed as a fort!'

Rossi was brought back into the side for the third game against the Cameroon, who were challenging Italy for the second qualifying spot, and though he looked sharper, he still couldn't score. True, it was Rossi's cross that Graziani headed home for a 1–0 lead, but any Italian euphoria was dispelled quickly as Cameroon equalized within a minute with an athletic goal from Gregoire M'Bida. Italy hung on to their draw to take second place in the group on a higher scoring total – two goals against Cameroon's one! But for Rossi and Bearzot, it seemed that an inevitable humiliation awaited them once they got in amongst the big boys in the second phase – and they didn't come much bigger than Brazil and holders Argentina who awaited Italy in Group C.

'In the beginning it was important not to lose, and to qualify for the next round,' Rossi remembers in defence of his team's cautious start. 'Because of this the team felt inhibited and unable to express itself. But from the moment we qualified for the second phase, we had nothing to lose – we were able to face Brazil and Argentina more openly. We could play at their level, because we knew we had a very skilful team.'

Fine words, but as a striker with no goals in three matches, Rossi's own form was handcuffed to the team's attitude to the forthcoming matches. If Italy were truly adventurous, they'd get the ball in the box more often, and Rossi would have some chances. But if they reverted to the cautious stereotype which had dogged Italy's teams ever since the 1960s, he was a goner.

Rossi didn't score against Argentina, but the Italian team's performance was a dramatic switch from collective anxiety to confident counterattacking. The key to Italy's 2–1 victory – apart from the goals by Tardelli and Cabrini – was the man-marking job Claudio Gentile did on Argentina's potential star, Diego Maradona. The majority view on this feature of the game was that Gentile couldn't have got much closer to Maradona if they'd been joined in marriage, but the controlled violence which the Italian used to suppress Maradona suggested that the relationship wouldn't have lasted anyway. What we saw was a specialist stopping display by

Midfield marker Claudio Gentile of Italy tries to swap shirts with Diego Maradona during their 1982 match. Italy won 2–1.

Gentile which pushed at the very margins of the game's laws. There wasn't an attempt to take Maradona out of the game at a single stroke, but a continuous barrage of bumps, nudges and grabs which must have left Maradona feeling like he was playing inside a wardrobe.

'Gentile was a very hard marker,' Rossi says of his team-mate. 'For him to play against Maradona wasn't easy but he did a good job, maybe committing a few fouls which were unnecessary. But with that Argentinian team, if you marked Maradona out of it, you stifled fifty per cent of their chances.'

Bearzot, who had watched Gentile snuff out Mario Kempes in the Group 1 match between the two countries in the 1978 World Cup, says that it was Gentile himself who volunteered to do a marking job in both games.

'In 1978, Kempes was the strongest

player they had, so I talked to the guys and asked, "Who feels like stopping Kempes?" Gentile stood up in the dressing-room and said, "Me!" On only three occasions did Gentile play by different rules, marking a forward, but it was his personal choice. I never forced a player to mark somebody. Kempes was a powerful player with pace, but he had a problem getting his runs started, so we needed to stop him there, and that's what Gentile did. So I never told Gentile to be dirty with Maradona because I hate violence. He just decided to play that way against first Maradona and then Zico in the next game. He never hurt anyone, no one was injured by him, he just used his arms to good effect. I don't think Argentina lost because Gentile destroyed Maradona. We just played better than them!'

If victory over Argentina had been Gentile's triumph, there was no doubt about who was responsible for seeing off Brazil – Rossi. The three and a half games he had played in Spain so far had gradually put an edge back on his running and his opportunism, and once his team felt liberated enough to attack in numbers, he was always likely to benefit. Against a Brazilian side which was playing with an even greater cavalier spirit than usual – they'd beaten Russia 2–1, Scotland 4–1 and New Zealand 4–0 in the Group 6 games, and Argentina 3–1 in Group C – Italy decided to shake off decades of defensive thinking and meet attack with attack. Bearzot had

Rossi redeemed: his hat-trick against Brazil in 1982 set him on the road to the Golden Boot, and Italy on the way to becoming world champions.

GARY LINEKER'S GOLDEN BOOTS

watched the Brazil–Argentina game with his squad, and had ruthlessly analysed the Brazilians' weaknesses.

'We could all see their defensive problems. And they didn't have such an unbeatable attack – they were playing with only one outright forward, Serginho, and the rest were half-backs, Socrates, Zico, Falcao, Eder, who pushed forward. But if you could stop them, they didn't have any other threat, and in defence, there was only Cerezo. Once Bruno Conti was face to face with their defenders, they had big problems. Of course, you can't use their weapons to beat them, just as we wouldn't use strength to beat the English. We had to use our own armoury and exploit their defensive problems. You can't be shy against Brazil!'

In an amazing start, Italy took the game to Brazil, and inside five minutes had the lead as Rossi angled home a beautiful header on the run from Antonio Cabrini's left-wing cross.

'It was a decisive moment for me to score after just five minutes. After a series of fairly disappointing games, it freed me psychologically and also increased my motivation. Like all strikers, once you get one goal, you want more as soon as possible. From that moment on the whole World Cup changed completely.'

Brazil, though, were agents of their own destruction. For after quickly equalizing through captain Socrates – a low shot on the run under Dino Zoff inside the near post – Brazil's defence went walkabout as they passed the ball lazily amongst themselves and Rossi pounced to intercept, before moving in to beat goalkeeper Waldir Peres with his shot. On the hour, Rossi was gifted another chance but missed, and eight minutes later Roberto Falcao equalized again for Brazil with a scorching left-foot shot from the edge of the Italian area. At 2–2, the Brazilians were safe – they would finish the group on the same points as Italy, but by virtue of their 3–1 win over Argentina, one ahead on goal difference. All Brazil needed to do was to keep the ball, and defend sensibly – but their inadequate defence, and their attacking instincts, wouldn't let them settle for this; they wanted to win the game.

With fifteen minutes left Italy won a corner and the ball was played into the crowded Brazilian box by Marco Tardelli, where Rossi turned in an instant to whip the ball home. Italy had a fourth goal disallowed, and Zoff needed to make a brilliant save from Oscar's header as the game reached a climax that matched its importance to the competition. Italy had won, memorably, and Rossi's reputation, not to mention Bearzot's judgement, had been comprehensively endorsed.

Perhaps more importantly for Italy, Bearzot's encouragement to his players to get forward was a dramatic cultural change, a departure from their normal defensive priorities. Bearzot was very pleased to point out how many defenders were involved in their decisive goal against Brazil. Grinning at me through a cloud of pipe smoke, he forcefully reminded me that, 'At 2–2 against Brazil, Bergomi, Tardelli and the sweeper Scirea were all getting forward. It was Bergomi who headed the ball into their defence, Tardelli's shot, then Graziani's flick before Rossi scored. We didn't score that one on the counterattack!'

The results in the other three groups meant that Italy would meet Poland again in the semi-final, after drawing 0–0 with them in their Group 1 game, while West Germany had edged out England, and France had eased past Austria and Northern Ireland. Poland, without their best player Zbigniew Boniek, had little to offer against a now rampant Italy, and Rossi bagged two more goals to take the *azzurri* to their first World Cup final since the traumatic 4–1 defeat by Brazil in 1970.

'The victory against Poland seemed almost a formality, even if it wasn't,' Rossi remembers, 'but we were a team that was really difficult to beat by then – we'd drawn three and won two of our

Two more for Rossi, as Italy beat Poland 2–0 in the semi-final, 1982. (*Inset*) Rossi is mobbed by his team-mates.

games. It just seemed like there was a twenty-day period when any team would have had real problems against us. My first goal against Poland came from a free-kick by Giancarlo Antognoni on the right. I ran in – it was one of my main qualities, to be able to get half a yard on my marker – and turned the ball home from about three yards. The second came from a wonderful movement on the counterattack. Alessandro Altobelli passed to Bruno Conti, who went right up to the edge of the area and put in an incredible cross, and it was actually easy for me to score with a diving header!'

The other semi-final contained all the drama, as West Germany came from behind to beat France in the World Cup's first penalty shoot-out. The Michel Platini-led French team, 3–1 up in extra time, were clawed back to a 3–3 draw by a mixture of their own nerves, Karl-Heinz Rummenigge's dramatic intervention as substitute, and the German goalkeeper Harald Schumacher's terrible foul on Patrick Battiston. The Germans won 5–4 on penalties, but their epic victory left them with just two and half days before the final on Sunday, 11 July.

Bearzot sensed that his team had a distinct advantage, despite a couple of the squad having sustained injuries, and he pumped his belief into the players.

'I knew that the Germans were a physically heavy but tired team, and that we were in excellent condition – slim, fast and calm, rating at only 38 heartbeats per minute – so I told my guys, "If you lose the World Cup, all of you deserve prison!" Those who are fast will always beat those who are strong.'

Rossi, on the top of his form, also felt confident, but in a tense first half Italy squandered a golden chance when Cabrini missed a penalty after Conti had been fouled. Bearzot remembers Cabrini breaking down in tears at half-time, and being worried that the game was slipping away from them.

'We were really worried during the interval, for many reasons. Gentile had been hit in the chest and had problems breathing; Graziani had already come off with his shoulder injury; the eighteen-year-old Bergomi had tendinitis. Thank God we had some players in the form of their lives – Cabrini, Tardelli, Oriali and Rossi.'

Rossi, however, had no sense of crisis about the way the game was going.

'After he missed the penalty, Cabrini was "gone" for about twenty minutes, but the team itself didn't feel demoralized. It was simply a question of a team playing on, knowing what it could do, and winning. When my goal came, on fifty-six minutes, it was just what we needed to put them out of it. There was a free-kick on the right, and Gentile crossed. I got off the mark a split second before my marker and got my head on to the ball. It was one of those two-in-ten occasions when you make the run and the ball actually falls right for you.'

Marco Tardelli's left-foot shot on sixty-eight minutes, after sweeper Gaetano Scirea had joined the attack, effectively finished the Germans off. The substitute

Top: The Italian line-up for the 1982 World Cup final. Bergomi, back row, third from the left, is still playing for Inter fifteen years on!

Bottom: Rossi, on the deck, dives in to head Italy's first goal, and his sixth of the tournament.

Altobelli had time for a third, before Paul Breitner got a goal for Germany that nobody can remember. At the whistle, Bearzot stood arms raised in triumph as Italy claimed their first World Cup win of the modern age. Rossi's goal in the final had left him with six for the tournament, clear of his pursuers. He was the outright winner of the Golden Boot.

'I had never really thought about it,' Rossi says, hand on heart. 'When you are in your national team playing in a World Cup, of course you imagine and hope that you are going to score goals. But what is more important is that the team gets the right results. Your goals may often be crucial to the success of the team, but it doesn't mean you're thinking about the Golden Boot. *Afterwards*, when the team's won, you can savour it a bit, but it's more of a personal satisfaction because it doesn't involve the others.

Enzo Bearzot is chaired off by his team, as they celebrate their 3–1 win over West Germany in the Bernabeu Stadium, Madrid.

'For a professional footballer to play in a World Cup is the greatest thing. To win it is the ultimate achievement. I went through two different sensations. When the final finished, I had a strange and wonderful feeling about our victory. The second emotion was sadness – that it had all finished, that it couldn't go on, that you could never again enjoy such intense emotions. To feel anything more would be almost impossible. And yet from that moment on, you're different inside, not only for yourself, but for what you've given the fans, and your country. The homecoming was extraordinary, crazy. It was something absurd and mad. I wasn't around at the end of the war for the liberation, but there must have been the same scenes and the same passion.'

Rossi is obviously in pole position to answer one of the questions which always intrigues football fans of other countries, which is why should Italians see football as so important to their lives.

'It's part of the people's culture. In Italy, you grow up from a baby with football. When you're a child, the mass media – television, newspapers – gives you football all the time. When you're older, everyone talks about football, in the bars and restaurants. And there is a rivalry about football at a very local level in every village, town and city in the country.'

After the World Cup, Rossi resumed his club career with Juventus, helping them to an Italian Cup victory in 1983, the European Cup-Winners' Cup in 1984, and then the European Cup in the nightmare of Heysel Stadium against Liverpool in 1985. He went to the 1986 World Cup finals with Bearzot, more for the squad's spirit than for football itself, and didn't get a game. Though Italy got through the first group stage, they were well beaten in the second round, 2–0, by Platini's dazzling French side, which many people thought should have made it to the final. Less than a year later Rossi retired with an injury at the age of thirty.

'When I finished my career, I needed a break away from football. I already had business interests in property which helped me get straight into work. I just felt I needed to get away from a culture that I had lived for the best part of twenty years, which had been very stressful and hard. I really needed to make my own life and enjoy myself a little. So I travelled, I took some holidays. Now I'm detached from football, and I don't even go to watch a game that often. I have a much quieter life than I did when I was playing. Professional football's unique, in that it can bring great popularity, success, money, but not always satisfaction. There are moments when it's not a great life, when you have to make sacrifices, when the tiredness overtakes the enthusiasm – but I did enjoy playing.'

For Bearzot, retirement in 1986, six years after his original contract had expired, was no dishonour for a man who brought pride and daring back to Italian football after the dark ages of the 1950s and sixties. He is still fêted wherever he goes. My interview with him in a hotel coincided with the last day of the Italian league's transfer period, and there were all these players buzzing around, all stopping to pay their respects to Bearzot, as though he was a great statesman, or a Mafia don. He no longer has an active role in football, but it gives him great pleasure that his assistant at the 1982 World Cup, Cesare Maldini, is the current Italian coach.

'He is my younger brother!' Bearzot shouts passionately. 'I think that the coaches of the national team have to grow up within its system. Those who come from the clubs know the football of clubs but don't have a clue about international football. When Maldini took over, Italy had already played three World Cup qualifiers, so a new coach from a club would have spent too long making his mind up over team selection. Instead Maldini knew the environment very well.'

So, too, did Bearzot's immediate successor in 1986, Azeglio Vicini, who, like most Italian national coaches, had spent many years in the system before assuming control. Vicini, in fact, had been at *five* World Cups from 1970 onwards, either as a trainer, an assistant or coach to the Italian Under-21 squad. Only Arrigo Sacchi of recent Italian managers had come direct from a major club, and his 'failure', at USA '94 and Euro '96, was deemed to be an endorsement for the old system of promoting from within the national training

Paolo Rossi as he is now – no need for the hair dye just yet!

A harbourside chat with Italy's 1990 World Cup manager, Azeglio Vicini. I have ordered the drinks, honest.

set-up. Vicini, like Bearzot, was a modest *Serie A* player – although Bearzot *did* win one cap – who ascended through the system.

'I believe that being a coach in a club is completely different from being a coach for the national team. You have to be clever in both cases but they are two completely different experiences. With the national squad you have to know the players very well, because when you call them up you know that they won't have too much time to play together, so they have to have some particular qualities. You don't just choose the best ones.'

This last remark is particularly apt for Vicini's most famous selection for Italy, that of Salvatore 'Toto' Schillaci in the 1990 World Cup. Like Rossi for Bearzot, the virtually unknown Sicilian striker was a huge gamble for Vicini to take, although it must be said that Bearzot virtually staked all on Rossi. Vicini, who had been growing up with a new generation of Italian Under-21 internationals – Walter Zenga, Gianluca Vialli, Giuseppe Giannini, Roberto Donadoni and so on – already had his basic First XI for Italia '90 in mind two years before the tournament, such was his familiarity with the players he'd coached and nurtured.

Back in Japan, waiting for the bullet train to shoot into sight. (*Inset*) Toto Schillaci, after training for his Japanese club.

'I had worked hard to make my mind clear, and the team for our first game of the European Championship in 1988 had ten players who also turned out for our first game of Italia '90 against Austria – Zenga, Bergomi, Maldini, Baresi, Ferri, Ancelotti, Donadoni, De Napoli, Vialli and Giannini, with Carnevale replacing Mancini in the forward line. So it was a team that I knew very well, which I'd created myself.'

Schillaci, who had played just one season with Juventus, scoring fourteen goals, after moving from second division Messina in Sicily for £1.7 million, was no spring chicken by the summer of 1990 – he was twenty-five, a late starter in the top grade of Italian football. He had made just two international appearances, but had obviously done enough to make Vicini include him in the twenty-two-man squad, albeit as a reserve striker after the first choices of Vialli and Carnevale, with Roberto Baggio about to be deployed as the free-floating attacking midfield player. Vicini denies that Schillaci was the last name to be added to his final squad, but the player himself says that he was the last to be called up and that it was a complete surprise to him.

I travelled all the way back to Japan to see Toto Schillaci, because that's where he plays his football now, in the J-League, as I did (when my big toe allowed!) from 1992–94. Having had two former Golden Boot winners, the J-League will probably be angling for Hristo Stoichkov next in order to complete a treble! Although most people think that European players who are past their sell-by dates are only going to Japan for the money, I have to say there was a bit more to it in my case. In the first instance, it's a fascinating country to live in, and in the second, the Japanese are so mad about football that it was an exciting experience to be in on some of the rapid growth which the game is making there. Don't forget that Japan has already been nominated as co-hosts with South Korea for the 2002 World Cup, which gives you some idea of the emotional drive and economic backing behind their football set-up.

So, although he readily confesses to the odd feeling of homesickness, Schillaci is relaxed about this exile from a Europe which hailed him as a new superstar at the start of the decade. But then Schillaci's late and sudden rise to world prominence, and equally swift exit from it, have probably left him with a pretty well-balanced view of life. Even when he was fatefully called up to the Italian squad in 1990, his feet stayed on the ground.

'It was a total surprise to me. No one expected it. I was just happy to get called up, but I didn't think I'd get a game because it was a strong and more-or-less complete squad. But everything that happened afterwards was down to me, because I really wanted to play and score goals. It was still a surprise, though.'

Italian tifosi anticipated a home victory in the 1990 World Cup. (*Inset*) And Salvatore Schillaci was the player who did his very best to achieve it, with six goals.

When Schillaci came on for Carnevale deep in the second half of Italy's first game against Austria, the Rome crowd were beginning to get edgy about the chances that the *azzurri* had missed. Holders Argentina had already been beaten by Cameroon in the opening match, so the big teams had all been put on alert for shocks. But within three minutes of bounding on, and having his short CV broadcast around a world which knew little about him, Schillaci had leapt into the global consciousness with a spring-heeled header from Vialli's cross into the roof of the Austrian net, followed by a wild-eyed celebration that resembled the look of a child who'd just opened the perfect present on Christmas morning.

Schillaci came on again as a second-half substitute for the game against the USA. The game had started as though it would be a goal-fest when Giannini scored early on, but with the USA keeping the score down to 1–0, Schillaci's goal instincts were needed. He didn't score in his thirty-nine minutes of play, but did enough to push for a start in the next game against Czechoslovakia. He didn't know what Vicini had been working on.

With two games completed, Vicini had decided to give up on the hapless Carnevale, especially when he was caught in a close-up on television mouthing obscenities about his substitution. Vialli, too, had disappointed, missing a penalty against the USA, but here there were mitigating circumstances since he was carrying an injury. So Vicini decided he would scrap his original line-up and pair Schillaci and Baggio as the front two, a bold but risky move considering how slight both men were. But Baggio had just signed for Juventus in any case and would be playing alongside Schillaci in the new season, so Vicini, cheekily, was giving Juve a very public preview of their expensive investments.

'Baggio was a very promising player, very talented, but he had a problem with stamina, and his recovery after matches. When he was fresh, he could bring lots of things to a game. Moving him up front meant he didn't have to run so much. As for Schillaci, he was quick off the mark and had good reflexes, and he'd got a goal, which was like an injection of optimism for him.'

The pairing worked like a dream, as first Schillaci and then Baggio scored goals, with Baggio's amazing dribble, run and shot seizing most of the crowd's attention. But Schillaci's reflex header off a rebound was just as impressive in its own way, displaying another aspect of the striker's arts – being in the right place at the right time.

Schillaci outpaces Ireland's Mick McCarthy in the quarter-final in Rome, 1990. Schillaci scored the only goal of the game.

Italy were easily through to the next, knock-out phase, with three wins. There, they encountered Uruguay who soon suffered from another shaft of Schillaci skill, the little man blasting home a left-foot half-volley on the run from twenty yards to put Italy 1–0 up. Aldo Serena scored a second, and Italy were into the last eight, cheered on by an increasingly hysterical home audience.

The 1990 World Cup semi-final: Schillaci gave his all against Argentina, but Italy were beaten 4–3 on penalties, exactly the same as England.

'It was like having twelve men,' Schillaci says of the knowledge that millions were willing Italy on to success, as they watched in their homes, bars and cafés. On match nights, Italy's streets would be utterly empty while the game was on, and then filled by a horn-tooting cavalcade on the instant that a victory was confirmed. Schillaci scored his fourth goal against Ireland, pouncing on Packie Bonner's error to slot the ball home for what proved to be the winner against Jack Charlton's resilient Irish side.

Next, they faced old enemies in Argentina who, despite an inadequate squad, were being driven on by Diego Maradona's almost demented will to win. In the quarter-finals, they'd scraped past a talented Yugoslavia on penalties after a 0–0 draw in Florence, having recovered from the Cameroon defeat with just enough points from a win and a draw to get through to the second round. There, they'd produced one of the all-time great burglaries in football, beating Brazil 1–0 with a Caniggia breakaway goal from a Maradona flick. Given all this, their reservoir of luck appeared to have been drained by the time they faced the hosts. Schillaci duly provided his fifth goal to settle the Italian nerves, but Caniggia equalized and the whole of Italy was stricken with dread as time lumbered on towards a penalty shoot-out, which Argentina ruthlessly won 4–3. The following night in Turin, England lost by the same method and the same margin to the Germans. England and Italy were united in mourning for the final that should have been.

'When Argentina made it 1–1,' Schillaci recalls with a haunted expression, 'and the game went into extra time, I felt we were going to lose. I knew we weren't good at penalties. It was the greatest disappointment of my life not being able to play in the final, because we would have definitely won.'

'Let's all have a disco!' The Italian lads join England in a celebration, after the third-place match in Bari – they won 2–1.

'I think we deserved a better fate,' Vicini reflects on the same misfortune. 'We had won five games and drawn one – but went out on penalties. After that match in Naples we travelled for 250kms to Marino in Rome. It was 2 a.m. or 3 a.m., and yet there were still crowds out on the streets clapping and supporting us. They understood the feelings that the squad had, and knew that their team had done as much as they could, with only circumstances depriving them of a place in the final.'

The third-place play-off game between England and Italy in Bari proved to be more of a spectacle than the grim final, as both sides decided to put on a show. Baggio got another goal after a bit of doziness in England's defence, while David Platt's header probably added another couple of noughts to his signing-on fee for Bari. When Italy won a penalty, Baggio graciously offered it to his new striking partner, knowing that if he scored he was more or less certain of the Golden Boot. Schillaci duly obliged and brought his total to six goals in seven games. Then it was time for 'let's all have a disco!'

Within a few months, however, the hangover was all Schillaci's. He struggled for form and goals with Juventus and the snipers got to work on his reputation.

'I had some problems,' he admits. 'A lot of bad luck, injuries and arguments with the Juve manager. Everyone was looking at me and saying, "Oh, that Schillaci, he's had his moment of magic." My life off the field stayed the same – same friends. The fact that I had become famous actually made me more mature. But the press can be very hard. They put you on a pedestal one moment and then destroy you the next. That's what happened to me.'

Schillaci was offloaded to Inter Milan but had little success there, and was eventually grateful to take up the offer of playing in Japan.

'Perhaps his popularity arrived too suddenly,' Vicini suggests. 'He wasn't able to manage it. His was a remarkable decline but he hasn't been the only player who played just one great World Cup. And most players would settle for that, anyway.'

'Schillaci was like a meteor,' says Sandro Mazzola. 'He arrived, did great things and then disappeared. He played by instinct, and while he was playing through instinct he was a great player. When he had to think about it, he lost his qualities, his unpredictability. Before he began thinking he was a great player, he was spontaneous, but the very moment he realized he was a great player, he lost that greatness.'

Nevertheless, by becoming only the second Italian player to win a Golden Boot – a trophy which depends on scoring goals – Schillaci helped keep Italy's momentum towards modern greatness alive, after a period in the mid-century when their early World Cup successes began to look like a fluke of history.

Sandro Mazzola tries to account for this dip in Italy's football power by pointing to the large number of *oriundi* who turned out in the azure blue shirts after the war.

'They often didn't have much desire to wear the *maglia azzurri*, didn't even want to play in the national team. It was a time when the general public lost interest, too. I remember in the 1950s, Inter won two titles but there was only an average of 15,000–20,000 at the games. It was a period of indifference, I think.'

The sterile, defensive tactics which spilled over from club football into the national team during the 1960s probably didn't help bring in the crowds, and nor did Italy's infamous 1–0 defeat by North Korea at Ayresome Park in the 1966 World Cup. (Perhaps that's why Ravanelli didn't settle in Middlesbrough?) 'We were ashamed of walking in the street,' Mazzola recalls.

Sandro Mazzola, one of Italy's greatest forwards, and now on the board at Inter Milan, tries to sign me in place of Ronaldo...

But Mazzola and others began to lead Italy back to the peak – Gigi Riva, a great goalscorer; Gianni Rivera, the sinuous midfielder; Roberto Boninsegna, a fluent dribbler. By 1970, Italy had regained their pride, beating West Germany 4–3 in extra time in the semi-final, before losing 4–1 to Pelé and Brazil in a glorious final.

Despite what England did to them in the qualifying group for 1998, Italy are now firmly established as one of the great powers of modern football, and for all the right reasons, too. They have caught up with their early history; but the successes of Rossi and Schillaci should remind all fans and coaches that tradition, history and popular expectation are not always enough. It still comes down to one or two exceptional players defying the odds.

1938	1962
Leonidas da Silva	Vava
8 goals	4 goals
1950	**1962**
Ademir	Garrincha
7 goals	4 goals

Brazil

There is simply no question that Brazil's World Cup tradition is the strongest and deepest of all the countries to have taken part since 1930. Winners a record four times – in 1958, 1962, 1970 and 1994 – they are the only country to have competed in all fifteen competitions to date; the only country to win the tournament outside their own continent; the only country to produce four Golden Boot winners…need I go on? Well, I do actually – they're the best, the benchmark by which all other footballing countries have to measure themselves, and the standard-bearers for the game at its most fluent and imaginative.

Each of the six nations to have won the World Cup so far has its own distinctive style of play, which may change in terms of formation and tactics, but doesn't change in essence – the Germans have a clear-sighted sense of the game as the product of team-work and organization; the Italians will defend systematically but will

ally this to wonderful, off-the-cuff attacking; the Uruguayans and the Argentinians play with strong defences, and passionate, almost neurotic surges on goal; England, under Glenn Hoddle, are going through a cultural change, from all-out, honest effort, to controlled, coolly intelligent football; but Brazil, apart from the odd dud vintage, hardly ever change. They play their football right through the team, seemingly with only one intent – to score more goals than the opposition.

These distinctive approaches to football make you realize what richness and complexity there is in such an apparently simple game, but then they are also the product of a national consciousness, shaped by all sorts of different cultural influences. All of the six nations to have won the World Cup bring different histories and traditions to their football. It's fair to say that all would express their love of football, but this is only

by degrees compared with Brazil, whose passion for the game borders on the obsessional. While Italy, Germany, Argentina and the rest can be defined as countries by other achievements – fashion, opera, engineering, politics, music, even food – only Brazil takes football so completely as its national identity.

Until this journey, I had never been to Brazil, having missed out on Bobby Robson's short summer tour in 1984 – the one where Barnesy scored *that* goal. Although I've played against them on three occasions, none of them was on Brazilian soil. So it was intriguing for me to arrive in a country about which I knew nothing but whose football I knew pretty well. I'd never really been able to connect with the country; all I had were the familiar, almost clichéd images of the Maracana Stadium, samba bands and Copacabana beach.

Well, I have to admit that at least one of these clichés seems to contain more than a deal of truth because, even in the autumn when I visited, the beaches of Rio de Janeiro were just full of football games – a bit like Hackney Marshes with a view. I even got involved in one of the impromptu, barefoot matches which mixes football with volleyball – a bit too much like training for my liking – and I could begin to understand how playing on sand not only strengthens the leg muscles but also makes you aware of your touch on the ball. It also encourages dribbling, which I was never good at and it's a bit late to start learning now.

But if I'd squeezed in a sociology degree while I was playing, I think I might have been able to come up with some fairly plausible theories about how beach football has created the Brazilian style of close control. I might not have offered the

Flying down to Rio – the view I got from Mount Corcavado, above Rio de Janeiro, with its famous statue of Jesus Christ.

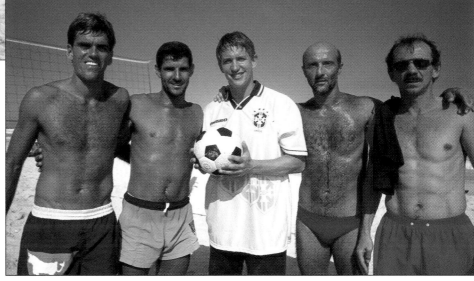

A quick game of beach volleyball with Rio's equivalent of the Arsenal back four. I got to keep the ball.
Below: Elsa Soares, famous singer and friend of Garrincha.

old standby of the football being connected to the samba, but one of my earliest witnesses insisted that there was a definite link between the music that Brazil dances to and the football the national team plays.

Elsa Soares is one of Brazil's most famous singers in the samba style, and she's also celebrated for her love affair with one of Brazil's great players of the 1950s and sixties, Garrincha, a Golden Boot winner in 1962. She loves football and music with equal passion and makes a convincing case for their connection.

'The importance of music to Brazilian football is because there is the same swing, the same dance, the same movement in both. I think that Brazilian players have this suppleness which comes from hearing the music, and I feel like a pioneer because I brought both worlds together when I started with Garrincha. When you see a Brazilian footballer he's playing and he's dancing. It's natural for Brazilians, this movement, and samba, the music that I sing, has the movement of football – you can play football dancing the samba!'

I'd have loved to have introduced Elsa to one of my old managers, the late Jock Wallace, whose idea of movement and football was something akin to a fixed bayonet charge at a brick wall! But seriously, I really do accept Elsa's theory that there's a kind of musical rhythm to Brazil's football, a fluidity of movement which makes us Europeans look stiff-limbed and awkward. On the occasions when I played against Brazil, they always communicated a sense of comfort on the ball and a flowing ease in their running. In England, I've seen Juninho at close hand producing those wonderful, sinuous runs with the ball under perfect control, that just look and feel different from anything our lads can do, even the good dribblers like Steve McManaman, Gazza or Chris Waddle.

I remember seeing a sequence in the 1982 World Cup film, in which the director cut between footage of the Italians and Brazilians warming up in training before their vital second-stage match. The Italians jog around the pitch with perfectly acceptable arm and leg movements, but it still looks hopelessly stiff when compared with the Brazilians, who are gliding across the turf, performing all their stretches and movements in harmony, just like a ballet troupe. Of course, Italy went on to beat Brazil 3–2 in that game, so clearly my theory isn't watertight – it's just one to think about when you watch Brazil in action in France this summer. So don't forget to listen to their fans beating out a rhythm with their snare-drums and maracas, and see if it sets up the rhythm of the team.

Having strayed into unfamiliar territory, I'd better get back to the real business of Brazil's Golden Boot winners, and the history of the country's football. Like most South American countries, Brazil had a distinct British influence in the development of their game. A Brazilian-born Englishman, Charles Miller, went to play for Southampton, and when he returned to Brazil he brought shirts, balls and boots so that he could start his own teams. These were linked to assorted companies – the English Gas Company, the London Bank and São Paulo Railways. By 1898 several small football clubs had been founded. Another group of Englishmen set up the Fluminese club in Rio de Janeiro, and it was there that I met Tim Vickery, an English writer who is based in Rio, sensible chap. Tim took me to the original Flumi

The original Fluminese ground in Rio reveals the club's upmarket beginnings.

nese ground which is startlingly similar to Trent Bridge cricket ground in Nottingham – all whitewashed stands and Victorian iron pillars – where he told me how much this elegant architecture reflected the upper middle class Brazilian control of football in those early days.

'It was very much their preserve,' Tim says, 'almost like the modern country club. The players all regarded themselves as gentlemen, to the extent that if the referee awarded a penalty, the player taking the kick would deliberately miss, so as to avoid an indirect accusation of ungentlemanly conduct being aimed at the player who'd conceded the kick!'

So obviously the British public have been wrong about Stuart Pearce, Chris Waddle and Gareth Southgate all this time – they're proper toffs, just like the Corinthians (a team full of former Oxford and Cambridge University graduates, which came out to Brazil in 1910 on a football tour, and made such an impact that a São Paulo club adopted the same name).

By 1914, the game had caught on to such an extent that Brazil were able to muster a team for their first national game at Fluminese Stadium against, of all teams, Exeter City! Apparently, the Exeter boys limped off in the second half complaining about the heat, but they were already 2–0 down by then. Later that year, Brazil played their greatest rivals Argentina for the first time, winning 1–0, and by 1916 the South American Championship was up and running.

So the attraction to Brazil of a first World Cup in Uruguay in 1930 was obvious – international competition was a means of expressing national identity, particularly in relation to other South American countries, and they didn't have too far to travel. But in contrast to their later contributions to the World Cup, Brazil's first appearance was an anti-climax: a 2–1 defeat by Yugoslavia and a 4–0 win over Bolivia meant that they didn't progress to the semi-final stage.

One aspect of their game that was rethought at this stage was the role of black Brazilians in the national team. Brazil had only emancipated its slaves in 1888, and so there was a formidable residue of racist attitudes spilling over well into the twentieth century. Players such as Friedenreich and Manteiga had managed to break through into the national team, but at club level the emergence of black Brazilians was still frowned upon. Tim Vickery says, 'Most of the black players were told to whiten their skins with rice powder and straighten their hair before going out to play.'

But a major social breakthrough arrived when another black player, Leonadis Da Silva, became Brazil's centre-forward in the mid 1930s, playing in Brazil's one and only game of the 1934 World Cup in Italy – a 3–1 defeat by Spain – but then leading the line to spectacular effect in the 1938 tournament in France. Leonidas was born in 1913 and actually played football for Uruguay as well as Brazil, so vague were the regulations in those days. But by the time of the 1938 World Cup, he'd become one of Brazil's first superstars with his supreme athleticism and eye for a goal. He is credited with being the player who invented the bicycle kick, that gymnastic manoeuvre in which footballers – with the exception of myself, I hasten to add – throw themselves into a sort of backward somersault, with both legs off the ground, and kick the ball back over their head. It's quite common in the game now – remember QPR's Trevor Sinclair winning the BBC's Goal of the Season award with his bicycle kick? – but still spectacular. Crowds love it, because it's both eye-catching and brave, and on the occasions when it comes off with a goal, it produces a genuine sense of excitement. But can you imagine how it must have been to see it done for the first time? No wonder Leonidas made such an impact on the Brazilian fans.

Leonidas da Silva launches into one of his famous bicycle kicks, which are commemorated in sculpture at São Paulo FC's museum.

In São Paulo, I met up with an old friend of Leonidas, who sadly is in poor health, a journalist and sportswriter, Luis Ernesto Kawall. At the museum of Leonidas's old club, São Paulo, they have a large model of their former player hanging by wires from the ceiling apparently in the act of one of his famous bicycle kicks. Mr Kawall, however, has been campaigning for years to get the sculpture changed because it shows Leonidas kicking the ball with his left foot, when he nearly always used his right for overhead kicks.

'It's unfortunate that it's wrong because the building and the idea of the memorial to Leonidas are beautiful. I keep telling the club's directors and the newspapers, but so far they haven't put it right. At least the statue reflects Leonidas's unbelievable agility. As well as the bicycle kicks, he could jump up to two metres for headers, and score with both feet. They called him "The Rubber Man", as well as "The Black Diamond", and it's good that he's been immortalized. Apart from Pelé, he was the best Brazilian player I saw in my time covering the game. We've had three players of genius in Brazil – Leonidas, Pelé and Garrincha.'

For the 1938 World Cup, Brazil travelled across to France by boat, trying to prepare physically on the journey, which evidently was not too successful. Nevertheless, Leonidas soon alerted the French spectators to his talents by scoring four goals in Brazil's first match in Strasbourg, a tight defensive affair against Poland, which ended up 6–5 to Brazil in extra time! Brazil were 3–1 up at half-time thanks to a Leonidas hat-trick, scored despite the fact that when the sole of his boot came off, he was forced to play barefooted for a while. But as many Brazilian teams have done since, they decided to make life difficult for themselves by keeping the game open when all the coaching orthodoxy is to close it up once you've got a decent lead. But

The Brazilian team keep fit during their trans-Atlantic crossing to the 1938 World Cup.

this instinct just isn't in the Brazilian footballing psyche, so the crowd were rewarded with an absolute belter of a game, with Poland pulling back to 4–4 after ninety minutes.

It should be recorded that a Polish forward, Ernst Willimowski, also scored four goals that day, and I imagine that he would have been pretty disappointed to finish on the losing side, after Leonidas and Romeu had scored in extra time for Brazil.

Leonidas was on target again in Brazil's 1–1 draw with Czechoslovakia in Bordeaux, with the match having to be replayed in order to get a result. But the first game was marred by some brutal tackling which left the 1934 Golden Boot winner, Oldrich Nejedly, with a broken leg. Two Brazilians and one Czech player were sent off. As Brazil would later show in their Battle of Berne in 1954 against Hungary, there was, and indeed is, a strong physical element to their football which can turn nasty if the drift of the game is against them. Fortunately, the replay was a calmer game, with Leonidas getting one of Brazil's goals in a 2–1 win. They were now in the semi-finals where they would face the holders, Italy.

What happened for this game is something of a minor mystery. We've heard from Italy's goalkeeper Aldo Olivieri that Brazil arrived in Marseille by plane, which they had already booked to take them to Paris for the final; and this apparent cockiness is supposed to have extended to Brazil's decision to 'rest' both Leonidas and their other main striker, Tim, for the final, so confident were they of beating Italy. But Luis Ernesto Kawall disagrees firmly with this reading of history, especially in the light of Brazil's eventual 2–1 defeat.

'Leonidas was injured. To say that he wasn't is absurd. Never, no way. He was already the top scorer in the tournament and it was in his interest, and Brazil's, to score more goals and become even more famous. So with the crowning moment of his career at hand, he wasn't about to feign injury, was he? If he'd been fit they'd have played him – it's logical. Later, back in Brazil, Leonidas sued one of his team-mates, the left-back Nariz, for suggesting that he'd been "bought" into not playing. Leonidas won the case.'

Whatever the truth of the story, there's no doubt about Leonidas's goalscoring achievements in the tournament. He scored a further two goals in the third-place match, in which Brazil beat Sweden 4–2 in Bordeaux, to bring his total to eight in four games.

Great acclaim awaited Leonidas back in Brazil, where any lingering racial resentment had been banished by his performance.

'He told me that he had never experienced any,' his friend Kawall reports, 'but he was a black man from another class, a rich and famous footballer. He used to say that there were certain hotels that other black players couldn't go into. Had this happened to him, he told me, he would have made a very public protest. But it didn't happen to him because he was so popular. In fact, people would be queueing up to buy him meals or drinks!'

Leonidas's name and face were soon adorning cigarillo packets as he cashed in on his fame in a small way.

Leonidas da Silva in his prime

The Second World War removed any chance of what should have been the 1942 World Cup in South America, and by the time the next one was staged in his home country in 1950, Leonidas was thirty-seven and considered too old for the squad, by some at least. But Kawall believes that Leonidas might have made the vital difference between Brazil losing and winning against Uruguay.

'Varela, their captain, was very strong in midfield for Uruguay. He dominated the entire pitch, shouting, kicking, knocking people over, but if Leonidas had been there, he wouldn't have allowed Varela to dominate everything on the field. If somebody whacked Leonidas, he always paid them back immediately, despite the fact that he wasn't so tall. He was the same with referees as well, which is probably why he was sent off for arguing on many occasions. He was a natural leader, you see, a captain, that's perhaps why he didn't get on so well with other players in the Brazilian team, because he was always demanding more effort from his team-mates.'

Two players who came into a later Brazilian team, and who went on to form a brilliant partnership with the 1950 World Cup top scorer Ademir, were Jair and Zizinho. Their early experiences with Leonidas drew a mixture of admiration and tetchiness as they tried to deal with their demanding team-mate.

'He was a very cunning player,' Jair told me as we talked on the terraces of the Maracanã Stadium. 'Sometimes with more cunning than football. He didn't get on with us, or socialize with us, or talk to us even. But on the field he was a beast.'

'It was very difficult to get on with him,' Zizinho added, 'because he would shout and swear at the young players, those starting out in the game. But though we were never good friends, he was a fantastic player. Even today when people choose an all-time Brazil team, Leonidas is the centre-forward. He had great ability and was very brave, even though he didn't have the physique to be so brave.'

Leonidas, despite his failure to be selected in 1950, remained a popular public figure and was able to develop a career in the media as a radio journalist, and also worked for the government's Department of Sports and Tourism. He is credited with starting up the Workers' Games in São Paulo, an athletics tournament organized on Olympic lines for trades unionists and manual workers. It allowed many people a glimpse of sport that they wouldn't otherwise have had. With business interests in property, Leonidas made a few bob for himself, and it was only when he reached seventy-five that his health began to decline.

A meeting with two of Brazil's great players of the 1950s, Jair (left) and Zizinho.

'He has Alzheimer's disease and trouble with the prostate,' Kawall reports. 'He's got a nurse with him twenty-four hours a day, so it's very sad for those of us who saw him play at his peak, but he's being well looked after. And all the other patients at the hospital treat him well too. "How are you, Leonidas?" they all ask him, and he shakes hands with them but he doesn't say anything because he can't remember anything any more.'

Alzheimer's is such a terrible disease for anyone to contract, but there does seem a particular poignancy when a sporting hero has to fade away without the comfort of his own memories of the achievements that thrilled millions. One of the most enjoyable aspects for me of undertaking this journey, compiling both the documentary series and this book, was the realization that I would be showing a new audience – perhaps those who think that football began with Ryan Giggs – some of the pioneering heroes of world football, among whom Leonidas da Silva can be safely numbered.

The 1950 World Cup tournament was awarded to Brazil for obvious reasons – war had devastated Europe, both physically and spiritually, so there was no apt venue and perhaps even no great appetite to stage a gathering of countries so close to such recent enmity. Also the last two competitions – 1934 and 1938 – had been held in Europe. It was fair and fitting that South America should get another chance, although by choosing Brazil, FIFA almost automatically offended Argentina to the extent that they withdrew from the qualifying stages. Brazil had been largely untouched by the war, and had a vibrant economy and a nation eager to prove itself on a wider stage. Brazil's biggest gesture was to build the fabulous Maracana Stadium in Rio de Janeiro, on a scale which reflected both the country's passion for football and its modernistic approach to the game. The great oval bowl would be built to hold 200,000 spectators – no messing about in Rio!

Brazil obviously also saw an ideal chance to register their first Jules Rimet trophy, knowing that the host nation had won the first two tournaments in 1930 and 1934. Flavio Costa, a successful player with Flamengo, who later became the team's coach, was charged with delivering the little gold statuette, having taken over as national manager in 1945. He was given four clear months to assemble and prepare his squad, so great was Brazil's eagerness to win the tournament for the home fans. They had learned from their half-cocked preparations for France in 1938 that a dedicated period of training and planning was essential for success.

The amazing 200,000 capacity Maracana Stadium, completed in 1950.

Flavio Costa, still rumbustious in his seventies, has mixed feelings about the 1950 tournament; Brazil came so near to winning their first World Cup with some fantastic attacking football and yet failed at the last gasp. So pride in the team's performance is tinged with a sadness that he will take to the grave about not getting Brazil the result for which it yearned. When I met up with him at his apartment, he was able to show me a more recent irony. His runners-up medal had only just been forwarded to him by the CBD – the Brazilian Football Association – forty-seven years after the final itself. Whether this was a snub, a tribute to the Brazilian postal service or a bureaucratic cock-up isn't clear, but Costa thinks that the publication of his autobiography was probably linked to the sudden appearance of this medal. Perhaps it's really a sign that after nearly half a century, he's been given a state pardon for not winning the trophy.

'I was really surprised by the guy who came and gave this to me, because there was no ceremony, it was just like getting a sandwich or something. But then I've always complained that the squad of 1950 and I got nothing for our defeat, not even a pat on the back or a "thanks for trying". It's the players I feel sorriest for.'

Trying to talk Flavio Costa through what is still obviously a fairly traumatic loss wasn't an easy business, but there are lots of positive things that I could pick up on, which deserve to be put on the record, not the least of which is that Ademir, Brazil's centre-forward, became the tournament's top scorer with nine goals. Of course, it probably wasn't much consolation to the team, nor to a devastated nation, but the fact that it happened is worth celebrating. I don't think that bad players have won the Golden Boot award because it's something that you can't fluke, and I'm pretty certain they weren't playing for bad teams either, otherwise they wouldn't have scored so many goals. So the achievement reflects both on the individual player and the team around him, despite their tournament placing.

So let's accentuate the positive which is that Brazil in 1950 were a wonderful, free-scoring outfit who put attacking football at the heart of their strategy. Not for them the nervous caution nor the tentative probing which afflicts most host countries,

Brazil's 1950 World Cup coach Flavio Costa shows me his runners-up medal, which he received forty-seven years after the final.

just two wins and eight goals in their first three Pool 1 games. First, a 4–0 win over Mexico, in which Ademir scored twice, then a 2–2 draw with Switzerland, followed by an impressive 2–0 win over Yugoslavia, with the attacking trio of Zizinho, Ademir and Jair brought together for the first time in the tournament, Ademir and Zizinho getting a goal each.

Indeed Zizinho performed what amounted to a party piece – moments earlier he'd scored only to find himself given offside, so he reproduced the same run and shot, scored again and this time the referee let it stand.

'I'd have tried it a third time if he'd disallowed that one,' Zizinho says, revealing some of the cavalier spirit which made him the youthful Pelé's favourite player. 'And when I went to get the ball out of the net, I kept kicking the ball back in, not in celebration, but in anger because that was a decisive game for us – if the Yugoslavs drew with us, we'd have been out.'

Zizinho played despite carrying an injury which had kept him out of the first two matches, but he wouldn't show any pain for fear of having to have a painkilling injection.

'I was terrified of any injection,' he says with a grim smile.

The understanding between Zizinho, Ademir and Jair da Rosa was at the heart of Brazil's progress. Ademir Marques de Menezes – just try and get all his name on the back of the shirt – was born in 1922, and started out as a left-winger, but became a prolific goalscorer for his two main clubs Vasco da Gama and Fluminese. Including his 1950 World Cup haul, he scored thirty-two international goals in just thirty-seven matches, which is some going, believe me.

'He had tremendous speed and was perfect with both feet,' Zizinho says proudly, recalling the friend and team-mate he describes as 'my brother', who only recently passed away. 'When I brought the ball forward from midfield, he would drop back towards me, and then he'd turn and I'd put the ball over the centre-back's head, and Ademir would be away, already five metres ahead of the defender. He was very difficult to mark because he could play all across the front line.'

Zizinho, still in mourning for his old pal Ademir, believes that their friendship off the pitch helped inform their play on it.

Zizinho, who was Pelé's favourite player as a child.

'We were great friends, we felt very connected. He always knew what I was going to do with the ball, so that he would make a sudden turn towards goal and just know that I would get the ball to him. Sometimes he played too much with his back to goal, which was a bit dangerous if the defenders wanted to kick him and break his leg, but he wasn't afraid to turn with the ball. And once he got a sight of goal, well, he was hallucinating because he just loved goals!'

In the matches of the final pool, which were structured on a league basis, Brazil clobbered a decent Swedish side 7–1, with Ademir scoring four times, and then beat Spain 6–1, with Jair and Zizinho both scoring.

'They were a good team,' Jair recalls, 'but when you looked at them out on the pitch they were white with fear, and after forty minutes, the game was ours.'

Meanwhile Uruguay had only managed a 2–2 draw with Spain and had scraped past Sweden 3–2. They had three points, Brazil four, so the home side only needed a draw in the match that was effectively the final to win the World Cup in front of 200,000 of their fans in the Maracana.

'The Brazilian public expected another victory against Uruguay,' Flavio Costa told me ruefully. 'But football is decided on the field, and on the field the Uruguayans, who were also good players, used a lot of caution in order not to lose. They had a very good attack but they were playing defensively. It was when Brazil scored the first goal that the Uruguayans had to attack. They found the hole on the left side of our defence and won the game. They scored two goals – and football is decided by goals.'

Reconstructing the bad memories of that 16 July day with Costa at his home, and then at an empty Maracana with Jair and Zizinho, was poignant stuff; they are all still haunted by the failure. They still point to their disrupted preparation for the final, when local politicians insisted on the team coming back into Rio de Janeiro to do a bit of glad-handing the night before the game. The reception not only disturbed the sleeping patterns of the players, but it also exposed them to the sights and the noise of people flying kites and flags, and setting off fireworks, in anticipation of a home victory the next day.

Yet when it came to the match itself, everything seemed to be in Brazil's favour. They had pushed Uruguay back on the defensive, and had laid siege to their goal, but had nothing to show for it by half-time.

'The pressure on Uruguay was so great,' Zizinho remembers, 'but we couldn't score, though we still felt we had the game in our hands.'

Two minutes into the second period, Friaca got on the end of a left-wing cross to force the ball past the defiant Uruguayan keeper, Maspoli.

'When Friaca scored, it seemed like we had a collective drop of pressure,' Zizinho recalls hauntingly. 'Our team just stopped playing, felt that we had done our duty, that our responsibility had ended with the goal. When a guy suffers a drop in pressure, he can't do anything, he feels bad.'

'The crowd were already celebrating the victory, after the goal,' Costa says. 'They were waving flags and handkerchiefs. But when Schiaffino equalized for Uruguay, there was a silence in the Maracana which completely terrorized our players. They felt responsible for this, seeing this vast crowd still and silent. They stopped, they froze. And Uruguay felt this and continued to attack.'

'We only really reacted once Uruguay made it 2–1, and then we started playing again,' Zizinho says, as if the images of the game were still alive in his mind. 'Ademir had the chances to win the game in the first half, but their keeper made at least four brilliant saves. The ball just wouldn't go in. Football is like that. You have your chances, but if you don't take them, they're not going to come again.'

'I was feeling very bad at that stage,' Flavio Costa recalls. 'There was this big hole in our defence, and there were no substitutions at that time. We had a defender, Juvenal, who just wasn't giving cover on the marking of Ghiggia. Perhaps he was worried about the crowd or something, but he hid from the game. If there'd been substitutions in those days, we'd probably have been all right, but we were stuck, with Ghiggia beating Bigode in midfield and then getting past Juvenal to the by-line. And of course, Ghiggia laid on the first goal for Schiaffino, and then scored the second himself.'

Juan Schiaffino, the elegant Uruguayan forward who graced two World Cups, as well as Italian football in the 1950s, recalls the vital equalizer in awed tones, because he still can't believe how Uruguay won, nor how the ball went in, which must make Brazil's agony even worse.

'If you want to know about that goal, I have to tell you God helped me, because I shot with a completely different intention. I hit the ball properly, but it just didn't go where I'd intended.'

Schiaffino became quite mystical about this goal when I talked to him in Montevideo, but what I think it boils down to is that when Ghiggia pulled the ball back to him from the right, he intended to drive the ball away from the goalkeeper inside the far post, but somehow couldn't get his foot round the ball and managed to put it inside the near post instead. I couldn't say it to Schiaffino's face, but I just wanted to get hold of him by the shoulders and say, 'Juan, it's a goal, in a World Cup final, which your team won! Stop fretting about it, will you!'

In fairness, part of Schiaffino's demeanour may be related to the sheer shock of what the Uruguayans achieved that day. Jair and Zizinho report that players from both sides were weeping with emotion, and Schiaffino himself says, 'The Brazilian players were crying as they came down the tunnel, and the crowd were almost silent, quiet and respectful. I've never seen anything like it in a football match. Everybody was crying, and I felt like doing it too because the atmosphere was terrible. We were happy about our triumph, but all around us it looked like a tragedy, a funeral.'

'Their centre-forward, Miguez, just came over and hugged me,' Zizinho remembers, pointing out the precise spot on the vast Maracana turf, 'and I think we stayed like that for several minutes. They just couldn't believe they'd beaten Brazil.'

The fact that the Uruguayans reacted with such untypical restraint, almost in sympathy with the Brazilian nation, earned them a great deal of respect in the aftermath of the game, with players from both sides becoming friends as a result of the intense experience which they had shared. For Brazilian coach Flavio Costa, though, the wounds have yet to heal.

'I can never forget that match because the people will never let me.'

A refashioned Brazil, with a new coach, Zeze Moreira, travelled to Switzerland for the 1954 World Cup but there was no Ademir, no Zizinho, no Jair da Rosa to add subtlety and grace to their attack. They

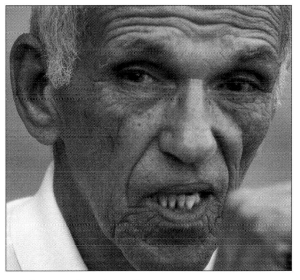

Jair remembers the 1950 final

beat Mexico 5–0 and drew 1–1 with Yugoslavia in their Pool 1 matches, but disgraced themselves against Hungary in the quarter-finals, not just by losing 4–2, but by kicking and punching on their way out of contention. But four years later, in Sweden, Brazil were finally able to achieve their Holy Grail, thanks in no small way to a seventeen-year-old prince of football by the name of Pelé.

Pelé wasn't brought in to the team until Brazil's third game, against Russia, when another new player, Garrincha, was also introduced. The combination of Garrincha's flying wing-play and Pelé's powerful goalscoring swept Brazil to the final against the host country. They'd beaten Wales – yes, Wales – by a single goal, courtesy of Pelé, in the quarter-finals, and the youngster then scored a hat-trick in the 5–2 semi-final win over France, eclipsing their free-scoring strikers Fontaine and Kopa. In the final itself, Pelé added a further two goals in another 5–2 victory, this time over Sweden. Brazil were finally world champions, in the style they would have wanted, although I'm pretty sure they'd have liked to have been nearer home than Sweden.

Now I'd quite like to have talked to Pelé, for obvious reasons, but he's a difficult man to pin down thanks to his duties as Brazil's Minister of Sport. But then again, Pelé's achievements are so huge, they would probably have swamped this chapter; and strictly speaking, I am primarily concerned with the top scorers of each World Cup, which is one of the few summits Pelé failed to conquer. All of which helps to explain the absence of any testimony from him in this section. Yes, he is *the*

Vava, on the ground, scores the first of Brazil's five goals against Sweden in the 1958 World Cup final.

footballer as far as Brazil is concerned, and always will be, but it's some of the others that my journey is concerned with – like Vava, for example.

Edvaldo Izidio Neto is his non-playing name, but as 'Vava' he has a tasty track record as far as the World Cup goes which most strikers would donate their left-foot for – two World Cup winner's medals in succession, and nine World Cup goals to his name, including a share of the Golden Boot award in 1962. Not bad, eh?

Vava recalls his World Cup exploits in a beautiful park along side the Maracana.

Vava had played in Scandinavia before – as an eighteen-year-old midfielder in Brazil's 1952 Olympic team in Helsinki. He was gradually converted to a forward as he developed as a player at his two clubs, first his home town team Recife, and then Vasco da Gama. It certainly helped that he was following the same route as Ademir, whom he effectively succeeded at both club and international level. The Vasco da Gama club, now coached by a recovering Flavio Costa, had about eight or nine internationals in the team. Costa, a demanding disciplinarian, had pushed Vava into the centre-forward role.

'He always wanted me to get in there and fight in the penalty area, so I adapted to this style. It's more difficult up front because of the physical contact. You have to fight for the ball a great deal. And a centre-forward playing in the penalty area doesn't have much space to operate. But I adapted well to it.'

Vava was soon nicknamed 'The Chest of Steel', in deference to his barrel-chested aggression and running. He didn't get into the Brazilian team in Sweden until they played the Soviet Union, having beaten Austria 3–0 and drawn 0–0 with England.

The seventeen-year-old sensation Pelé (second left) scores Brazil's third goal against Sweden.

But Vava secured his place for the rest of the tournament by getting both the goals in Brazil's 2–0 win, which enabled them to head Pool 4 by two points from England.

'One goal came in the first half, from a pass by Didi. He played me in, and I was face-to-face with their keeper, the great Yashin, but I got the goal. The other one was when I got hurt. It was a fifty fifty ball, Pelé went on a run, knocked the ball back and I went in for it, and as the covering defender came across I got there first and scored. But I was lucky that he didn't break my ankle when he caught me. I just got a cut near the ankle, but I couldn't have stitches because it would have meant I'd have been unable to play. So I just had to be bandaged up for the next games.'

Vava missed the quarter-final against the gallant Welsh team, with the injury, but was able to return in the semi-final against France, and got another goal.

'Garrincha pulled the ball back from the wing and I hit it with my left foot. Garrincha had bags of speed, even with his dodgy legs. He used to make short bursts, short sprints, and then take the ball past a defender. He was a very good colleague – humble, calm, never wanted to show off. But it was Pelé who got all the headlines in that game – three goals at seventeen. God gave him qualities that I never saw in other players. He was just an extraordinary player.

'The final against Sweden – also 5–2 – was quite easy, because our team was well trained, consistent and very sure of itself. We had prepared well, having spent three to four months in a training camp, and it was all worthwhile. The management had definitely learned from the 1950 shambles, dragging the team up to meet politicians on the very evening before the final! One of the first things our squad did was to get out of Rio and distance ourselves from all that nonsense. We rationed press access to the camp, too, because in Brazil every journalist is always writing about picking a player from his city or region, trying to do the manager's job. So we avoided all that. Even today, I believe that since 1958, Brazil have organized the team well, and this is why Brazilian football has won so many titles. Brazilian football is good, but it didn't have rules, it didn't have discipline. Everyone went about things their own way, everyone wanted to discover gunpowder!'

Surprisingly, after all this effort had been rewarded with football's ultimate prize, Vava found himself taking victory fairly calmly.

'To be honest, I didn't feel that much after the game. I'd grown up in a winning, professional environment at Vasco which, as the team of the Portuguese descendants, was always a serious team, almost a national team in its own right. We landed in my home town, Recife, on the way back due to bad weather, and had a party there, but there were some dangerous things going on as the people celebrated – I saw a bridge just packed with people and I was convinced it was going to collapse. Later, there was constant attention from people on the street, which became a bit tiring. But the result was a good one because it lifted the gloom after 1950 and 1954, and the whole country began to feel good about football again.'

Brazil, strong favourites along with Russia, repeated their World Cup success in Chile in 1962, surviving the loss of Pelé in the second game to beat England 3–1 in the quarter-final, Chile 4–2 in the semi-final, and Czechoslovakia 3–1 in the final itself. Vava and Garrincha were Brazil's star performers, notching four goals apiece to finish joint top scorers along with four other players.

'It was the same preparation, the same feeling,' Vava told me as we talked on the terrace of his country house. 'Even losing Pelé, the team didn't suffer that much

England full-back Ray Wilson tries to tackle Garrincha during the 1962 World Cup quarter-final in Vina del Mar, Chile. Brazil won 3–1.

because Amarildo came in and got goals. There was a bit of pressure from the journalists doing their usual stuff of trying to pick the team, but the squad had a lot of confidence.'

Vava didn't score in any of the Group 3 games, in which Mexico were beaten 2–0 and Spain 2–1, while the Czechs, who resurfaced in the final, held Brazil to a goalless draw. But in the quarter-final, Garrincha with two goals and Vava with the other destroyed England's hopes of progress.

'I remember my goal against England,' Vava says, trying not to smirk. 'Garrincha took a free-kick and the keeper [Ron Springett] let it bounce up, and I headed it into the goal.'

If the goal sounds fortuitous, don't believe it. Bobby Charlton, who was playing in his second World Cup, says that the Brazilians 'knew exactly what they were doing. Vava turned as soon as Garrincha struck the ball because he knew he'd get it on target, and it was hit in such a way that a rebound was almost inevitable. They were very smart, those two lads.'

Garrincha later confirmed his shooting skills by swerving a long shot past Springett, having somehow

Golden Boot winner, Vava, heads past England's Ron Springett.

managed to get in a spring-heeled header from a corner to give Brazil the lead in the first half. Gerry Hitchens got England's only goal after Jimmy Greaves's header had come back off the bar. In the semi-final, the double-act worked again, as Garrincha and Vava got two apiece in a comfortable 4–2 win over Chile. Vava says that he played throughout the tournament still recovering from a form of anaemia, so I suppose the other teams should be grateful that he wasn't in full-blooded form.

'I knew my main job was to score goals, and to do that you need to find space in the penalty area. The centre-forward has to play in a funnel, sometimes making runs to create space for someone else, so the centre-forward has a lot of work.'

Garrincha's two goals were a twenty-yard, left-foot shot and another flashing header from a corner, and then Vava's two headed goals kept Chile at bay in front of a passionate crowd of over 76,000 in Santiago. The only sour note was Garrincha's dismissal for a kick on Rojas, for which he also received a head wound after being hit by a stone thrown from the crowd. Strangely, considering today's rules on totting up yellow cards and instant punishment for red ones, Garrincha was still able to play in the final.

The durable Czechs had made their way past Hungary in the quarters (1–0) – a goal by Scherer, no relation I presume! – and had beaten Yugoslavia 3–1 in the semis, with two more by Scherer – he *must* be a relation, surely? But they were no match for the Brazilians, even without Pelé, as Amarildo, Zito and Vava scored the goals. Vava's goal was actually a gift from the Czech goalie, Schroiff – a bit like my third against Poland in 1986 – who dropped the ball at his feet from a cross. But it

Pelé, unable to play because of injury, hugs his replacement, Amarildo, as Brazil celebrate their 3–1 win over Czechoslovakia in the 1962 World Cup final.

was just another thing that Vava can be proud of – three goals in two World Cup finals, talk about being a big occasion player.

Zizinho, who meets up regularly with Vava, Jair, Didi and others for paella dinner parties, praises his compatriot as 'a marvellously creative midfield player, who had to change all his characteristics when he was moved to centre-forward, but became a really brave player. As for Garrincha, he was just spectacular. He could demoralize a team if you didn't mark him well. He would risk everything for the team.'

Despite his apparent disability – he had badly distorted legs after childhood polio – Garrincha, 'the little bird', was able to develop fantastic dribbling skills, as well as a powerful shot. Elsa Soares, who became Garrincha's lover in the early 1960s and later his wife, was the woman to whom Garrincha dedicated his World Cup win in 1962. She says that 'he was a very beautiful person, very calm. I was at the 1962 World Cup as a sort of mascot for the Brazilian team. I met Louis Armstrong there, too. When Garrincha was hit by a stone at the Chile game, I went running to help him, but the police dogs chased me away. Garrincha, or Mane as I called him, just loved football. He had no malice, he was like a child really, which is why he was such a joker with the team. Garrincha was a star, in my opinion the biggest in Brazilian football, and he was the most exploited. I think he deserved a much happier ending.'

Garrincha eventually died of alcoholic poisoning at the age of forty-nine in 1983, having contributed a brief cameo – a wonderful goal from a swerving free-kick against Bulgaria – in Brazil's traumatic World Cup of 1966, when they were beaten 3–1 by both Hungary and Portugal and knocked out of the tournament in the first stage. Pelé was very nearly crippled by some ruthless Portuguese tackling, but I guess that this experience made him all the more determined to win the World Cup four years later in Mexico.

Now this is hardly a controversial opinion, but for me, the Brazil side of that 1970 World Cup was just the greatest ever. I was only nine years old at the time, but I remember watching it, disappointed by England's defeat against the Germans, but thrilled by what the Brazilian players did with the ball. And they had not just Pelé, but Rivelino, Gerson, Tostao and the fantastic Jairzinho in the team. Gerd Müller may have won the Golden Boot at the tournament, but Jairzinho took a unique honour by becoming the first player to score in every round of a World Cup – two against the Czechs, the winner against England, one each against Romania, Peru and Uruguay, and then another in the final against Italy. And he was only supposed to be a winger!

I met up with Jairzinho on a Brazilian chat show while I was there. It was all about football of course, with Branco, once briefly of Middlesbrough, Raul Plassman, a former Brazilian goalkeeper and Suzana Werner who's one of Brazil's most glamorous models and just happens to be Ronaldo's girlfriend. Jairzinho, like many ex-internationals in Brazil, now runs a football school, which is doing good business because the hunger to be a player is stronger than ever now that the financial rewards are so great. His current claim to fame is that Ronaldo was a pupil at his school, so if the young Inter Milan forward *does* end up as 1998's Golden Boot winner, don't forget to give credit to Jairzinho.

The great Jairzinho, a hero of Brazil's 1970 World Cup-winning team, invites me on to his TV chat show.

Jairzinho still remembers his own vital statistics from 1970 – 'six games, seven goals, against everyone!' – but is a bit embarrassed about his Afro hair-style whenever they show clips, as they did on this programme.

'It was all the Americans' fault – black power!' he says with a smile. He still thinks that his goal against England 'was the goal that won the title for us, because both England and Brazil were in great form, in all aspects of the game, emotional and tactical. And we knew that whoever won this game was going to the final, even though it wasn't a knock-out situation.'

They replayed Jairzinho's goal, making me suffer all over again as Tostao pulls the English defence around before Pelé gets the ball and feeds Jairzinho on the right of the box.

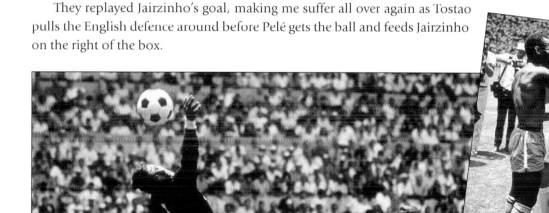

The epic England–Brazil game in Mexico in 1970: Felix claws the ball away as Geoff Hurst waits to pounce. (*Inset*) Two of football's gentlemen, Pelé and Bobby Moore exchange shirts after Brazil's 1–0 win.

'There's an important detail about that goal,' Jairzinho told me as he forced me to watch. 'Pelé brought the ball down and there were three English players on top of him, including my marker, Terry Cooper. And when Pelé gives me the pass, everyone bets that I win, that's why I'm in good shape, and everyone thinks I'm going to hit the ball first time. But I didn't. I *feigned* to hit it. Cooper fell over, and then I lined it up seeing that Banks was coming out, so I put it into the top corner!'

Jairzinho's perspective on Brazil's overall success is a potent one – 'What existed in 1970 was a strong group of players in which everyone played his part. We were all in good form, so the chances seemed to come naturally. There was always specific marking for Pelé, which is why defences forgot about me, Tostao and Rivelino. When they woke up, it was too late!'

'For a team to win a World Cup, lots of things have to come together,' Branco says, having himself been a member of the 1994 squad. 'You can't have people thinking they're stars. Everyone is equal. From the moment that the twenty-two players are called up, you have twenty-two first-choice players. Okay, eleven are picked…but everyone must feel they're in with a chance.'

Of course, Pelé stood out in that tournament, too. It was his coronation, slightly delayed, as the world's best player; his four goals weren't sufficient reward for his all-round play. Remember the shot from the halfway line against Czechoslovakia? Remember the dummy he pulled on the Uruguayan goalkeeper, Mazurkiewicz? He didn't score on either occasion, missing by inches, but the daring and the imagination he showed lives on.

The unmatchable Pelé gets Italy's defence in a spin, as Brazil romp to a 4–1 victory in the 1970 World Cup final.

The final against Italy, in the Aztec Stadium, was really a parade once Brazil had taken a 2–1 lead with Gerson's swerving shot. Pelé's first-half header was Brazil's one hundredth World Cup goal, a fair measure of their attacking power over the years, and the other goals came from Jairzinho (of course) and Carlos Alberto (unlikely). I went to meet Carlos Alberto at his ranch which backs on to a wide lake with a mountain range in the distance. Besides scoring that final goal – a thumping right-foot drive from Pelé's deft flick – he was also the team captain, the man who lifted the trophy.

Brazil's 1970 captain, Carlos Alberto, collects the Jules Rimet trophy. (*Inset*) Carlos Alberto still smiling today.

'I was lucky to be captain of that team,' he says in perfect English, 'but I was captain of Santos, so I suppose that counted in my favour. We had a great squad of players and worked really hard for several months in isolation before the tournament. That was the key to it all – preparation and a happy squad.'

Carlos Alberto still insists, and not out of politeness, that England were Brazil's most dangerous opponents.

'It was a big game for us. You were world champions, don't forget, and we knew we'd have a battle on our hands, both physical and tactical. I had to sort Francis Lee out after he'd kicked our goalkeeper, but after that incident the game was wonderful – great football, Banks's miracle save, Jairzinho's goal. We really needed that goal against England, because I thought you should have won.'

Carlos Alberto failed to list Jeff Astle's horrible miss, which was the main reason why we didn't get anything out of the game, but it wasn't a knock-out, so it didn't really matter, I suppose, except in terms of confidence and prestige. Brazil took that with them from the game, while England couldn't, and we all know what happened next against West Germany...

'The England game was the best match,' Carlos Alberto insists. 'The Italians were very tired in the final because they had been to extra time to beat the Germans 4–3. We also knew how they played, and the altitude of Mexico City didn't help them. Anyone could have scored the goal I got [I don't think so!]; it was the movement up to the goal that was important. From that moment on we knew that the trophy was ours. You know, people still call me Captain?'

Despite Brazil's dazzling success in 1970, they didn't really build on it. The squad for West Germany in 1974 was aggressive and short of flair, though they were

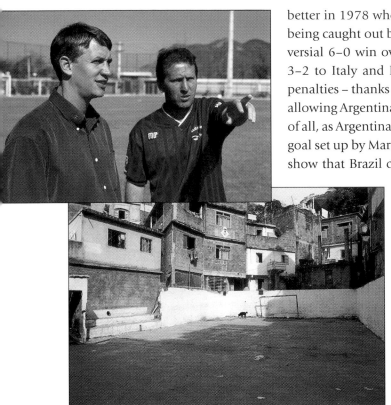

better in 1978 when they finished third without losing a game, after being caught out by Argentina's leap-frog over them with the controversial 6–0 win over Peru. In 1982, they committed suicide to lose 3–2 to Italy and Rossi, and in 1986 probably deserved to lose on penalties – thanks to poor Zico's miss – to France in the quarter-finals, allowing Argentina in for another win; and 1990 was the most painful of all, as Argentina nicked a win in the second round with a breakaway goal set up by Maradona and scored by Caniggia. All of which goes to show that Brazil can't always achieve perfection, which is why their 1994 victory, hard work though it was, has been so vital to the country's self-confidence.

'We were free to play how we wanted in our day,' Carlos Alberto says. 'Now the coaches talk too much about tactics. In 1970 nobody told us the things that we did. We need to discover our flair again, to forget the coach and play by instinct. This is the secret of Brazil's football!'

I'm not sure there'd be too many managers and coaches who'd agree with Carlos Alberto – they have to protect their jobs and their self-importance after all – but I know what he means. It seems particularly important for Brazil, for whom self-expression in the game is almost the first object. Believe it or not, there were a lot of Brazilian football people I talked to who weren't that happy with the 1994 win, feeling that it had lacked style, which just goes to show the high standards they expect of their football.

Another Brazilian great, Zico, shows me around his soccer school. *Below:* Football in the favelas of Rio.

I canvassed opinions from some of the more recent Brazilian heroes to find out just what powers Brazilian football and maintains its style. Zico, whom I played against in Japan when I was there, now runs his own football 'ranch' back in Brazil and he believes that 'it all comes down from other generations, a tradition and a passion for playing with style. We are a big country, don't forget, with a population of over one hundred million, but football touches everybody, poor and rich. The more people you have playing, the more chances you have of producing quality players. And in Brazil kids and boys play football on wasteland, on a patch of sand, on the beach, on the pavement – everywhere. That's why more great players are produced. Beach football in particular has brought out some good players like Junior and Paulo Cesar, and I have a sand pitch here at my training camp. It gets you in good physical shape and sharpens technique. But the rhythm of our game comes from Africa. Brazil is such a mix of people, and playing football is a form of music for us.'

From the latest generation of players, I was able to catch up with Bebeto and Juninho at their respective houses, while they waited to return to the Spanish league season, and they *both* picked up on the fact that Brazilian kids get some form of expert coaching in the game at an early age.

'We work with kids here from the age of eight,' Bebeto told me, as his own children played around the family pool. (The toddler is the baby Bebeto celebrated with his famous cradling gesture at USA '94!) 'And because football is a passion, more of them stick at it than in other countries.'

Juninho told me that he 'started playing on small-sized pitches at the age of six' – he doesn't look that much older now! – and that 'all Brazilian kids dream of is playing football for their country'.

This may sound like insufficient explanation for Brazil's success, but you have to think about how much of a grip football has on the whole of the nation. In Britain, we're only just getting used to the idea that the middle-classes like football, while in Brazil it's been the sport of all people since the 1930s.

To get some idea of the reservoir of passion and commitment which continues to feed into Brazilian football, I met up with an English painter, Bob Nadkarni, who lives in one of the

Bob Nadkarni introduces me to JJ, the man who teaches football to a 'new harvest' of favela kids.

favelas overlooking Rio de Janeiro. Now a favela – literally a place where you plant beans – is a kind of spontaneous housing development on public land, a sprawl of flats, alleys and houses. It's not a shanty town, but it is the sort of place where the best escape is still football. Bob drove me down from his favela to the shore-line where, in the public parks, a famous old player, 'Jota Jota', conducts matches and coaching clinics for the favela kids for absolutely no charge. The operation is called 'new harvest', for obvious reasons. JJ, as he is known, is in his mid-sixties, but is as fit as a butcher's dog, and thousands of kids take part in the games he stages on shallow sand pitches. He coaches them as they play, and he gets involved himself. You can see from the children's faces how much it means to them. Even if a professional career is not on the cards, they can still get pleasure out of playing the game.

'It's Brazil's religion, football,' Bob Nadkarni told me as we watched, and I could believe it. Later JJ introduced me to one of his kids who *is* on the way to making his dream come true – a twelve-year-old boy who goes by the name of Leonardo (they all adopt nicknames, some derived from other players, in Brazil). Leonardo is a product of JJ's school, and now he's been signed by Feyenoord in Holland as a junior, travelling over to Europe each winter to complete both his academic and footballing education. He thought he recognized me from a TV programme he'd just seen about what he called 'old footballers' – the young can be so crushing at times.

But looking at Leonardo and sensing the great adventure that lies ahead of him, I couldn't help thinking back to something Zizinho had told me in our conversation. It was only a throwaway remark, but it suddenly came into focus when I was chatting to JJ and his pupils. 'For every boy in Brazil,' Zizinho had said, 'the first present he gets is always a football.'

Germany

CHAPTER FOUR

We all know that German teams are the most organized and competitive in world football, but the details need spelling out. Since 1954, Germany have qualified for every World Cup. They have won it three times and been runners-up three times, as well as twice reaching the semi-finals. Even in the years when they 'failed' – 1962, 1978 and 1994 – they still reached the quarter-final stages. All this means that they have played in five out of the last eight World Cup finals. Convinced? Having lost out to them in 1990 in the semi-final, I can testify to their collective resilience. They just don't know when they are beaten, even when it goes to a penalty shoot-out. I think I'm right in saying that they've only lost one of those, to Czechoslovakia in the 1976 European Championship final. Oh, and they've won that competition three times and twice been runners-up. So, as my good friend Des Lynam might say, 'How do they do that?' This chapter, while telling the story of Golden Boot winner, Gerd Müller, will also attempt to answer that question.

The 1934 German World Cup team gives the Nazi salute before their second-round match against Sweden in the San Siro Stadium, Milan. The Germans won 2–1.

It wasn't always so easy for the Germans. Like the majority of European countries, they didn't go to the first World Cup in 1930, but they were quick off the blocks in entering the 1934 tournament, and got as far as the semi-finals before losing to Czechoslovakia 3–1 and beating Austria 3–2 in the play-off for third place. Their contribution to the 1938 tournament was more controversial, in the light of Germany's annexation of Austria in March of that year – *die anschluss* – which ultimately involved absorbing many of the top Austrian players, survivors from Hugo Meisl's *wunderteam*, into the German line-up. They fielded four Austrians in their match against Switzerland, but were held to a 1–1 draw. In the replayed match – the first round was staged as a simple knock-out rather than a collection of group games – Germany had three Austrians in the line-up, but after taking a 2–0 lead, they were overcome by a defiant Swiss side. The Swiss, who had refused to give the Nazi salute during the pre-match anthems, eventually ran out 4–2 winners. Adolf Hitler was said to be not best pleased with his country's early elimination, so it was a surprise he didn't end up invading Switzerland for their cheek!

Even in that humiliating defeat, Germany had sown the seeds of future achievements with the appointment for the World Cup of Sepp Herberger as national coach. Born in 1897, Herberger had enjoyed a professional career as a player, although at that time all of Germany's football was organized as a regional competition rather than a national league – the *Bundesliga* wasn't founded until 1963. Herberger was to reign as German coach for twenty-five years, eventually retiring after the 1962 World Cup in Chile. With the Second World War, the splitting of Germany into East and West, and FIFA excluding German teams from the World Cup until 1954, Herberger had plenty of time to work out his style and his tactics.

Horst Eckel, who became a post war international for what was then called West Germany, runs a lucrative car dealership these days, and his showroom boasts a huge mural print of the 1954 World Cup-winning team of which he was a leading member. When I spoke to him about what state German football was in after the war, he said simply, 'We were on the floor, just like our economy and our political life.'

Edmund Conen, who scored four goals for Germany in the 1934 tournament.

Germany's master coach Sepp Herberger, on the extreme left, sits with members of his 1954 World Cup squad.

Horst Eckel had direct experience of Herberger and calls him 'a great football scientist. I would even go so far as to say that he knew everything about football. He was a great teacher, and was able to prepare every individual player, and the team in general. He used to have separate talks with each player before a game, detailing the player's duties and telling him about the opposition. Our captain, Fritz Walter, was like the extended arm of Herberger, stretching out on to the field.'

1954 World Cup winner Horst Eckel shows me the replica trophy in his motor showroom.

As you will read in the chapter on Hungary, it is generally accepted that Herberger outwitted the strongly fancied Hungarians in the 1954 World Cup in Switzerland, first with the ploy of fielding a weakened team in the group match between the two countries, and second with his tactics in the final, when the Germans man-marked some of Hungary's key players and scored a shock 3–2 win. Strong on discipline and organization, Herberger effectively hammered out the template for the German teams which followed, and their remarkable record of consistency since remains a testimony to his pioneering work.

Germany's progress to their first World Cup win was helped by the strange group system used in 1954. Although there were four teams in each pool, the teams played only two matches rather than three. So once West Germany had beaten Turkey 4–1 in their first game, and Hungary had beaten South Korea 9–0, they knew that if they lost to Hungary, they would only have to play off against Turkey or South Korea to go through. Herberger fielded a side with six or seven 'reserves' against Hungary and his side was duly walloped 8–3 by the wonderful, and full-strength, Hungarian team.

Eckel says that this calculated loss was devised before the tournament by Herberger at the German training camp in Munich.

'We still wanted to look good, so the defeat was very depressing for us even though we knew we were under-strength.' Nevertheless, the Germans bounced back as planned to thrash Turkey 7–2, and go through to an easier quarter-final and semi-final than Hungary. Yugoslavia were beaten 2–0, and then Austria 6–1, while the Hungarians had to get past much tougher South American competition: Brazil in the quarter-final (4–2) and Uruguay in the semi-final (4–2, after extra time).

Even at full-strength, the Germans knew that Hungary would be difficult to beat. Eckel recalls the feelings in the German camp.

'We had played very well against Austria, and that was when we knew we might have a small chance against Hungary in the final. We felt that if we reached half-time at 0–0, we would be right in there, but they went quickly into a 2–0 lead, and in our heads, we thought it could be another 8–3. We were lucky to get a goal back very quickly through Max Morlock [West Germany's top scorer with six goals] and then Helmut Rahn scored an equalizer before half-time. It was like a jolt through the whole team; we were determined to hold on till the interval and then go into the second half with a will to win the World Cup.'

In that second half, the German goal enjoyed a charmed life, and eight minutes from time Rahn scored his second goal to put West Germany 3–2 up. Even then they had to survive the drama of a last-minute goal by Puskas which was disallowed. So the instant the game was over, you can imagine both their relief at surviving and then disbelief at winning.

'When we became world champions it was a wonderful feeling,' Eckel says with a misty look in his eyes. 'When that final whistle blew, we knew we had won, but didn't know what

Above: Captains Ferenc Puskas and Fritz Walter exchange pennants before the 1954 World Cup final in Berne, Switzerland.

Left: Max Morlock gets a vital goal back after Hungary had taken a two-goal lead.

awaited us. It wasn't until we returned to Germany and there was an incredible number of people on the streets to welcome us, all cheering, that we suddenly realized we'd done it! It didn't change my life to any great extent, but as a World Cup winner you are more in the public eye. I tried to keep my feet firmly on the ground and stay the person I had always been. I've managed it so far and I don't think I did too badly.'

Eckel, as the youngest player in that 1954 team, also enjoyed a second World Cup campaign in Sweden in 1958, and was proud to reach the semi-final where West Germany were beaten by the host nation, 3–1.

'I wouldn't say that the Swedes were the better team, because we were leading 1–0 when they equalized with a goal that was clearly handball. In the second half one of our defenders, Juskowiak, was sent off and then we lost Fritz Walter with an injury, so we were down to nine

The victorious German team seem almost unable to believe their 3–2 win over Hungary.

men and just couldn't hold on. I didn't play in the third-place match because Herberger wanted to give a game to those players who hadn't been used, and we lost 6–3 to France.'

Eckel remains convinced that the work that Herberger did, and the knowledge he passed on to his successor Helmut Schoen, helped create the successful dynasty that modern German football has become.

'Herberger was always far-sighted, and always said that we must try not only to play in one position but search for players who can play in all positions. He had this vision back in '54 and he always tried to find such players and build them into his team. That's how Germany became the best tournament team – and in all of them, there was always strong discipline, which is why we stay one step ahead. We also have the ability to improve our performance from game to game in a tournament, which is another of our biggest strengths.'

Herberger signed off with a 1–0 quarter-final defeat by Yugoslavia in Chile in 1962. With players such as Uwe Seeler, Helmut Haller, Willi Schulz and Karl-Heinz Schnellinger gaining valuable experience, new coach Schoen inherited what might be called a going concern, but then he had already been working with Herberger as his Number 2 since 1955. The German intention to make continuity a corner-stone of the national team had been well and truly signalled. Schoen had been a decent player in his time, winning sixteen caps as an inside-forward before the Second World War, and the team he brought to the 1966 World Cup in England was a bright mixture of youth and experience, with the odd prodigy like Franz Beckenbauer thrown in for good measure.

The Germans finished top of Group 2, having beaten Switzerland (5–0) and Spain (2–1) and drawn with Argentina (0–0). They cruised past Uruguay (4–0) in

The West German and England teams line up before the start of the 1966 World Cup final at Wembley.

the quarter-finals and snuffed out Russia in the semi-final at Goodison Park (2–1). The final itself is discussed in greater detail in the chapter on England – well, it was *our* big day – but from the German point of view, perhaps the key point for the match was Schoen's decision to deploy Beckenbauer, who'd been playing as an attacking midfielder, as a defensive marker on Bobby Charlton. The strategy obviously has echoes of what Schoen's mentor Herberger did against the Hungarians, when specific creative players such as Hidegkuti were targeted for man-marking.

This time it didn't work, not in the wider sense of crippling England's invention at least, but Charlton was definitely stifled and the Germans' sheer determination allowed them to extend the game into extra time, during which the famously disputed third England goal finally ended their resistance. I wonder how many experts of the time, if they'd been asked about who would go on to be the stronger World Cup force, would have opted for West Germany rather than England? After all, including that 1966 final, England had never been beaten by the Germans in eight encounters between the two countries.

Shortly after the disappointment of July 1966, Helmut Schoen gave an international debut to a stocky, twenty-year-old forward whose goals had just helped Bayern Munich achieve promotion from their regional league into the *Bundesliga*. His name was Gerd Müller, and over the next eight years Müller would prove to be instrumental in the fates of both West Germany and England. There is a common misconception about Müller – most fans know that he was top scorer at a World Cup and that he gained a winner's medal when West Germany beat Holland 2–1 in 1974, so they assume that both happened at the same tournament. But no, Gerd Müller's Golden Boot arrived in 1970 in Mexico. He scored ten goals, his team

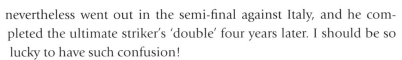

I finally meet my boyhood hero Gerd Müller, at work with Bayern Munich. (*Inset*) Müller in action in the 1970 World Cup in Mexico, where he scored ten goals.

nevertheless went out in the semi-final against Italy, and he completed the ultimate striker's 'double' four years later. I should be so lucky to have such confusion!

This is confession time for me – for although Müller's winning goal against England in 1970 had the nine-year-old boy Lineker in tears, I have to admit that as I began to score goals at schoolboy level, *Der Bomber* became a bit of a hero of mine, probably because he managed to be both small and successful. So despite the passing years, which have given him a greying beard, bi-focal glasses and a spreading waistline, Müller was instantly recognizable to me when I turned up at Bayern Munich's training camp to talk to him. Müller is on the staff of the club with whom he won so many honours and I'd imagine it must be a great thrill for the young German strikers whom he now coaches to have such a great player passing on his wisdom. For Müller's record is quite outstanding. In just sixty-two international appearances he scored sixty-eight goals for West Germany; 365 goals in 427 appearances for Bayern Munich; and his combined total of fourteen World Cup goals over two tournaments is still the highest in history, and is unlikely to be threatened unless his compatriot Jürgen Klinsmann, currently on eight World Cup goals, goes berserk in France this summer.

I asked Gerd first about how he became involved in football, and more particularly how he ended up at the sharp end.

'I started kicking balls around at the age of six,' he told me in a break from training. 'At school, I scored 190 out of a total of 218 goals scored one season, and so I joined a local football club at eleven, and at fourteen was taken on by TSV Nordlingen where I played for four years. I scored goals in my first match wearing somebody else's boots. I always dreamed of playing higher up in the League, but never for one moment thought that I'd play in the *Bundesliga*. My hero when I was a boy was Max Morlock, who played for the 1954 World Cup-winning team, and I can remember listening to the match against Hungary on the radio. Morlock scored one of the goals. He was little, like me, which is probably why I modelled myself on him.'

Gerd's big break came late in 1963 when Bayern Munich signed him up although they were then nothing like the force they later became in German and European football. The Bayern coach, Tschik Cajkovski, hadn't liked the look of a player he dubbed 'a baby elephant', and both he and a subsequent Munich coach, Branco Zebec, insisted that Müller cut his weight down by dieting. But there was obviously enough goalscoring talent there to make Bayern persist with him. Their faith was rewarded with promotion to the national league in 1966, and later the same year Gerd won his first cap for West Germany against Turkey. He didn't score on that occasion but he made amends by notching four in his next international against Albania.

'I always had a talent for scoring goals, both at school and youth level, and I kept improving my standard through training. I was strongest inside the penalty area rather than outside it. I'd start with my back to goal, then turn in the penalty-box and get a shot in. I practised this technique for half an hour every day with Zebec.'

Müller's progress was helped considerably by the recruitment of another young player to Bayern, Franz Beckenbauer, who played in three World Cups before managing West Germany to their 1990 success in Italy.

'Franz and I understood each other perfectly,' Müller says with a smile. 'If he made a precise pass and it landed at my feet, I was to turn and shoot. If he passed me a "soft" ball, he wanted to play a one–two, and if my pass to him didn't work, he'd give me a right telling off!'

These two players were at the heart of West Germany's rising success in the late 1960s and early 1970s, building on Schoen's 1966 achievements with his World Cup squad. They qualified with relative ease for the 1970 tournament in Mexico and, along with England and Italy, were regarded as Europe's strongest challengers. But before the competition could begin, Schoen had to sort out a little local difficulty between the young Müller and the squad's senior striker, Uwe Seeler.

'There was a bit of a dispute between Seeler and me during the build-up. I went to see Schoen and asked him to decide who should be centre-forward because I didn't think it was working with both of us up front. So even at the beginning of that World Cup I didn't know if I'd be playing or not, until it was decided with two days to go that both of us would be in the team.'

The wily Schoen had helped solve part of the problem by making Seeler and Müller share a room, so that in the run-up to the tournament and during it, they could sort things out themselves rather than spend time bickering behind each other's backs. Throwing them together on the pitch had much the same effect, and in the first three group games, Müller and Seeler scored nine goals between them, with Müller claiming seven. He scored one in their 2–1 win over Morocco, and scored two hat-tricks in succession against Bulgaria (5–2) and Peru (3–1), to make an early pitch for the Golden Boot.

Then came that infamous game which is etched on the heart of every Englishman of a certain age, the quarter-final between England and West Germany at Leon on Sunday, 14 June 1970. Look away now if you can't stand hearing about it again! My own tearful reaction aside, my co-author, Stan Hey remembers trying to get his French A-level paper cancelled the next day on the grounds of national mourning.

A nightmare moment – Müller blasts West Germany's winning goal past Peter Bonetti in the 1970 quarter-final in Leon.

England scored through Alan Mullery after thirty-two minutes, and then Martin Peters added another early in the second half. With just over twenty minutes left, Alf Ramsey brought Bobby Charlton off and even as that substitution was about to take place, Franz Beckenbauer strolled forward to drive a shot under the body of stand-in goalkeeper Peter Bonetti. Eight minutes from the end, Müller's partner, Seeler, arched a back-header over Bonetti and the game went into extra time at 2–2, with England tiring rapidly from their earlier exertions.

Eight minutes into extra time, substitute winger Jürgen Grabowski got the better of England's left-back Terry Cooper, and slung in a deep cross which was headed back across goal for Müller to volley home what turned out to be the winning goal.

'It was lucky for us that Ramsey took Bobby Charlton out of the game so early,' Müller remembers, with just the trace of a smirk. 'That handed the game to Franz Beckenbauer on a plate!'

However, England fans were soon able to experience the German concept of *schadenfreude* – the enjoyment of the misfortunes of others – when West Germany were beaten 4–3 in extra time by Italy in a barnstorming semi-final. Müller winces at the mention of it.

'I can't bear watching that game on TV any more. I just get annoyed with Sigi Held, our winger, who lost the game for us when Burgnich levelled the scores at 2–2. There was a free-kick and Held, who didn't have much technical skill, tried to take the ball in mid-air in the penalty area, jumped up and missed it by three metres. Burgnich collected to score.'

Müller, who scored his ninth and tenth goals of the tournament in that match, was probably unlucky not to finish on the winning side, although even he doubts that West Germany would have beaten the brilliant Brazil in the final.

'Franz Beckenbauer was injured in that game, and played part of it in a sling, so he wouldn't have been fit for the final. We'd also played two lots of extra time, against England and Italy, so I think Brazil would have won. That's why the Italians went to pieces in the final, sheer exhaustion.'

Despite Brazil's flying winger Jairzinho scoring in every game and racking up seven goals, Müller was a clear winner of the Golden Boot award with his ten goals. All he had to do now was claim a World Cup winner's medal, and as hosts in 1974, West Germany were well placed to fulfil his dream. But, as Müller admits with a curl of the lip, 'We played appallingly in the first three games of the 1974 tournament. We beat Chile 1–0, Australia 3–0 [Müller one goal] and then lost 1–0 to East Germany. The team just wasn't right. Franz Beckenbauer and I put our heads together and changed the whole team around.'

This example of 'player power' was confirmed to me by West Germany's mighty centre-half of '74, Georg Schwarzenbeck, when I spoke to him in the newsagent's shop he runs in Munich.

'Beckenbauer, Müller and Overath were able to exert considerable influence on Helmut Schoen for the remaining games. The whole squad was assembled and Beckenbauer practically had a hand in choosing the team. Schoen was a good listener, and

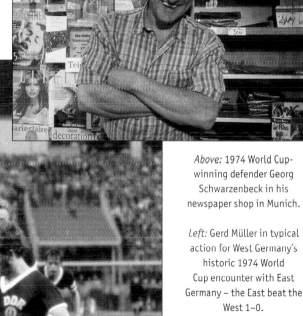

Above: 1974 World Cup-winning defender Georg Schwarzenbeck in his newspaper shop in Munich.

Left: Gerd Müller in typical action for West Germany's historic 1974 World Cup encounter with East Germany – the East beat the West 1–0.

talked with the senior players without being offended by it. In fact he actively encouraged discussions. He was very calm.'

The reshaped West German team began to show stronger form in the next stage, Group B, beating Yugoslavia 2–0 (another goal from Müller), Sweden 4–2 and Poland 1–0 (Müller again). There are still strong suspicions that they 'chucked' the game against East Germany so as to avoid going into Group A, against Holland, Brazil and Argentina; but as Holland won that group easily, the West German team couldn't avoid them any longer, and the final on 7 July 1974 brought the two greatest exponents of 'total football' together for a memorable showdown in the Olympic Stadium in Munich.

Most pundits had Holland down as favourites, despite playing with most of the crowd against them, and that assessment looked spot-on, so to speak, when the Dutch got a penalty in the very first minute when Johan Cruyff was sent crashing in the box by Uli Hoeness. The other Johan, Neeskens, smashed home the penalty, and a Netherlands win looked odds-on. But Müller remained confident, despite the shock start by the home team.

'Once they got their lead, the Dutch completely underestimated us. They thought they'd won the game. But we got lucky and scored an equalizer [a Paul Breitner penalty after Holzenbein had taken a tumble in the area]. We were not afraid of them; tactically, we had to make sure that we didn't let Cruyff into the game, which Berti Vogts achieved admirably.'

With just two minutes to go in the first half, the Germans worked a low cross in from the right and Müller's greatest moment had come.

Above: Müller and Schwarzenbeck celebrate West Germany's 2–1 win in the final against Holland.

Right: Gerd Müller turns away in triumph after slotting home the winning goal.

Left: The German coach, Helmut Schoen, lifts the new World Cup trophy after the 1974 final.

Below: Uli Hoeness, a member of the 1974 World Cup team, now on the staff at Bayern Munich.

'It is always fantastic scoring a goal, but in this case three Dutch defenders did something rather stupid in front of goal. I took a step forward, and they went forward, but then I stepped back and was able to aim the ball between their feet into the far corner of the goal.'

West Germany's 2–1 victory gave them their second World Cup, twenty years after their first, and was due reward for Müller's goalscoring skills, Beckenbauer's supreme leadership and tactical awareness, and Helmut Schoen's coaching services to his country. Immediately after the game, Müller announced his international retirement at the age of twenty-nine, having decided to go out at the top. He continued to play for Bayern Munich, winning two more European Cups in 1975 and 1976, before leaving in 1979 to play for Fort Lauderdale Strikers in the American League.

Despite Müller's achievements and records, opinion about him is still some-what divided. His team-mate Schwarzenbeck says, 'Gerd was simply the best centre-forward ever, he was always in the right place. If anything he was more important to the German team than Franz Beckenbauer, because of his goals.'

Uli Hoeness, another former team-mate from 1974 who is now general man-ager at Bayern Munich, also sings Müller's praises, 'because he scored over 300 goals in the *Bundesliga*, and some incredible goals for the national team, he must be the best goalscorer of all time. I can't imagine that there is anyone to beat him today.'

But some of those who played *against* him take a slightly more sceptical view. Sandro Mazzola, who was in the Italian team for that epic 4–3 semi-final win over West Germany in 1970, says, 'Müller was a typical penalty-area player. In Italy we call these players "robbers", players who don't run a lot, and only help their team-mates a little. But he just had an incredible flair for scoring goals, and although he was small, he was a great header of the ball.'

A meeting with the great Karl-Heinz Rummenigge, who can still smile despite twice being on the losing side in a World Cup final, in 1982 and 1986.

Bobby Charlton, who has more cause than most to rue Müller's skills, sums Müller up thus: 'I would never look at Gerd and say there was a world-class player, but he was a phenomenal finisher. He wasn't interested in anything else, just scoring goals.'

I can't sit on the fence for this one – goals are the point of football and for someone like Müller to score so many at the highest levels of the game makes him a great, even unique, player in my opinion. What matters most, perhaps, is that his play inspired some of the best German strikers who followed him into the national team. Karl-Heinz Rummenigge is a German with the unusual distinction of losing in two World Cup finals, 1982 to Italy and 1986 to Argentina, but he was a top-class player without a shadow of a doubt, and remembers Müller's contribution to his own game.

'I played with him at Bayern for five years after I joined the club at eighteen years old. It was incredible to watch him, not just during a game but also in the training sessions, and I learned a lot of things from him.'

Jürgen Klinsmann, Germany's most potent goalscorer of the 1990s, appreciates what Müller's special skills taught him.

'He had a fantastic instinct, which all the best strikers must have, for where the ball was going to go. He would watch his team-mates, and get ready to play the one–two, and he would attempt goals from almost impossible positions, reminding you that the element of surprise, the early strike, is always one of a striker's best weapons.'

If further evidence were needed, it comes from examining West Germany's form after Müller retired. They still had tremendously resilient players, but without what you might call a 'volume goalscorer', they weren't quite good enough to win another World Cup until 1990. Three goalless draws in their matches in Argentina in 1978 spoke volumes of their plight, and they were effectively out of contention before Austria produced a shock 3–2 win against them in the quarter-final group stage.

Four years later in Spain, Rummenigge was on the verge of becoming the best striker around, as he hit four goals in West Germany's first two matches – although one of them was in a 2–1 defeat by Algeria! – but once he was injured, they struggled. Rummenigge came off the bench for the semi-final, clearly only half-fit, but

Tottenham's Jürgen Klinsmann, one of the stars of Germany's victorious 1990 team, pays tribute to Gerd Müller's 'fantastic instinct for goal'.

still managed to wrestle that emotional game off France, Germany coming back from 3–1 down in extra time to win on penalties. But in the final against Italy, he couldn't force his way into the game.

'They were the better team, anyway,' he reflects, 'but we had only two days to recover after the French game, and were too tired. It was the right result, though.'

West Germany struggled for goals in 1986, too, drawing with Uruguay (1–1) and losing to Denmark (2–0). They were lucky to survive the first round, and beat Morocco in the second by only 1–0, before getting past Mexico 4–1 on penalties in the quarter-final after a goalless draw. They beat a tired France 2–0 in the semi-final, but were 2–0 down to Maradona's Argentina before a late flurry by Rummenigge and Völler got them back to 2–2.

'We were a strong team in 1986, but our tactics, and dealing with the altitude and climate, weakened our challenge,' Rummenigge recalls. 'We approached the final not thinking that we could win it, but surprised Argentina and ourselves before they got the winner.'

By 1990, however, West Germany had the balance right, with Klinsmann coming in to partner Rudi Völler up front. Nine goals in their first two games intimidated their later opponents, especially Holland, who lost their collective rag in a quarter-final which Klinsmann graced with a wonderful goal and a sustained display of attacking football after his partner got himself sent off with Frank Rijkaard in a pretty sleazy exchange of spittle, insults and violence.

They eased their way past Czechoslovakia in the quarter-final, doing only as much as they needed to win, before meeting England in that memorable semi-final in Turin. They may have been lucky to get their goal – Andy Brehme's free-kick taking a vicious deflection off Paul Parker – but once the game went to penalties, there was only one winner. They spent hours practising penalties after training,

World Cup win number three – the West German squad celebrate their 1990 victory over Argentina.

having chosen exactly which five players will take the kicks and in what order. In contrast, we practised penalties as an after-thought, inevitably ending up in some training-ground laughter, and then *still* had to find a volunteer, the unfortunate Chris Waddle, to take the fifth penalty on the night.

The German win over Argentina wasn't the greatest game, but it was unquestionably the right result, and they became only the second European team to win the World Cup three times, after Italy. The Germans' is probably the greater achievement, because their wins have come in the modern age – 1954, 1974 and 1990 – while two of Italy's victories were pre-war.

There's no doubt about the reasons for the German success – meticulous planning and training combined with a consistent playing system and a built-in continuity of coaching. They've only had five coaches since 1938 – Herberger, Schoen, Durwall, Beckenbauer and Vogts. England have had four managers in the last eight years – Bobby Robson, Graham Taylor, Terry Venables and Glenn Hoddle!

What's more, underpinning the organization is the single authority of the DFB – *Deutsche Fussball Bund* – and the requirement that all *Bundesliga* coaches take a two-year coaching and management course before receiving their licence to train.

Tony Woodcock, the former Nottingham Forest and Arsenal striker who played forty-two games for England, went to play for Cologne in the early 1980s and has stayed on to make his home there. He took the course at the DFB's special campus in Cologne and has no doubt about its benefits to the German national system.

'Without the licence, you cannot work in professional football in Germany. So you come to the college and it's eight in the morning to six at night, five days a week for two years. It covers everything from tactics to coaching routines to diet and psychology. It's exhausting, but it feeds the system with one logical step following the

The secret of German success is out – Horst Eckel shows me the delights of human bar-football.

previous one and so on. That's exactly how football is played in Germany. In England, there are three different bodies – the Football Association, the Premier League and the Football League – saying what gets done, and you can get a coaching badge in two weeks, not two years!'

England, I believe, have only just caught on to the advantages of a fully coordinated system for the coaching of football throughout the country, so that the kids coming into the game learn the same things that will stand them in good stead for when they make it as professionals or even internationals. It's not that we have worse players than the Germans – despite recent results suggesting otherwise – but their preparation and planning gives them the extra edge when it comes down to the wire. Even a mediocre German team will be organized and competitive because of the system that all the players have grown up in. If they happen to enjoy a superiority in goalscoring talent, that practically makes them unbeatable.

When they lost to Bulgaria in the 1994 World Cup quarter-finals, the Germans for once looked as though they were running on empty. Two years later, they bounced back winning Euro '96, beating England in the semi-final in yet another penalty shoot-out. They were prepared for that eventuality and we, sadly, hadn't learnt the lesson of 1990.

One small detail from their successful Euro '96 campaign gives a clue to the German mentality – even during the group stage of matches, the training pitch at their hotel in Cheshire was marked out to the exact dimensions of Wembley. They leave nothing to chance! So is it more than an unfortunate coincidence that the German squad are sponsored by Mercedes-Benz, the makers of the world's most reliable cars, while England are still backed by a national breakdown company?

England

Now we come to England, which in their short history of World Cups have embraced both triumph and turnips – I'm not quite old enough to remember the win in 1966, but I can remember all the other ups and downs, especially the two I was involved in as a player, in 1986 and 1990, not to mention the 1970 defeat by West Germany which had me in tears. In between, we had the wilderness years when we didn't qualify for either the 1974 or the 1978 World Cups – unlike Scotland, I am asked to point out – and everybody was disappointed not to be at USA '94.

Even from this brief summary you can see that England's World Cup byword has not been consistency, either in qualifying or indeed in performance levels at the tournaments themselves. It's possible to argue that this reflects a natural cycle in the production of top-class players. No nation possesses the secret of producing them on a regular basis. Brazil seems to do best of all, but as suggested already, that's to do with culture, climate and the size of the population. Certainly it's no coincidence that England's win in 1966 involved three players who were world class by anybody's standards – Gordon Banks, Bobby Moore and Bobby Charlton.

In the absence of such players, teams have to fall back on organization – which should be good in any case – and it's here that I think England have let themselves down compared with Italy and West Germany, the two other European nations to become World Champions. For close on fifty years in Germany's case, and perhaps thirty for Italy, both countries have enjoyed the benefits of a national coaching system – that is, a continuity in playing style and a continuity in the role of the national manager, not to mention a single, dedicated training centre for the team. The Germans and the Italians have these systems running in a planned partnership with their élite leagues – the *Bundesliga* and *Serie A* – which means that there isn't a clash of cultures or egos between the two.

How many of England's World Cup campaigns have been ruined by club versus country rows, or overtaken by the sudden appointment of a mildly successful league manager to the position of national coach? How many times has there been a drastic change in playing style and personnel when a new England manager has taken over, bringing his own assistants in with him? How long has it taken us to realize that the international prestige of the Premiership, and our football's self-esteem, is directly linked to the performance of the national squad?

Right, I'll stop moaning now – for a short while anyway – but I would like to suggest that England's recent revival, both in Euro '96 and in qualifying for France '98 under Glenn Hoddle, has at least something to do with the greater time allocated for the preparation of the national squad. Now, in terms of organization and the way they are playing, England are getting there, and there is a great opportunity for Glenn Hoddle, as a young man – well, I played with him! – to establish himself and his system for perhaps ten or even fifteen years, which will make a big difference from all the usual chopping and changing.

Going further back, I suspect that a great deal of the confusion over England's international status was down to a combination of colonial arrogance and blinkered, bureaucratic thinking, the legacy of which has only just faded. England didn't actually enter the World Cup until the fourth tournament in 1950, having withdrawn from FIFA in the late 1920s in a silly row over payments for players. There was also, I guess, a suspicion of what 'Johnny Foreigner' might be up to, and a feeling that because we invented the game, we must therefore be the best at it. There was, too, the social snobbery that permeated the Football Association, guardians of the amateur game and all its codes, towards the professional leagues which entertained the working masses.

As a result of this package of thinking, England for a long period regarded international competition as rather beneath them – they had little option while out of FIFA – and concentrated on a fairly repetitive cycle of matches against the other home countries, and friendlies against the likes of Belgium,

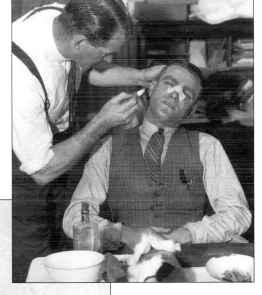

England's first home game against Italy at Highbury in November 1934. England beat the new world champions 3–2, but left-half Eddie Hapgood (*inset*) knew he'd been in a tough match afterwards.

France and Austria. England didn't play Italy until 1933, and our 3–2 home victory over the world champions a year later no doubt reinforced the FA's view of our world dominance. The first game against a South American team didn't come until the 1950 World Cup when England played Chile in Brazil. That's half a century after many British league sides had been on South American tours, spreading the appeal of the game!

Don't get me wrong – I'm not knocking the players of the 1930s or 1940s. There were some real stars among them, but just how much better would they have been if they'd enjoyed genuine international competition?

Of course, all of this isolation came home to roost with a vengeance in a four-year spell at the start of the 1950s, after England had rejoined FIFA and appointed Walter Winterbottom as 'Director of Coaching to the Football Association' – not that Winterbottom was allowed to pick the team, this duty remaining the privilege of an FA committee. Three traumatic defeats shattered official complacency – the 1950 World Cup loss to the USA, the 3–6 home defeat by Hungary in 1953, and then the 7–1 thrashing by the same side in Budapest in 1954. Sir Tom Finney, who was one of England's greatest-ever internationals in my opinion, played in two of these humiliations and witnessed the other. So I made the relatively easy trip up to Preston North End FC, where Tom is the club's President.

You might expect Tom to write off these games and bluster on about how good England used to be, but he's a sharp cookie and

Top: Billy Wright leads England out for their fateful match against Hungary at Wembley on 25 November 1953. The Hungarians won 6–3.

Bottom: Stan Mortensen is beaten to the ball by Hungarian goalkeeper, Gyula Grosics.

knows his football thoroughly. So when I asked him about the experience of the 1950 World Cup, he answered honestly, summoning up the sense of bewilderment he felt at the time.

'I knew nothing at all about the World Cup until the 1948–9 season when there was talk about us entering the competition for the first time. Apart from what we read in newspapers and magazines, we knew very little about Brazil and the other South American countries. We played European teams almost exclusively up till then, so in terms of both the football and the travel, going to the World Cup in 1950 was a journey into the unknown. The preparation was just ten days together, starting in London and including the trip out to Rio de Janeiro. In fact, if I remember rightly, it took us about two full days to get there. The plane broke down, and we had to stop at a place called Recife overnight before going on to Rio. When we got there, we were in a hotel right on Copacabana beach, which was a bit of an experience because even in those days it was alive all night. It was an education but we didn't think it was funny at the time because we got very little sleep.

Sir Tom Finney shows me around Preston's Deepdale ground.

'The other thing that struck us was the fact that it was so hot and the pitches were very hard. We saw the new Maracana Stadium, and Brazil's first game against Mexico, which they won 4–0. It was quite an eye-opener, I can tell you, because the Brazilians had some fantastic skills, even in those days. The thing that struck me most was that they were playing in these lovely lightweight boots, more like slippers really, while all we had were those old, big brown boots. Later on we were given a pair of the lightweight ones each by the shop who made them, and I used them for several years.'

Despite having seen Brazil at their mesmerizing best, Tom remembers thinking that 'England could qualify for the later stages because of the group we were in, with Chile, USA and Spain.'

England comfortably won their game against Chile in Rio by 2–0, with the goals coming from Stan Mortensen and Wilf Mannion. But then they flew up to the coastal resort of Belo Horizonte to play the United States, and duly suffered one of England's most humiliating defeats.

'It was one of those games that can happen to any team. We must have hit the woodwork four or five times, and then they broke away and had two efforts at goal and scored one. They were really excited after the game, jumping about and dancing whereas we just trooped off. You wanted the ground to open up and swallow you. There were no excuses really, but the pitch wasn't up to much. It was a great embarrassment – probably the biggest of my career. The English press had been writing us up as possible winners of the tournament, so we knew this wouldn't look

England's first World Cup game, against Chile in Rio de Janeiro, 25 June 1950. Tom Finney waltzes past Chilean defender Roldan. (*Inset*) Sir Tom tells me about that first World Cup experience.

too good back home. I mean, we still had a chance to qualify if we'd won our third game against Spain, but we lost 1–0, and had what looked like a decent goal by Jackie Milburn disallowed in the first few minutes of the game. One of the Spanish full-backs was standing on the line, but the referee still gave offside. We played quite well, and I think we were unfortunate to lose. But teams like Spain were expert at closing up at the back once they'd got a lead.

'The next thing we knew we were on our way back, which I always thought was a big mistake, because we could have learnt some things about the modern game if we'd stayed on a few days. Spain went on to play Brazil in the next stage and got

The 1950 England World Cup team lines up before losing 1–0 to Spain. Future manager Alf Ramsey is second from left, back row.

beat 6–1, so that says something about our relative merits, I suppose.'

Zizinho, one of the Brazilian players from the 1950 tournament to whom I spoke on my travels, actually watched the England v. USA game on television, because England were apparently one of the teams they feared most. Zizinho recalled his reactions to what was a shock defeat.

'Flavio Costa had made the trip over to England to watch them play and came

Nat Lofthouse and Tom Finney caused Uruguay some problems in their 1954 quarter-final, but Uruguay came out on top, winning 4–2.

back saying wonderful things about the English team. So when they lost to the United States nobody could believe it, it was impossible! I saw England play and they were a really good team, but they were lacking something. It was a machine with no heart, good team, good players – Tom Finney, Stanley Matthews, Billy Wright and Alf Ramsey – but they didn't have the desire to grit their teeth and score a goal to win the game.'

'He's probably right in a way,' Tom admitted when I relayed these remarks to him, 'because in a game like that, once it starts to go away from you, you *do* begin to lose confidence. Perhaps the worst thing to come out of it for me was when I met Pelé much later on, and he told me that his dad had taken him specially to that game because he thought England would be a great team! That really hurt. Even today I get people coming up to me asking if I was involved in that game, and I have to tell them that I was.'

But Tom did bring some happier memories back with him, images of the way Brazil played football which influenced the way he saw out the rest of his career.

'They used the short ball a lot, kept possession and passed it around, both at the back and up front. This was the style I'd always wanted to see in our game, with skill and dribbling and pace being given a premium throughout the team, rather than the sudden long ball.'

Tom's next session of footballing education came with the two games against Hungary in 1953 and '54, about which he speaks in detail in the following chapter. This time it was a combination of skill *and* tactics which proved to be the eye-opener, with Hungary deploying Hidegkuti as a deep-lying centre-forward.

'Those two games definitely changed things for us,' Finney insists. 'People realized that there must be something wrong in our game to get beaten by such scores, and began to understand that we weren't the best team in Europe, not by any stretch of the imagination. The general attitude had always been that we were the best, but that couldn't be sustained any longer.'

Even so, Finney says that England's squad approached the 1954 World Cup in Switzerland 'feeling quietly confident that we'd do reasonably well'. But in their first game in Pool 4, they threw away a 3–1 lead over Belgium by letting them come back to level 3–3. Bizarrely, extra time was played even though this wasn't a knock-out game, and the same pattern emerged again, with Nat Lofthouse putting England 4–3 up before an own goal gave the Belgians the equalizer and a share of the points.

A 2–0 win over hosts Switzerland nevertheless allowed England to qualify at the top of the pool, but in a free-scoring quarter-final, they were beaten 4–2 by a fluent Uruguay side who had yet to be beaten in any World Cup – oh, all right, it's not as impressive as all that because they'd won the trophy in 1930 and didn't play again till 1950, when they won it again.

'They were a very strong physical team,' Finney recalls, 'but they were also tremendously skilful, and again they had these ball-players in the defence, like Brazil had.' One small consolation for Tom, was that he scored his first World Cup goal in that game. Once again, England were whisked quickly home – presumably to save the FA money – rather than staying on to watch and learn from the final stages of the tournament.

As the domestic game rapidly expanded and English club sides were contemplating European club opposition for the first time, the England team, fortified by a strong element of Manchester United's 'Busby Babes' – Tommy Taylor, Roger Byrne and Duncan Edwards – lost only one match in 1956 and 1957, and even beat

England v Uruguay in the 1954 World Cup quarter-final in Basle. Nat Lofthouse, watched by No. 7, Stanley Matthews, wins the ball, but Uruguay won the game 4–2.

Brazil 4–2 at Wembley. Tragically, the Munich air crash on 6 February 1958 killed all three Manchester United internationals and several other promising players. Bobby Charlton survived and although he went to the 1958 World Cup in Sweden, he didn't get a game.

'They would have made quite a difference, I'm sure,' Sir Bobby reflected sadly, when I nipped down from Preston to interview him at Old Trafford. Bobby's time would come later, but 1958 at least allowed Tom Finney a World Cup swan song, while for at least two other England players in that tournament, Don Howe and Bobby Robson, the taste for international competition they acquired there would be something they never lost.

England were unlucky not to make the quarter-final stages in 1958. After drawing with Russia, a game in which Tom Finney scored a late equalizer from the penalty spot – 'I didn't know whether to hit it with my right foot or left,' he says, disarmingly testifying to his own skills – England held the eventual champions Brazil to a goalless draw. They were the only team to stop Brazil scoring. England went on to draw 2–2 with Austria and finished in joint second place in Pool 4, on the same points and with the same goals total as Russia. In the play-off in Gothenburg, England lost 1–0 to Russia. Tom Finney had been injured in the first game and was ruled out of the rest with knee ligament trouble. He stayed on to watch, and his appetite for the World Cup tournament, despite disappointment in three competitions, remains undimmed.

England's leading goalscorer of all time, Sir Bobby Charlton

'It's changed tremendously of course, it was far more open in my day, there were more pure dribblers around, but it's the best stage there is for footballers. The pace of the game has increased hugely, and technique has improved all round. But England have got some fine young players and must have a chance in 1998.'

England qualified for the 1962 World Cup in Chile out of a relatively easy group containing just Portugal and Luxembourg. They won all their games apart from a 1–1 draw in Portugal. Once there, they found themselves in a tough Group 4, which included Hungary, Argentina and Bulgaria.

Bobby Charlton remembers feeling 'it was a long way from home. We played a couple of matches on the way there, but Walter Winterbottom more or less had his team set out, and for the players who weren't picked, boredom was a big factor.'

England were beaten 2–1 by Hungary, but helped their cause enormously by defeating Argentina 3–1, a game in which Charlton scored his first World Cup goal. A 0–0 draw against Bulgaria – 'the worst game I've ever played in,' according to Charlton – put England through to the quarter-finals where they again faced Brazil, albeit without the now injured Pelé. Vava and Garrincha more than made up for Pelé's loss, sharing the goals between them in a 3–1 win which sent England home.

'It was that game which convinced me that we could win in 1966,' Charlton says forcefully. 'We got to 1–1 and caused a lot of problems for them, so I knew when they became champions again that we weren't too far behind them and that with some good players coming through, we'd give a good account of ourselves in 1966.'

1962 marked the end of Walter Winterbottom's sixteen-year reign as England coach, and Alf Ramsey, who'd just taken Ipswich Town to the First Division championship, was appointed, famously predicting that England would win the World Cup in 1966.

'Winterbottom was a theorist, but he'd never played the game as a professional,' Bobby Charlton reflects. 'I thought that when Alf told you something it was as one professional to another. We could work in more detail. Walter was a terrific person, but it was just that extra professionalism that he didn't quite have.'

During the build-up to the 1966 World Cup, English clubs began to make their first impact on European competitions, with both Spurs (1963) and then West Ham (1965) winning the European Cup-Winners' Cup. The emergence of such players as Bobby Moore, Martin Peters, Jimmy Greaves and, later, Geoff Hurst, helped build up the squad, while Liverpool were also becoming a force in both domestic and European football, largely through the goalscoring skills of Roger Hunt. In Leicester

An England international scorers' conflab: me (forty-eight goals), Bobby Charlton (forty-nine) and Geoff Hurst (twenty-four).

City's Gordon Banks, England had the makings of a world-class goalkeeper. The other advantage of being hosts, apart from not having to qualify, nor to travel and acclimatize, was that the England squad was given a two-week holiday at the end of the domestic season in 1966, before returning to prepare for the tournament.

Bobby Charlton remembers how well this was received by the squad.

'You really do need a break between one season and another. You can't continue playing football, so this holiday put the lads in a great mood and went down fantastically well with all concerned. Alf gaves us a date on which we should report to Lilleshall for training, and then off we went. It didn't impress the papers who all seemed to think we should get to it right way, but Alf's intention was to have us fresh rather than tired. The training itself wasn't very hard because Alf knew how fit we'd all be after a season of football. So we just worked on light training, and the rest of the time was spent talking about tactics and such.'

When England's opening game against Uruguay ended in a goalless draw, however, the press critics thought their objections had been vindicated.

'Uruguay were a very disciplined team, very organized at the back. And they just wouldn't let you get past them, giving you a little nudge or a push if you tried it. But we were patient enough not to lose. The spirit inside the camp stayed very good despite the result, and we all still felt we were going to win. We had a great team, which had hardly lost a game in the previous year or so. We weren't afraid of anyone.'

England showed more form in their 2–0 win over Mexico, marked by one of Bobby Charlton's specials from around twenty-five yards, and comfortably beat

France 2–0 to top Group 1 from Uruguay. At this stage, Jimmy Greaves had played in all three games but hadn't had much of a sniff at goal, which worried Alf Ramsey in terms of scoring power, but Roger Hunt at least had got three goals.

'My goal against Mexico got us going,' Bobby recalls. 'We felt suddenly that we were off and running which is why I jumped up a lot when it went it in.'

Despite qualifying for the next stage, there was no euphoria in the England camp, nor much chance of it being imported by press or fans.

'Alf kept us away from everyone. We were never really allowed out on our own. If we wanted to do something – like going to the pictures or a visit to Pinewood Film Studios – we did it as a team. Nobody was allowed to pursue any individual excursions. After a match it was straight back to the hotel. He'd let us have a drink, but again it was as a team, all together. Newspaper people and others were kept at a distance. Alf had strict rules about giving them access. They had it when he felt it was right, and they didn't like it of course. It was probably one of the things that eventually brought him down.'

England's quarter-final opponents were Argentina, who finished second behind West Germany in Group 2, winning two matches – against Spain and Switzerland – and holding the Germans to a goalless draw at Villa Park. They met at Wembley on Saturday, 23 June, in front of a 90,000 crowd, and the game became notorious for the wild behaviour of the Argentinian captain, Antonio Rattin.

'I was fouled,' Bobby remembers, 'and then there was this big hullabaloo around the referee because he'd given the free-kick our way. Rattin started arguing with the ref, and he kept touching his armband as if to say, "I'm the captain, I have the right to speak to you." But he went on and on and you could see the referee waving for him to go away but he wouldn't. In South America, I think it's common practice to berate the referee, to push him. The game was going on and Rattin was running round after the referee still shouting at him until the ref had had enough and sent him off. Then, of course, he took for ever to leave the field, and walked around the pitch very slowly, making everything worse for himself. I thought it was stupid for a captain to do that and end up back in the dressing-room leaving his ten team-mates to battle it out in a World Cup quarter-final.'

Geoff Hurst heads England's match-winning goal in the tempestuous 1966 World Cup quarter-final against Argentina.

While Rattin threw all the toys out of the pram, England kept their concentration.

'Rattin was such a mammoth figure for them, that I think it had an effect on Argentina when he was sent off, although it took us for ever to get the goal.' It was Geoff Hurst, in for the unfortunate Greaves, who headed home England's winner in the second half. 'I think Alf wanted more of a target man than Jimmy could be, someone who was stronger and who could hold the ball up. There was no big fuss. The manager just gave the decision to the team on the bus, and nobody was given an explanation. There was no dissent, because we all respected Alf, and we all thought he must know better than us.'

Ironically, after all the fuss, Charlton and Rattin later became quite close friends and regularly keep in touch.

'He's always ringing me up,' Bobby says, 'especially before a World Cup.'

England now faced Portugal, and the awesome goal-scoring power of Eusebio, in the semi-final at Wembley on a steamy summer night. It was probably one of Charlton's greatest games; he scored both goals to take England through to a World Cup final for the first and, up until now, only time.

'I had this great feeling for Portuguese teams. I always played well against them for some reason. So I expected to win. I had a stiff neck in the afternoon, but I forgot that as soon as we kicked off. By this time, I had so much confidence in our defence that I couldn't see Portugal scoring, so it was simply a question of us getting a goal. Eusebio was the only danger, but Alf had designated Nobby Stiles to look after him. He shook him up early on, and Nobby never left his side really. When Alf said, "I want you to mark Eusebio," Nobby said, "Where do you want me to mark him, boss?" That's the story, anyway. People underestimated Nobby's skill. He was a great reader of a game, really fast, sharp and quick; and tough, too. So he was the perfect man for the job – a world-class player in his own right.'

Charlton's two strikes – one after Roger Hunt had chased down a ball which the Portuguese keeper José Pereira fumbled clear, and one from a lay-off by Geoff Hurst – closed the game down for England, although Jack Charlton's reflex hand-ball allowed Eusebio to pull one back from a penalty close to the end. England were in the World Cup final!

Although football culture has changed emphatically since 1966, I think I can guess what it must have been like for the England squad of the time, with three and a bit days to wait for the biggest game of your life. In my experience, time takes on a new speed limit on these occasions. You can't wait for the game to start, but equally, you want to pack as much preparation in as possible, without too many demands from the press and photographers. I asked Sir Bobby how the mood in the England camp changed once they knew they were in the final.

'Once we'd got to the semi-final, the whole country was alive, so reaching the final had an enormous effect. We weren't allowed to take a lot of phone calls from outside because Alf wanted us left alone. We were as well prepared as we could be for every match. All the little superstitions started to come out in each player, everything had to be done according to them. I mean, I'm not superstitious but I had to fall in with them all to keep everybody happy. Then came the morning of the match, and the game seemed hours away. We just didn't know what to do with ourselves. The girls were coming down that night for the official function so Ray Wilson [the left back] and I got permission to go into Hendon to buy a shirt.'

The 1966 Golden Boot winner, Eusebio of Portugal, is watched by England's Nobby Stiles in their semi-final game. England won 2–1.

Sociologists will no doubt want to log this revelation to prove beyond all doubt just how exciting the sixties were! More seriously, this brief escape into the real world revealed to Charlton – if he didn't know it already – just how World Cup crazy the country had become.

'Everybody who saw us in town couldn't believe we were there. They were all asking what we were doing and why we weren't at the hotel and what was the match going to be like. We had to tell them the bus wasn't leaving till 1.30 p.m. Eventually the time passed, we read all the good-luck telegrams, had our team meeting, and then got on the coach for Wembley. All you could see were flags and crowds waving. Even a firestation was done out with Union Jacks. It was such a relief when the game got started.'

But England soon went a goal down, as Ray Wilson mis-headed a clearance and Helmut Haller pounced to tuck a right-foot shot past Gordon Banks. It was just the start that the England team, and the watching millions, must have dreaded. Yet according to Bobby, the team took the setback in their stride.

'It wasn't the end of the world. We felt we'd played our toughest match against Argentina. We'd analysed every German player and we just thought that we were a

better team than them. Really. As for being marked by Beckenbauer, I reconciled myself to it. I thought that it would probably hurt them more than us, because England without Bobby Charlton would still be better than Germany without Franz. Alf had told me to stick with him. He was young and fast, and I was the only one who could keep up with him. I had good legs, and I was quite fit and sharp, so there was no chance of him getting away from me either.'

Date with destiny: England line up before their 1966 World Cup final against West Germany, and (*inset*) captains Bobby Moore and Uwe Seeler toss up.

With two of the teams' best players effectively cancelling each other out, it was left to others in the midfield to provide the necessary edge. Alan Ball had a fantastic game down the right side, while Martin Peters' free-floating role meant that the Germans could never really pick him up. England soon equalized when Bobby Moore took a quick free-kick and found Geoff Hurst's well-timed run into the box. Hurst had all the time in the world to plant his header beyond Tilkowski. Charlton recalls the moment when England calmed their supporters' nerves.

'There was quite a bit of noise in the stadium when the Germans scored, because they had a lot of fans following them. But Bobby Moore always knew where Geoff would be, from playing together at West Ham, which was one of the benefits of selecting little groups of players from the same club. Once we'd equalized, I wasn't bothered at all then.'

Martin Peters gave England the lead in the second half, and with just seconds to go, it looked like England were home and about to get very drunk. But the Germans won a disputed free-kick outside the area, and when the ball was played in, it ping-ponged around for what seemed like ages before Wolfgang Weber stretched out at the far post to turn the ball past Banks. Bobby Charlton says that he didn't realize how close England had been to winning.

'I thought there was about ten minutes to go. I never look at the touchline to see what they're signalling, and I didn't have time anyway. But when they equalized and the ref blew as soon as we kicked off, I realized how close we'd been. I still felt we'd win though.'

Surprisingly, Sir Bobby had only watched a full recording of the 1966 final for the first time quite recently, and ironically in view of what happened in the match itself, he did so with Franz Beckenbauer.

'He still moans a bit about the third goal, but I just say we'd have beaten you anyway, whether it was allowed or not. Franz did admit after watching the game with me that it was the first time he'd realized "how much England were better than Germany on the day". We were on top, we were better, we were fitter, we were better organized, we had more chances. So it's not fair to suggest that we only won because of a linesman's decision! When we came off at the end, it was such a thrill to be able to say that we were now the best in the world.'

It was later that the magnitude of the team's achievement, not just for the players themselves but for the whole of England, began to sink in.

'It was after the match, when the team coach was on its way to Kensington for the function, that we saw every window open in every house we passed, with somebody hanging out waving a flag. It was sensational. That's when I thought to myself, "What would have happened if we'd lost?"'

The formal celebrations at the Royal Garden Hotel – with each semi-final team

With seconds left to full time in the 1966 final, Wolfgang Weber puts the ball past Gordon Banks to level the game at 2–2. But England scored two goals in extra time to win the World Cup for the first time.

The England players celebrate their historic victory. Bobby Charlton holds the Jules Rimet trophy

present – took an unusual twist for many of the England team when they became stuck in a lift because of the sheer hordes of people who were thronging the lobby and the bars.

'There were about twelve of us squeezed into a little lift, trying to get down to the basement because we couldn't get out on the ground floor, and it broke down between floors. We had to prise the door open and climb out. I did think at one point what it might look like in the papers – "Twelve World Cup Heroes Suffocate in Lift". But we got out and went off for a couple of drinks. It was nice and I knew it would be nice for ever.'

Obviously, the German master-plan came into operation twenty-four hours too late…sorry, that's a joke. Four years later, the laughs were on us in one of the most painful episodes of English football. England had reached the quarter-finals of the

England's Martin Peters tussles with Dobias of Czechoslovakia during their 1970 Group 3 match. England won 1–0.

1970 World Cup in Mexico, having beaten both Romania and Czechoslovakia 1–0, and lost narrowly to Brazil, also 1–0. That was an epic match, about which the Brazilian captain Carlos Alberto says 'that was our final'. Banks's save from Pelé, Jairzinho's wonderful goal, Bobby Moore going head-to-head with Pelé, and the two embracing each other in respect afterwards – it's up there with all the best World Cup matches for the sheer intensity of the play and the raw intelligence which informed it.

'It was like a chess match,' Bobby Charlton says, still smiling in remembrance at an example of football at its best, though he contradicts what many pundits have tried to assert, that the England team of 1970 was stronger than the one in 1966. 'I can't go along with that, simply because we didn't win in 1970.'

That brings us to the fatal game at Leon – with Gordon Banks out with a dodgy tummy, and England bravely going two goals up despite this reverse, everything suddenly began to go 'Herr-shaped', as it has done ever since, really. Alan Mullery had put England ahead in the first half, and Martin Peters stole in to poach another goal at the far post from Keith Newton's cross. With half an hour or so to play, England looked comfortable. Then Alf Ramsey took Bobby Charlton off. When I spoke to Gerd Müller, who scored the winning goal that day, he confessed to being 'amazed that England would even consider taking Charlton off, because it allowed Franz Beckenbauer to take over the game'.

'Well, I was getting on a bit and it was quite hard physically. But I must be honest, I felt full of running. Alf must have thought let's save things a little bit, not burn our boats in this.

'I was still on the pitch when their first goal went in. I was being called over to the touchline where Colin Bell was waiting to come on for me, when Beckenbauer went forward and scored. I was really disappointed to go off, because I felt I could run for ever.

'With all due respect to Peter Bonetti, the bigger tragedy was not my substitution but Gordon Banks's illness earlier in the day. Banks was the best goalkeeper in the world by miles. We could never get a shot past him in training. So there was that, and I also think it was fate as well, the ball just dropped for them that day – for Seeler's goal, he was just heading in the general direction but it floated in. So we were out, and that was my last match for England!'

Geoff Hurst goes close with a header in England's dramatic quarter-final against West Germany in Leon, 1970. *(Inset)* Manchester City's Francis Lee takes on the defence in bustling style.

Astute readers will no doubt draw parallels between my final substitution against Sweden in 1992 in the European Championship and Bobby's in Mexico in 1970, and it does seem a bit odd that England's first and second top scorers should bow out in the same fashion on a traumatic losing day. Maybe that's our fault, too, for hanging on too long – leaving the game is a matter of good timing, and few of us have the power to get it exactly right.

Even with that departure, Bobby retains his affection for the World Cup, not least in his role as one of the team campaigning for England to stage the tournament in 2006.

'There is nowhere else in football that you can truly measure yourself. Take George Best, he didn't make it on to a world stage. Although he was a great player, he didn't get the chance to prove it. If you're a footballer with any ambition, it's the only event to play in.'

Well, quite. Only England didn't manage it for another twelve years after 1970, thanks to Poland getting their outrageous draw at Wembley in 1973, and Italy qualifying on a slightly better goal-difference in 1977. It must have been particularly sad for a whole generation of English players, whose careers spanned those twelve years, that they never reached the World Cup finals, and it makes me feel very privileged to have made it on two successive occasions. When you think of some of the great players like Kevin Keegan, who only played that last bit of the decisive England v. Spain game in 1982 – and missed the best chance, to boot – you realize how fine a margin there is between a fulfilled career and a frustrated one.

At which point, I suppose, it's time to go on to my own contribution to the history of Golden Boot winners. It obviously wasn't practical, nor indeed modest, for me to interview myself, even though I do mutter a bit to the mirror when I'm shaving in the morning. So my old chum Alan Hansen posed the questions when we sat down for a natter in the *Blue Peter* garden at the back of the BBC's Television Centre, alongside a statue of Patch, or was it Petra? Anyway, here I've linked up all the answers to give some kind of account of my career, with particular references to the two World Cups in which I played.

Alan Hansen gives me the Scottish Inquisition in the 'Blue Peter' garden.

As is probably well known, thanks to a certain brand of crisp which shares the same name as a Tottenham goalkeeper, I was born and brought up in Leicester, and supported the local team. My two favourite players were Frank Worthington, for his style and his extravagant finishing, and Peter Shilton because I thought, and still do, that he was the best. I'd loved football from an early age, and liked scoring goals, but there was one particular year, when I was ten or eleven, when I scored something like 160 goals in a season for the school team, and that started me thinking about playing for real when I grew up. I enjoyed cricket very much, too, but I suppose if I'd taken that up I might have blighted David Gower's career…!

It was a great thrill when I joined Leicester at sixteen, even though Jock Wallace was a tough manager to work for. My pace, which was always my best asset for most of my career, eventually brought me a few goals and I managed to get into the first team during the early 1980s. I won my first England cap in 1984, when I was still at Leicester, coming on as a substitute against Scotland. I moved to Everton in 1985, and by the time I was called into the 1986 World Cup squad, I'd won thirteen caps and scored six goals, three of which had come in

A hero, a team-mate and a pal: Peter Shilton, England's goalkeeper in 125 internationals.

a World Cup qualifier against Turkey at Wembley.

So I wasn't exactly the finished article but Bobby Robson must have seen something to make him persist with me and take a risk on a World Cup place. True, I'd got a lot of goals in my single season with Everton, and had won both the PFA and Football Writers' Player of the Year Awards in 1986, but the World Cup was a

Left: 'The boy Lineker' in the early years at Leicester City.
Above: Back to Barcelona to talk to Bobby Robson.

different proposition – better class of defenders, more likely to run into a sweeper system which would negate some of the long ball goals I'd scored at Everton, not to mention the sheer nervousness of being on a world stage in front of millions of viewers. But I was developing my own style, and I knew my limitations as a player, which basically meant that as a striker my best chances were to pounce on defenders' mistakes and to make runs into space in the hope that the ball would come to me. I reckoned that about two times out of ten this would happen and I'd get a chance on goal. But the percentages are certainly different at World Cup level – you might only get one chance a game, and it was my job to be there and to take it when it came.

As is well documented, England didn't get off to the best start in the 1986 World Cup, losing 1–0 to Portugal and drawing 0–0 with Morocco, a game in which we lost Bryan Robson through a shoulder injury and Butch Wilkins through a silly dismissal. This meant changes for the vital game against Poland. Perhaps the most crucial as far as I was concerned was the replacement of Mark Hateley with Peter Beardsley. I'd played quite well with Mark, but it was very much a classic English attack with me feeding off his headed flicks, and that didn't work out so well when you have a sweeper to deal with them.

With Peter Beardsley, however, he would drop back a lot more and push me up to the front, on the backs of defenders, and try and play me in with little passes

which would allow me to exploit my pace. We also had a bit more width in that game with Steve Hodge coming in on the left. The team's confidence hadn't been too good after two bad results, but as Bobby Robson recalled when I spoke to him in Barcelona, he and Don Howe had 'a long discussion into the night about the best team, settled on a formation, and decided to trust the players'.

Not that this stopped Bobby from producing his flip-chart in the team meeting, on which he'd written down every possible permutation of results which would keep us in the competition. But we knew the basic situation against Poland – only a win would do. So there was a lot of determination to get it right. When Peter Shilton made a good early save, we began to think it might be our day. Sure enough, as I got the ball on the left and then laid it square – much to the dismay of BBC commentator Barry Davies – Gary Stevens' run on the right was picked up and he crossed the ball low into the box. I'd decided to make a run for that space anyway,

The three goals that changed my life, Mexico 1986.
Top: Celebrating the first against Poland.
Above: Spot the ball – volleying the second past Josef Mylnarczyk's right shoulder.
Right (and inset): Mylnarczyk drops a corner onto my left foot, and England have won 3–0!

got half a yard on my marker, and was able to hit an instant shot into the goal. It was probably the biggest goal I've ever scored because of its importance to the England team's morale, not mention my own. I hadn't scored in six internationals, which is long time for a new boy hoping to keep his place.

Now suddenly there were chances coming thick and fast, and from Steve Hodge's cross I got my toe on another and it went into the top corner. Shortly afterwards, the Polish keeper dropped a corner at my feet, and I was even able to turn it home with my left peg, so easy was the chance. I had a first-half hat-trick to my name, and England were through to the quarter-finals.

I have to confess here that I was aware of the Golden Boot Award, mainly because my dad had backed me to win it at odds of 16–1. I hadn't dared speak to him after the first two games, for obvious reasons! The result lifted my confidence as well as the team's, and I was, to use a familiar expression, in cloud cuckoo land. Mind you, I was out on my feet in the second half due to the heat, the altitude and the humidity. We'd prepared for some of this by training in the mountains of Colorado and doing hour-long exercises in a steam room, but even that doesn't take into account the nervous energy you use up in a real match. I probably also took a lot out of myself with the goal celebrations, wasting energy charging around looking for someone to kiss.

With our midfield now containing Glenn Hoddle as the passer and Everton's Peter Reid as the holding player, it felt like we had decent balance, and a style to suit those conditions. You really couldn't go all out like in an English league game – you had to be patient, keep possession and then move quickly when a chance was created.

I got two more goals against Paraguay in our 3–0 win, but this header wasn't one of them!

The second-round game against Paraguay followed a similar pattern to the Poland game – a good early save by Shilton and then Glenn Hoddle's pass set me up for a goal. I fell over in the first attempt to score and just managed to poke the ball home when it came back in, with Peter Beardsley waiting behind me if I missed. Peter got a goal for himself in due course, while I was off for attention after getting a Paraguayan elbow in the throat. Peter took my position at a corner – a couple of paces off the goalkeeper – and was able to turn and shoot home when the ball was played in. Watching from the sidelines, I felt that I'd been robbed of a goal that would have been mine if I'd been on the pitch. But soon enough a cross from the other Gary Stevens (of Spurs) allowed me to tap home my second of the match and fifth in the World Cup. I think the total 'yardage' of all of these goals wouldn't have been much over fifteen, but that was the sort of player I was – a 'box player' in trade terms.

We were now through to the quarter-finals where we faced Argentina and Diego Maradona, who was playing right on the top of his brilliant form. Naturally, Bobby and the players discussed what we might do to stop him, but as English players didn't go in much for man-to-man marking we decided that the best way was to try to crowd him out with numbers and force him to play deep. We felt that while Maradona was exceptional, there wasn't much in the rest of the Argentinian team to be frightened of, or that we couldn't handle...apart from Maradona punching the ball into the net! Let Peter Shilton describe that terrible moment when our World Cup fate was decided by a supreme act of deception.

'Everybody in the ground knew what had happened. When Maradona went up for the ball he put his hand up, but he flicked his head as well to make it look like that was where the contact was. A few people still ask me whether he did handle it, but there are pictures to show that's what happened. Besides which, as a keeper, I just knew what he'd done.

'It was a fifty-fifty ball – I could have stayed on my line, but I think Maradona would have just pulled it down and blasted it past me, so I had to go for it. In that situation I'd normally make sure that I'd get the ball and hit the forward as well, but because I was stretching I just couldn't quite get close enough to him in time. He knew that, which is why he used his hand to flick it over me.'

Bobby Robson, sitting aghast on the touchline, waiting for a linesman's flag that never came, recalls the sickening feeling of having been cheated.

'I knew it wasn't a goal the instant he did it, and for about three seconds I didn't worry, and then I realized that the linesman and the referee were running back to the halfway line, and that the goal had been given. What annoyed me most, though, was the way Maradona jumped up and down to the public in celebration, pumping the air, as if to say what a great goal he'd scored. And that still sticks in my throat...'

My own abiding memory of the incident, from an up-field viewpoint, was of Shilts and the rest of the England defence chasing the referee waving their hands at him, and then realizing that he'd still given the goal against us. What riled me most was all this 'hand of God' guff afterwards.

But if there were moral and legal doubts about Maradona's first goal, there could be none about his second. It began just inside his own half with a turn which took Peter Reid right out of the game – no big deal you might think, but the turf in that Azteca Stadium in Mexico City was actually very loose and not very conducive to ball control, which makes Maradona's subsequent run on the England goal even more impressive. To be able to move at such speed and still have the ball under control was the hallmark of a great player, and I have to admit that I think this goal was probably the best I ever saw scored against a team I was playing in.

We were on our way out, 2–0 down, but Bobby Robson's decision to bring John Barnes on completely threw the Argentinians' defensive cover, as their manager Carlos Bilardo admitted. It was from John Barnes's left-wing cross that I scored my

England goalkeeper Peter Bonetti came in for some harsh criticism when Engand lost 3–2 to West Germany in the quarter-finals of the 1970 Mexico World Cup, and he was never selected again. But, for the record, his previous six international appearances have happier statistics – all six games won, ten goals scored and only one conceded.

Above: Substitute John Barnes takes on the Argentinian defence.

Left: The goal that won me the Golden Boot – a header from Barnesy's cross. But Argentina went through 2–1.

sixth goal, a free header from four yards out, right up my street. I learned from my talk with Bilardo that this goal had saved him a couple of thousand dollars, as he'd promised each of his central defenders a reward if they stopped me from scoring!

A few minutes later came the incident which I still can't fathom, even though I've watched it over a thousand times. John Barnes had got to the by-line again and his cross beat the goalkeeper and was travelling along the Argentinian goal-line when I threw myself at it, completely convinced that I would score. I ended up in the back of the net but when I looked around the ball wasn't with me – it had somehow missed both me and the defender who'd been climbing all over me, and I still don't know how. I strongly believe that if we'd equalized we'd have gone on to win that game, and then who knows what would have happened?

In the end I was left with the depression of defeat, the sensation of having been cheated, but the personal consolation of leading the goalscorers' table. As we returned home, and the disappointment subsided, I became anxious about keeping my lead in the hunt for the Golden Boot, even though there was nothing I could do about it. When Maradona scored two against Belgium in the semi-final to bring his total to five, I was convinced that he'd get at least one more in the final, and probably two, knowing him. So I watched the Argentina–West Germany final not caring who won the game but very much caring who scored, and miraculously Maradona was kept off the score-sheet. I was left out on my own as top scorer. I felt a genuine sense of history and achievement which ultimately led me to research the stories of all my fellow winners of the Golden Boot.

In the four years until the 1990 World Cup I had the Barcelona experience, which unquestionably improved me as a player, and I also returned to English football with Spurs. In that time I developed some ideas of my own about the game, about having a ball-player in defence, and about my own way of playing. I had to, of course, because one of the consequences of such a public achievement is that all the best markers are deployed against you – the Mark Lawrensons as opposed to the Alan Hansens! I'd grown used to man-marking in Spain where I'd had to change the angle of my runs, away from the sweeper. I passed this kind of information on to the likes of Glenn Hoddle, Bryan Robson, Chris Waddle and even Gazza; they picked up on it when we were playing together and learnt to adapt to the new way in which I was playing.

The ecstasy before the agony – my last World Cup goal draws us level against the Germans in the 1990 semi-final in Turin but, as we all remember, they went through 4–3 on penalties.

I thought we had a great squad for 1990, probably the best in my time, so although we struggled in the group games against Ireland, Holland and Egypt, there were some positional changes, like the deployment of Mark Wright as sweeper, which I felt would make us into a better team. The senior players had talked to Bobby Robson about this change and he'd admitted that he was thinking along those lines, too. The best managers are the ones who listen to the players.

The press coverage was more volatile than ever in 1990, I'm afraid, and a touch personal too, but you have to put that aside once you're on the pitch. After that sticky start, our World Cup was transformed by David Platt's late extra-time winner against Belgium; the whole squad was flying then. Just look at my face on the TV replays and you'll know how we were all feeling. I felt we deserved our win nonetheless.

I'll admit we were fortunate to get past Cameroon, who were a really tough team, and skilful with it. We needed both the penalties I scored once we were 2–1 down, because I don't think we would have scored in open play. Although it was an unsatisfactory way to win, it was still part of the game proper, rather than a shoot-out. For the first one, I could almost see the challenge coming in. I thought that if I took the ball on, the guy would hit me, which is what he did. Same thing with the second really, letting the keeper come at me and then not moving my legs once the ball had gone so that he was bound to hit me. I suppose I was too honest when I was younger! Still, I had to score both penalties. I opted for power rather than placement in both cases, and tried not to think about how many millions of people were watching me.

This put us through to the semi-final against West Germany. You probably know the story of that game, and I've lived through it a million times since that sweaty night in Turin. Suffice to say that I thought we would win when I equalized, because England were in a groove and playing well. But the Germans, as we know to our cost, they just won't stay down. When Chris Waddle's shot screamed past their keeper but hit the post, I have to admit that the old alarm bells began to ring. So it was on to penalties – it was scary but not as bad as against Cameroon, because if we'd lost to them we'd have been slaughtered. My own rule is always take the first penalty – which I did, and scored. The one you don't want to take is the fifth, which is what poor Chris Waddle had to do, after Stuart Pearce had missed. It's a strange business, the shoot-out. You focus on yourself to begin with and then worry about the others, praying they don't miss. But you have to hand it to the Germans; Shilts didn't have a chance with any of their kicks.

Needless to say, we were all devastated by the result. As Bobby Robson says, 'We really fancied we could have beaten Argentina, and got one back on Maradona.' After about an hour, the numbness faded and we all began to realize that we had no need to go home hanging our heads in shame. I now had ten World Cup goals to my name, appearances in a quarter-final and a semi-final, a Golden Boot trophy, and a lot of playing friends around the world. I'd have swapped it all for a World Cup win with England, of course, but that will be somebody else's pleasure, perhaps even this year.

1954

Sandor Kocsis
11 goals

1962

Florian Albert
4 goals

CHAPTER SIX

Hungary

I have devoted a whole chapter to the two Hungarian winners of the Golden Boot, partly because Hungary has such a rich footballing history, and partly because the national team in which Sandor Kocsis excelled was, along with Johan Cruyff's Dutch team in 1974, the unluckiest and best regarded of World Cup runners-up. The Dutch were beaten in two finals, in 1974 and 1978, while Hungary lost 4–2 to Italy in 1938 and, most traumatically, to West Germany 3–2 in Switzerland in 1954. But at least the Hungarians had, in this latter case, the small consolation of providing an outstanding winner of the Golden Boot, Kocsis scoring eleven goals in just five matches. The Hungarians scored twenty-seven goals in those games, a fair measure of the brilliant attacking football they brought to this fifth World Cup competition. To score so many as a team, and also to have the highest scorer in Kocsis, and yet end up as losers must have been one of the biggest sickeners of all time. I felt bad enough in 1986, getting six goals and going out to Argentina in the quarter-finals!

The 'Man with the Golden Head', Sandor Kocsis.

Yet the Hungarians deserve not just our sympathy, but also our deep respect, for theirs was undoubtedly one of the most magical teams to grace football in any era. Just look at some of the names in that team, apart from Kocsis – Ferenc Puskas, perhaps the most powerful striker Europe has ever produced; Nandor Hidegkuti, another goalscorer whose deep-lying centre-forward role revolutionized football's tactical thinking; Zoltan Czibor, a winger of such speed and trickery, who supplied crosses for Kocsis, but who could also score himself; and Josef Bozsik, a classic wing-half with immense power and authority.

Of course, all of these names are particularly etched on to the English footballing consciousness for more than their World Cup performances. Hungary's two devastating victories over England – 6–3 at Wembley in November 1953, 7–1 in

Left: The Hungarians prepare to unveil their magic against England at Wembley in November 1953.

Below: England goalkeeper Gil Merrick manages to block a shot by Kocsis, but Hungary went on to win 6–3.

Budapest in May 1954 – were twin bomb-shells for English football's sense of its own superiority, nurtured over half a century during which pride in our role as the game's originators swelled into a complacent belief in our divine authority. At least two significant figures in later English football history, Alf Ramsey and Don Revie, openly admitted to having their horizons expanded by the Hungarians' performances. Revie borrowed freely from their tactics both as a player for Manchester City and as manager of Leeds United, while Alf Ramsey, who played (and scored) in the 6–3 defeat at Wembley, used the humiliation of that day as one of his motivating forces in driving English football back to world respectability with his World Cup-winning team of 1966.

Billy Wright, who was the England captain for both games, later spoke in glowing terms of what the Hungarians had unveiled.

More Magyar misery for England, as Puskas scores in the 7–1 win in Budapest in May 1954.

'The reason for our defeat that day at Wembley was not our bad football. Often it was very good. The Hungarians beat us because, quite simply, they were by far the better side. And even though we were beaten, and beaten very easily, there was something supremely satisfying about that game. The "Magnificent Magyars" they were called and not without good reason.

'Puskas, Hidegkuti, Bozsik, Kocsis – they are names fit for any sporting Hall of Fame, worthy of any and every superlative. The margin of their victory and the manner in which it was achieved inspired the biggest most critical examination and reassessment our game has probably known.'

Kocsis didn't manage a goal at Wembley – Hidegkuti with three, Puskas with two and Bozsik did the damage – and Wright particularly remembered Puskas's first goal as a demonstration of the Hungarians' vision and technical skills. It was a goal that made everybody who saw it gasp.

'Puskas suddenly bobbed up in front of me with the ball,' Wright recalled. 'I moved into the tackle firmly, quickly and with my eyes on the ball. Nine times out of ten that tackle would have won possession. But this was the tenth time. Puskas dragged the ball back with his studs and my striking leg met just air. In the same incredibly quick movement the great Hungarian pivoted, his left foot flashed and there was the ball nestling in the back of the net!'

Perhaps Wright, and the English football establishment, shouldn't have been so surprised by the Hungarian wizardry. They had become the Olympic football champions in 1952, and by the time of the 1954 World Cup were unbeaten in internationals for over four years. The back-to-back victories over England merely confirmed what the rest of Europe already knew – not only was this the first outstanding national side to emerge after the Second World War, but they also looked like absolute certainties to win the 1954 World Cup.

Sandor Kocsis, sadly, is no longer alive to give his account of those wonderful four or five years when Hungary were the world's

A river runs through it: the beautiful city of Budapest and the pleasures of the Danube.

GARY LINEKER'S GOLDEN BOOTS

top side. In 1979 he died at the wastefully young age of fifty in Barcelona, having settled there after playing for my old club in the late fifties and early sixties. But fortunately for us, several key members of Hungary's 1954 team are still hale and hearty, and I travelled to the beautiful city of Budapest to talk to them, both individually and as members of a sports dining club which meets regularly to chew over the past. They also hang out in a place called the '6–3 Bar' – forty-five years later, and they're still rubbing it in!

But anyone who thinks that Hungarian football didn't exist before the 1954 team, should think again. The Hungarian Football Association was founded in 1901, and soon had a national team entering the Olympic competition. A Scottish émigré called Jimmy Hogan expanded their football base in the years immediately after the First World War. (Hogan was the Hungarians' guest of honour at Wembley in 1953, so he must have been double-chuffed to see England beaten!) Hungary entered a team for the 1934 World Cup in Italy, featuring Dr Georges Sarosi in attack, but although they beat Egypt 4–2 in the first round, they lost 2–1 to the powerful Austrians in the second.

Four years later in France, however, they made it all the way through to the final – having beaten Dutch East Indies 6–0, Switzerland 2–0 and Sweden 5–1 – before losing 4–2 to the sharp-passing, strong-tackling Italians. The Second World War and its after-effects kept Hungary out of the 1950 World Cup in Brazil, but by the time of the 1954 competition, the new internal politics of Hungary had built up a sports system to deliver a strong national team.

As discussed in the chapter on the Golden Boot winners from Eastern Europe, the principle mechanism for communist parties to advance their sporting prowess was the so called 'army' or 'police' teams. Hungary was no exception, and their best players were gradually brought together under the single banner of Honved, the Budapest-based army side.

Sandor Kocsis was a typical example of the state system's machinations. A youth-team player with one of the famous Budapest clubs, Ferencvaros, with whom he won a national championship in 1949, Kocsis was enlisted by Honved in 1950, along with wingers Budai and Czibor. Puskas found himself travelling a similar route from his original club, Kispest. By the early 1950s, Honved had become in effect the national team in club form. But these players still needed a good coach to get the best out of them and Gustav Sebes seemed to be the man to do the job.

A friendly handshake with Nandor Hidegkuti in the bar which still celebrates the 6–3 win over England forty-five years ago.

I met up with Nandor Hidegkuti at the 6–3 Bar to talk about the building of this great team, and also about his late colleague with the 'golden head', Sandor Kocsis. Now seventy-six, Hidegkuti, recalls how Sebes set to work.

'There were a lot of great players coming through the Hungarian system by the early 1950s, thanks to a good coaching system which employed lots of former Hungarian internationals who could demonstrate what they wanted from their players. Sebes was basically trying to hone a national squad of about sixteen players. Early on in his career as national coach, we suffered a big defeat by the Czechs, 5–2 in Prague, in which a lot of our players were asked to fill positions they didn't play in for their clubs. Sebes rearranged the team to suit the players' abilities, and invented this role of the deep-lying centre-forward for me because that's roughly where I played for my club (MTK). The 4–2–4 system evolved, with me and Bozsik in the middle, Budai on the right wing, Czibor on the left, and Puskas and Kocsis as the two strikers.'

The system worked well enough in the 1952 Olympics, and in the friendly internationals around Europe which followed. But its ultimate vindication came at Wembley on Wednesday, 25 November 1953, with England's first home defeat by foreign (i.e. non home countries) opposition. While it is wrong to overplay the 'Wembley as a fortress' angle – Scotland had beaten England there 5–1 in 1928, and only three foreign teams had played England there before Hungary (Argentina, Austria and Belgium) – the defeat was nevertheless a potent symbol of the new order of international football overtaking the old.

'That 6–3 win gave us enormous confidence,' Hidegkuti recalled over a local beer, 'because England had not been defeated by anyone else at home. It was a world sensation. After the match, when we arrived in Paris, there were thousands of people waiting to greet us at the station. We all went to watch a French game, and the crowd yelled for us to get out on the field and take on both sides! As we returned

Hungarian keeper Gyula Grosics in action as the Germans fight back in the dramatic 1954 final.

home through Switzerland and Austria, there were people at every railway station cheering us, such was the sensation we had created.'

Hungary's 7–1 win over England in Budapest the following May naturally enough made the team strong favourites for the forthcoming World Cup. Preston North End's Tom Finney, one of England's greatest-ever players with seventy-six caps and thirty goals, was unfortunate enough to be in the second England side to be pasted by the Hungarians within six months, but he still has good memories of them.

'I couldn't play in the Wembley game because I'd been injured on the Saturday beforehand. But I went to Wembley anyway, and I was asked to make comments on the Hungarians for an article in the *Daily Express*. Well, the Hungarian team came out about twenty minutes before the kick-off and started to warm up with all these passes and flicks and little tricks with the ball. I'd never seen anything like it in my life. But the lads in the press box were all saying that they couldn't possibly do this stuff in the real match – by half-time the Hungarians were 4–1 having done exactly what they'd been doing in the warm-up. They were just amazing – nobody on the England team had any idea how to cope with Hidegkuti, who got three goals, while Puskas looked as though he could score whenever he got the ball. They completely foxed us. The English game was never the same again afterwards, so big was the impact they made in terms of ideas and skill.'

The parallel universe which Tom and his England colleagues had seen that afternoon, in which football was played but not as we knew it, revealed itself again in Budapest on 23 May 1954. This time Tom was right in the thick of it, and was no less impressed with what the Hungarians were doing.

'To be honest, it was a case of racehorses playing cart-horses that day. The England team was a much inferior side to the one at Wembley, and they just murdered us. Kocsis, who hadn't scored at Wembley, got two this time, and he was an outstanding player with some wonderful skills. But then they all had this: the way they controlled the ball and passed it was just an eye-opener. Puskas and Hidegkuti ran the game – we were never in it. I can honestly say that in all my England career they were the best international team I ever played against.'

Less than a month after this stunning victory, the fifth World Cup got under way in Switzerland with Hungary installed as almost unbackable favourites, such was the awe in which they were held. Nandor Hidegkuti says, 'We felt no pressure. We were a team who had played so much together that it really made no difference who played in what position, and we were fairly confident.'

When I later spoke to Ferenc Puskas at his trophy-lined home he, typically, made no bones about the hopes that had built up around this wonderful team – 'The country expected us to win, and so did we.'

Trying to unravel what went wrong for Hungary in 1954 may be reduced to a simple phrase that English teams have had to learn – 'never underestimate the Germans' – but within the chess game that the modern World Cup had become even by that early stage, we can detect two or three crucial moves which conspired to deny Hungary their World Cup crown.

At home with a legend – Ferenc Puskas, scorer of eighty-three goals in eighty-four internationals.

One theory we can dismiss right away is that the Hungarians had somehow left their best form behind them in the friendlies before the tournament. In their first two games they scored seventeen goals – nine against South Korea (Kocsis getting three), and then eight against West Germany (Kocsis getting four). But within that 8–3 win over the Germans, there were two sub-plots. One concerned the precise strength of the German team which their coach Sepp Herberger put out, and his reasons for doing so. The other sub-plot was simply whether Werner Liebrich's kick on Puskas was a deliberate attempt to put him out of not just the game, but also the whole competition.

Let's look at the German team issue first. Their line-up for the first game was as follows: Kwiatoski, Bauer, Kohlmeyer, Posipal, Liebrich, Mebus, Rahn, Eckel, F. Walter, Pfaff, Herrmann.

For the World Cup final itself it was: Turek, Posipal, Kohlmeyer, Eckel, Liebrich, Mai, Rahn, Morlock, O. Walter, F. Walter, Schaefer.

I make that five changes between the two selections, which certainly looks like an attempt to play a weakened team in the first game, rather than a case of rotating the squad to see who was in form. What adds to the suspicions, though, is the fact that by strategically losing the game, the Germans were not only disguising their true strength, but also getting themselves an easier run to the final – playing Yugoslavia in the quarter-final, and Austria in the semi-final, while Hungary were left to battle first Brazil and then Uruguay.

Puskas isn't so sure that this was the German intention – 'I don't think so – conceding so many goals to us must have hurt them.' But Hidegkuti is in no doubt that the Germans planned for their own defeat.

'When we played them first, Herberger definitely substituted a few of his best players, he wouldn't let them play us. The defeat meant they had a really smooth ride to the final, beating Yugoslavia 2–0, and Austria 6–1. But we had to play *two* finals just to get to the World Cup final itself!'

West Germany's Horst Eckel tells me how they beat Hungary in 1954.

One of the Germans who played in both games against Hungary, Horst Eckel, confirms that some 'calculation' took place, but denies that the first match was thrown.

'During our preparations in Munich, Herberger had told us that we could only get through that first group by way of Turkey, and that we would play the Hungarians not with our strongest team, but with reserves and maybe three or four players from the main team. We still wanted to look good against Hungary, but the game did not go as we had imagined and the 8–3 defeat was actually very depressing for us, for Herberger and for the whole of Germany. People talked of "our great shame", and to lose by that margin was awful for us. Anyone who is a footballer goes into a game to win. We knew that it would be difficult against Hungary, but we wanted to put on a show. They were much too strong for us, though, and we had no chance.'

Because of the defeat, the Germans were required to play off for second place in the group against a Turkish team they had already beaten 4–1 in their first match. The rematch went exactly to plan as West Germany thrashed the Turks 7–2, and were able to take advantage of the bizarre structure of the tournament whereby the four teams which finished top of their groups – Brazil, Hungary, Uruguay and England – battled for one place in the final, while the four teams finishing second – Yugoslavia, West Germany, Austria and Switzerland – played for the other. This naive 'seeding' effectively meant that mediocrity was guaranteed a reward, and that a final which reflected the true status of the teams – Hungary v Uruguay, say – was denied to the fans. Nowadays, the group structures are always geared to reward a team finishing top with a fixture against a team finishing second, although as we have seen with Argentina in 1978, that system can also be abused.

The other controversial element from Hungary's first game against West Germany was the kick Liebrich applied to Puskas's ankle, which caused him to hobble off fifteen minutes from time, with Hungary 5–3 up, forcing him to miss both the quarter-final and semi-final matches, and then play in the final some way short of full fitness.

Puskas generously says that he 'doesn't think it was deliberate. I went first for the ball, Liebrich was running after me, and I don't think it is that easy to kick someone's ankle from behind. I can't imagine that it was intentional. It wasn't that bad an injury because ten days later I could play again.'

Similarly, Hidegkuti acquits Liebrich of any crime.

'I've met Liebrich several times since that game and he is not a man who would deliberately kick another player. You can see it in the films of the game. It was a correct tackle, and quite accepted in football. He was just trying to tackle Puskas, who strained his ankle. But that is part of football!'

What wasn't in any doubt by this stage of the competition was the potency of Sandor Kocsis who had rattled up seven goals in his two games, several of them coming from his remarkable heading ability.

'Sandor had unique ability in the air,' says Hidegkuti. 'But he was also a very good technical player. Whenever he got the ball, he would bring the team into play.

The Hungarian World Cup keeper Gyula Grosics in action.

The strategy was to keep Kocsis permanently up front since he was one of our slower players, but he was able to keep the ball, hold it up for Budai, Puskas, Czibor or myself as we came up to join the attack. He really was excellent with his head when he got the chance, and his role in the team was to score goals from the crosses which Budai or Czibor put in. I remember in one game against Austria back in 1948 or '49, he twisted backwards in the air to get in a header and still managed to score, and even the Austrian players congratulated him on the goal!'

Kocsis headed two more goals in Hungary's 4–2 quarter-final victory over Brazil, but the match was destined to be remembered as 'The Battle of Berne' for the sustained outbreaks of violence which saw two Brazilians, Nilton Santos and Humberto Tozzi, and one Hungarian, their captain Josef Bozsik, sent off for fouls and fighting. The fisticuffs even spread into the tunnel and the dressing-rooms after the game had ended, as the Brazilians went on a sour rampage.

'That Brazilian team had left home feeling they had the World Cup in their pocket,' Nandor Hidegkuti observes. 'Nobody doubted their excellence, because they had some really extraordinary players on their team. But we were better. So when we started scoring early, they got aggressive straightaway and the game became very violent. At the end, when we were going back to our dressing-room, they threw bottles at us and started a fight in the corridor, so the police had to be called to restore order.'

Nevertheless, Hungary had shown that they could still pack a punch, so to speak, even without the injured Puskas, and they advanced into the semi-finals to face Uruguay, who had ended England's excellent run with a 4–2 win in Basle. The Hungary–Uruguay match was in complete contrast with the previous

Hidegkuti dives in to head Hungary's second goal in their 4–2 extra-time win over Uruguay in the 1954 semi-final.

GARY LINEKER'S GOLDEN BOOTS

Europe–South America encounter, as both teams settled to play stylish, intelligent, attacking football, although Hidegkuti had to put some media-inspired fears aside beforehand.

'After the Brazil game, some of their journalists came to our hotel and told us that, compared to Uruguay, Brazil played really gentle football. They said that the Uruguayans were even prepared to shoot players on the pitch! But really it was a very fair game, a beautiful one even. We could easily have lost it because Uruguay played brilliantly at times.'

The thrilling narrative of this match, which is still remembered with great affection by those who either played in it or watched it, embraced a typically sharp Hungarian start as they went two goals up in the first half through Czibor and Hidegkuti. But Uruguay came back, inspired by Juan Schiaffino to get two goals in the last fifteen minutes from Hohberg.

'It was raining throughout the match,' Hidegkuti recalls, 'so we had to play on a deep, soggy pitch. But in the half-hour of extra time, Kocsis found the strength to head two more goals to put us in the final. Everybody was exhausted by the time we got to the dressing-rooms, we hardly had enough strength left to undo our boot laces.'

Hidegkuti gives due praise to Kocsis, but insists that 'that wasn't his best game because he was playing equally well in all our matches, and getting his share of goals.' From the opposition point of view, the Uruguayan star, Schiaffino remembers 'almost losing a boot in the water that was lying on the pitch, but even the conditions couldn't stop Kocsis. He was an excellent player, and Hungary were truly a great team.'

The exhausted Hungarian team had only three days to rest before the final, where West Germany now awaited them after thrashing Austria 6–1. Hungary's night before the final was bizarrely disturbed by a brass-band competition staged outside the hotel – not another German strategy, I understand, just a quirk of fate and bad planning by the Hungarian management.

'We couldn't get any sleep at all,' Hidegkuti laments, 'and the whole team was really tired by the following morning. We should have stopped it, or moved to another hotel. The square outside was small and surrounded by houses, so the brass-band music just echoed around the enclosed space. It was dreadful all night!'

Battling against fatigue and injury, Hungary prepared for the World Cup final in Berne as best they could, agonizing until the last minute over whether Puskas was fit to play.

'Both Sebes and the team doctor advised me not to play,' Puskas says, before adding defiantly, 'but I insisted and I think I was able to play really hard.'

Puskas proved his fitness by scoring Hungary's first goal on six minutes after a Kocsis shot had been blocked by Turek in the German goal. Two minutes later, Czibor cut in from the right wing and made it 2–0, and Hungary had a dramatic early lead. But Germany quickly got one back through Morlock before Rahn tucked the ball home after a corner to make it 2–2. Hungary got their second wind and laid

GARY'S GOLDEN NUGGETS

In Hungary's 1934 World Cup match against Egypt, the goalkeeper they faced really was called Moustafa Kamel!

The dramatic 1954 final: Hungary took a 2–0 lead, but eventually lost 3–2 to West Germany. (*Inset*) Ferenc Puskas, denied a late equalizer by an offside decision, sportingly shakes hands with Fritz Walter, the German captain.

siege to the German goal, with Hidegkuti firing in a shot that hit one post and then bounced off another before Turek grabbed the ball. Kocsis hit the bar, and the German defender Kohlmeyer cleared Miska Toth's shot from the line with his knee. In what now seems typical German style – especially if you're English and you remember that game in Leon in the 1970 World Cup in Mexico – Rahn scored a second goal to give Germany a 3–2 lead. Even then, there was time for one last, fateful twist as Puskas squeezed the ball home for an apparent equalizer only to see that the linesman had flagged for offside.

'The referee had given the goal,' Puskas recalls with some bitterness, 'and was heading back to the centre circle when he finally saw the linesman's flag. I still think of that moment often – I will never forget it.'

Hidegkuti's memories have mellowed somewhat, blaming the fatigue brought on by extra time against Uruguay as the key factor, but he still believes Germany had the crucial advantage of an easier run to the final.

'The final outcome had really been decided by Herberger's ploy to lose the first game against us. He knew who they would play if they lost. But we could not afford to be beaten – if we had lost that game, we'd have easily beaten Yugoslavia and Austria and maybe saved our energy, rather than having to battle against Brazil and Uruguay, but it wasn't our style to lose games. There was one other factor – Sebes dropped Budai and brought in Toth, so Kocsis didn't get his usual service from the wing, and that's perhaps why he didn't manage to score in the final.'

Horst Eckel, of the victorious German team, gave me some insight into how Herberger had planned to stop the Hungarian goal machine, and reverse the trauma of their earlier 8–3 defeat.

'Herberger allocated each individual in the team to a Hungarian player with similar skills, so Karl Mai was put on Kocsis, Werner Liebrich marked Puskas again, and I was told to play on Hidegkuti. In this way, these three great footballers were as good as excluded from the game. They were the key to Hungary's game, and Hidegkuti was often left unmarked because he dropped so deep. But I moved well forward to pick him up in his own half. We were able to cut them off from the play and become world champions!'

Hungary were left to reflect on what might have been, or rather should have been, and to deal with the huge disappointment which they knew their defeat had caused back home.

'When we lost,' Hidegkuti remembers, 'someone rang us from the government in Hungary and told us not to come home but to stay in Switzerland. So we stayed on for a week, playing friendly matches, and then a government minister came out to escort us home on a private train. We got to Tata where our training camp was, and stayed until midnight before being taken back in separate cars to our flats. They were afraid of the public's reaction. There'd already been some rioting, with trams and cars smashed up, and the windows of Sebes' house were broken. The police warned us not to go out on to the streets. When the Hungarian championship resumed later in the summer, the spectators would whistle at us loudly. It was unjust really – we'd been undefeated for four years and all our matches had been followed by hundreds of thousands of spectators, but because of losing this one match, the World Cup final, there was all this anger directed against us. A long series of wins counted for nothing because we had lost this one vital game.'

'You could say that the people were not whistling happy,' Puskas remembers, 'they were shouting at us and cursing us, so we stayed off the streets until it calmed down a bit. And there was a lot of harsh criticism in the newspapers.'

Puskas shows me around Budapest from which he was exiled for over twenty-five years.

Italy's World Cup-winning manager Enzo Bearzot played his only international game against Hungary in 1955, and lost 2–0. 'We were happy to lose only 2–0,' he says, 'because they really were a great team.'

The Hungarian players' attempts to pick up their footballing careers were generating a new momentum – there was another World Cup in 1958 to anticipate, after all – when the political uprising which provoked a violent Soviet backlash took place in 1956. The Honved team – with Puskas, Kocsis and Czibor – was abroad playing friendlies at the time of the Russian repression, which gave the players a terrible dilemma about whether they should return to their country or not. It wasn't an easy decision and it divided the players not just in terms of loyalty to their country but also in their attitudes to their families. Puskas and Hidegkuti ended up representing opposite sides of the argument. Puskas and Kocsis remained in Spain, while Hidegkuti stayed put in Hungary.

'I had two children,' Hidegkuti points out. 'My father-in-law had to have his leg amputated, so he was unable to work, and my parents were also elderly. I couldn't leave these people behind; being there was the only way to help them. Besides, my playing career was more or less over anyway. I was thirty-four and nobody around the world wanted a player of that age. I managed another two years, a few more games in the national team [Hidegkuti played one match, against Wales, in the 1958 World Cup] before I retired at thirty-six. I didn't envy the likes of Puskas and Kocsis. They were among the best and most popular players in the world, so they had a strong base for their future. It was down to individual choice, I suppose. For example, the whole Hungarian Youth Team left the country, so our football came to a standstill, and a whole generation was lost to us.'

For Kocsis, and especially Puskas, life was very different as, banned by the Hungarian Football Association, they signed for Barcelona and Real Madrid respectively, and enjoyed various levels of success. Kocsis became one of Barca's best-loved *extranjeros* (foreign players) and if you ever visit the club's museum, you'll see his picture up there on a huge wall alongside the likes of Steve Archibald, Diego Maradona, Mark Hughes and, er, me. Puskas meanwhile had dramatic success with the great Real Madrid side which won the European Cup for the fifth time running in 1960 when they beat Eintracht Frankfurt 7–3 at Hampden Park, a wonderful game in which he scored four goals. Puskas even went on to change his nationality and played for Spain in the 1962 World Cup.

Food of the gods – a celebratory lunch with the surviving members of the 1954 Hungarian team. At current transfer values, about £50 million worth of talent!

For Kocsis, life wasn't quite as sweet as Barcelona lost the 1961 European Cup final 3–2 to Benfica, although he and his Hungarian team-mate Czibor scored Barca's goals. Kocsis was apparently always one of the quieter Hungarian players, despite his successes, and after he finished with Barcelona he settled in the city and opened a small bar. In 1974, with bitter irony, he had to have a foot amputated after a domestic accident, and he was later diagnosed as having stomach cancer. After more than twenty years of exile, he visited Hungary in May 1979 for specialist treatment, but nothing could be done, and the following month he threw himself from his hospital window in Barcelona, getting his retaliation in first before the cancer could bring him down.

Puskas was eventually able to return to Hungary after a quarter of a century of footballing travels, but he has always been one of football's great survivors. I was truly honoured to meet up with him, Hidegkuti, and the 1954 goalkeeper Grosics, along with a few other players from that wonderfully gifted squad. We drank and ate well, and talked football for hours, not just about the past but the present, too. They had no doubt that had their great friend Sandor Kocsis lived his full span, he would have been there with us. Somebody in the restaurant summed it all up – 'In football, if a striker is a great scorer, it cements a firm friendship, even with defenders. Kocsis was a great goalscorer. And that Hungarian team knew only one style of football – attack!'

There haven't been too many occasions to cheer for Hungarian football since the great days of the 1950s, with the country gripped by political turmoil and not really enjoying freedom until the early 1990s. But one small highlight was the form of Hungary's other Golden Boot winner, Florian Albert, who scored four goals to finish joint leader in Chile in 1962. Albert made a great impression on English fans, without scoring unfortunately, during Hungary's brief success in the 1966 World Cup. In what seems a typical Hungarian destiny, given their ability to snatch defeat from the jaws of victory, Albert raced to four goals

One of Hungary's most stylish forwards, Florian Albert, tells me about his heyday, and (*inset*) in goalscoring action in the 1960s.

The Ferencvaros stadium in Budapest.

in Hungary's first two Group 4 games in Chile – one against England in a 2–1 win, three against Bulgaria in a 6–1 win – and then found the coach, Lajos Baroti, resting him for the game against Argentina, which ended in a goalless draw.

'He wouldn't allow me to play against Argentina,' Albert laments as he sits in his offices at Ferencvaros, the club he graced as player in the 1960s, 'but in the very next game we got knocked out by the Czechs, 1–0, who went all the way to the final. It was very painful for me, because I knew all about the Golden Boot. I followed all the World Cups from 1954, and always knew the scoring lists. It would have been nice to have been an outright winner.'

Bizarrely, because the 1962 Golden Boot award was shared by six players – Albert, Leonel Sanchez of Chile, Ivanov of Russia, Drazan Jerkovic of Yugoslavia, and Vava and Garrincha of Brazil, each with just four goals – a dinner was held after the World Cup, during which the six names were put into a hat, and the trophy was awarded to the first one drawn. No, it wasn't Albert, but Garrincha of Brazil.

Florian Albert, still a striking figure at fifty-six.

'I didn't know about this,' Albert says with a shrug, 'but he deserved it anyway for his performances, because he was the main star for Brazil once Pelé was injured. I mean, Garrincha looked as though he must be disabled with those twisted legs of his, but when he was on the field it was fantastic what he could achieve. My other memory of 1962 is really a feeling of how lucky we were as players. My generation was allowed to travel abroad, and we played Chile and Uruguay as well as the World Cup games. For us, just young kids, it was great to travel the ocean and it was fantastic to see another world, another way of life – it was an unforgettable memory.'

Albert was born in the Hungarian countryside, but moved to Budapest in 1952, and saw the emerging side of 1954 play some of their early games. 'The Golden Team' he calls them with genuine affection. He used to try and get into the huge Nepstadion when the Magyars were at home, buying a student ticket for two florins. But he couldn't get in for the 7–1 win over England, having to watch the game at an open-air cinema nearby.

Later as Albert began to build his club and international career, he faced the same dilemma as that which plagued the 1954 players – to flee abroad, or to stay in Hungary and make the best of it.

'I could never consider leaving without permission, but the Sports Ministry just said no whenever any of us were approached about playing abroad. It was regarded as a defeat for the system. I have to say that my heart ached when I spent three weeks at Flamengo in Brazil, training and playing. They wanted me to stay for two years, but the Hungarian authorities wouldn't let me have the chance.'

Nevertheless, Albert proceeded to become one of Hungary's most elegant and admired forwards, and his displays at Goodison Park – another one of my old grounds – in the Group 3 games of 1966 earned him a great deal of public acclaim, not the least of which was the very Scouse chant of 'Albert!' in which the 't' in his name was not left silent as it should have been.

'I have the fondest memories of those few weeks. The fact that neutral teams – us, Portugal, Brazil and Bulgaria – played there meant that the Merseyside people could be enthusiastic about the football. They clapped and cheered almost all the time. It was a special joy to win in such an atmosphere.'

Win Hungary did; after being beaten by Portugal in their first game, they overpowered the champions Brazil 3–1 with a great display of attacking football. The names Bene, Farkas and Albert became as familiar in Liverpool as Roger Hunt and Alex Young. They also beat Bulgaria 3–1 at Old Trafford to qualify for the quarter-finals, but were beaten 2–1 by a strong Russian side at Sunderland's Roker Park.

'When the Hungarian team – even in the era of Puskas – played against the Soviet Union, it was often suggested that we had to let them win because of the political situation. But as a player you simply cannot think that way. Playing already has a risk of losing, without contributing to it further. We lost to a stronger team that day, on the threshold of the semi-final, and it was very painful.'

That was the end of Albert's, and indeed Hungary's, World Cup dreams. They have rarely threatened since 1966, even if they have managed to qualify, and will again be missing from France in 1998 after being thrashed by Yugoslavia in the European play-offs. The prevailing logic of modern football suggests that Hungary will struggle even to get close to the standards set by the 1954 team, but then who ever thought logic applied to such a beautiful uncertainty as the game of football?

Albert outjumps the Russian defence in the quarter-final tie at Sunderland's Roker Park in the 1966 World Cup; but the Soviets went through 2–1.

1934	1962	1994
Oldrich Nejedly (Czechoslovakia) 5 goals	Drazan Jerkovic (Yugoslavia) 4 goals	Hristo Stoichkov (Bulgaria) 6 goals
1962	**1974**	**1994**
Valentin Ivanov (USSR) 4 goals	Gregorz Lato (Poland) 7 goals	Oleg Salenko (Russia) 6 goals

Eastern Europe

The not inconsiderable factor of post-war Soviet communism directly links all of these Golden Boots winners and certainly affected their lives and the footballing histories of the countries they represented. Hungary, too, was affected but Hungary, I felt, merited a chapter all to itself. The story of football in Eastern Europe cannot properly be told without due reference to the spread of communism from post-revolutionary Russia, especially after the end of the Second World War. Even players such as Oleg Salenko and Hristo Stoichkov, who played for theoretically democratic states in the 1994 World Cup, began their careers under the shadow of communist cold war politics, which as far as football was concerned meant clubs dominated by the special interests of the party in various guises – police, national army, secret police, factory – with players enjoying material benefits but existing as chattels of the state and being denied individual liberty. Modern concepts such as freedom of contract and freedom of movement certainly didn't figure in the communist view of football as a means to project the virtues of the ruling political system. 'Monsta, monsta' agent Eric Hall would probably have been put up against a wall and shot if he'd tried to operate behind the Iron Curtain!

Czechoslovakian football at least had several decades of freedom before first the Nazis, and then the Russians, took control of their country. Their game developed in the late nineteenth century, helped considerably by a Scottish coach, John Dick. Celtic played a friendly in Prague in 1906, while two years later England played Bohemia in an international, winning 4–0. A Czech team reached the final of the 1920 Olympics in Antwerp, and with two clubs, Slavia and Sparta, thriving in Prague, the Czechs had sufficient quality to send a strong team to the 1934 World Cup in Italy, strong enough to have beaten England 2–1 in May of that year. Their captain, Frantisek Planicka, was regarded as one of the best goalkeepers in Europe, and in Antonin Puc and Oldrich Nejedly they had gifted goalscorers who would make their mark on the tournament.

> **GARY'S GOLDEN NUGGETS**
>
> The World Cup has yet to be staged in Eastern Europe, having been confined so far to Italy (twice), Spain, Switzerland, Sweden, England, Germany and France. Russia seem to be the likeliest candidates from the former communist bloc, but their earliest chance to be hosts looks like being in 2014.

Nejedly was born in Zarbrak in December 1909 and played for the Rakovnik club for five years from 1926, before joining Sparta Prague in 1931. He won his first international cap against Poland in June of the same year and then quickly established himself as both a fluent inside-forward and a consistent goalscorer. In forty-three internationals for Czechoslovakia he scored twenty-nine goals. Three of these came against England: one in the 1934 win in Prague, two in the Czechs' 5–4 defeat at White Hart Lane. Most significantly, five of his goals came in the 1934 World Cup, for which he finished top scorer.

In the first round, the Czechs beat Romania 2–1 (Nejedly one goal); and in the second round, they beat Switzerland 3–2 (another for Nejedly). Nejedly claimed a hat-trick as Czechoslovakia beat Germany 3–1 in the first semi-final in Rome, taking them through to a final against hosts Italy. There were fairly widespread rumours that Italy had 'made sure' that they would win and fulfil Mussolini's dearest wishes, and considering these suspicions the Czechs did brilliantly to take Italy to extra time at 1–1, before eventually losing 2–1. Indeed, Puc gave them the lead with only twenty minutes to go, and the Italian equalizer from one of their imported Argentinians, Raimondo Orsi, was deemed to be a bit of a freak goal because of the ball's unusual swerve over Planicka and into the net.

Nejedly was also in the Czech team that competed in the 1938 World Cup in France, but after scoring in their 3–0 win over Holland in the first round, Nejedly had dramatically mixed fortunes in their second-round match against Brazil. The game ended in a 1–1 draw, Nejedly equalizing with a penalty after Leonidas had given Brazil the lead; but the bare statistics disguise a disgraceful spectacle in which three players (two Brazilians, one Czech) were sent off, Planicka had his arm broken, and Nejedly his right leg. With Nejedly's World Cup career over, Brazil won the replay 2–1. Nejedly managed a last international in December of 1938 against Romania in Prague, but football was about to become an irrelevant sideshow as Hitler's Nazis reached out across Europe.

The Czech team lines up before their first game in the 1934 World Cup finals in Italy. (*Inset*) The 1934 Golden Boot winner, Oldrich Nejedly.

Postcards from Prague.

Sadly, Oldrich Nejedly died in June 1990 at the grand age of eighty, but I was able to track down a friend of his to provide testimony of his skills. Josef Bican played in the 1934 World Cup for Austria, Hugo Meisl's so-called *wunderteam* – they were beaten 1–0 by Italy in the semi-final – but then fled to Czechoslovakia when Hitler staged a 'friendly' takeover of Austria in the spring of 1938. Bican became a Czech national and played for several years for Slavia Prague, rivals of Nejedly's Sparta, but this didn't stop him becoming great friends with 1934's Golden Boot winner.

I travelled to Prague to meet Bican, an alert and extremely fit-looking eighty-four year old, to hear not just about Nejedly but also Bican's temporary escape from oppression, as German occupation gave way to Soviet rule. Bican's story may well be typical of many football players who had the misfortune to be in Central and Eastern Europe during the long years of war and repression which afflicted that area, but it also underlines the universality of football as both a childhood pastime and a grown-up career. I asked him first about his own early influences and experiences.

'As a boy, like thousands of others after the first Great War, I wanted to be a footballer. There was terrible poverty in Europe, little boys had nothing. I didn't know a single one who had a scooter or a bike. The only thing we had was a rag-ball which we kicked around all day long. That's why there were so many good footballers in the 1930s.'

Bican's father had died following a football accident – a kick in the kidneys – but that traumatic loss didn't put the youngster off the game. At the age of seventeen, he was taken up by Rapid Vienna's youth team; after scoring seven goals in a practice match, Bican found himself elevated into Rapid's first team. Then, in a game against the Austrian national side, Bican scored four times in a 5–3 victory, which prompted a 'rapid' selection for his country, and a short trip to Italy for the World Cup.

Austria had beaten Italy 5–2 away in a friendly six months before the World Cup, and had reasonable expectations of a place in the final; but Bican quickly became aware of the effect Mussolini's desire for a home win was having, both on the referees and the teams who stood in Italy's way.

'Before we played Italy in the semi-final, Mussolini invited the Swedish referee to see him, and according to Meisl our coach, the ref was bribed and swayed the game in favour of the Italians. It was the same referee in the final when Nejedly and the Czechs also lost to Italy – he damaged them a lot, too. I knew and trusted Swedish people, but when we saw him – Mr Eklind – in the final, we knew he had been bribed again.'

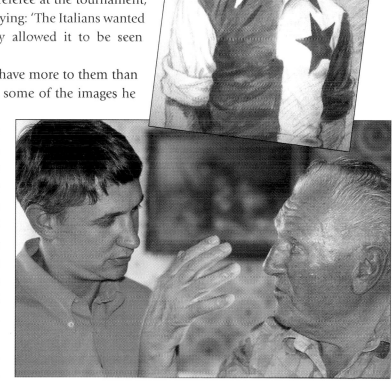

Austrian international Josef Bican talks about the 1934 tournament, and (*inset*) a portrait of Bican from 1934.

Not unreasonably, I asked Bican if he had any evidence for this charge, but he said simply: 'We knew it in advance. The Italians did another shocking thing as well. Just a fortnight before the World Cup they brought in top players from Argentina, who became Italian overnight.'

Without evidence, I can't support Bican's allegations, but he *was* there, and what is certainly acknowledged by most football historians is the pressure that the referees were under in the face of Italy's lust for victory. The Belgian referee at the tournament, Jean Langenus, was later reported as saying: 'The Italians wanted to win, which was natural, but they allowed it to be seen too clearly.'

Bican's memories, therefore, may have more to them than just a losing player's resentment, and some of the images he recalled were fairly alarming.

'I have a picture of the way Italy scored their one goal against us, with five Italians practically carrying our goalkeeper into the net! There were even moments when the referee played for the Italians. When I played a ball out to the right wing and one of our players, Zischek, ran for it, the referee headed the ball back to the Italians – he jumped up and headed the ball back to stop Zischek getting it, I swear!'

Before an international football dispute could be sparked off, I decided to steer Bican on to the less controversial territory of his Czech friend Nejedly's skills and received a glowing response.

'He was one of the best players in the World Cup. He was a fine man, too – elegant, good, honest. The whole of the Austrian side were sorry to see Czechoslovakia end up the same way as we did. Nejedly was their inside-forward and was very quick, and he could shoot with either foot. But the Italians managed to stop him scoring in the final. That was probably the main footballing reason why they won.'

Bican's flight to Prague to be with his grandparents as the Nazis moved into Austria, presented him with a chance of playing for the Czechs in the 1938 World Cup. Bican had grown in stature since 1934, representing a Central Europe team in a match against Western Europe in Amsterdam in 1937 – Nejedly was also in the line-up – but the Czech Football Association stayed loyal to their existing World Cup squad.

'Nejedly and I would have made a great partnership for Czechoslovakia, so I think they made a great mistake in not putting me in the team. I'd have been like Ronaldo and Nejedly would have been like Puskas!'

Bican can enjoy his jokes now, but as he and Nejedly cemented their friendship through playing football for the two main Prague teams, the way Mussolini may or may not have blighted their World Cup experiences was replaced with the fear generated by the German occupation, and after that with the suffocation and brutalism of Soviet communism.

Bican, a living witness to the suffering endured by those whose lives were ruled by state communism.

'My family had two houses and a factory here in Prague but lost everything overnight. They took the lot. Had I joined the Communist Party, I would have been all right, but my wife and I didn't want to do that. It was like life back during the war, with food shortages and so on. Those who were talented and qualified never got into top positions where they could earn a lot of money, but those in the Party had everything. I don't want to cast suspicions on Nejedly, but he had a good position with the railways, had good money and built a house. It's possible he was a member, but we never spoke about it – all we talked about was football. I was made to do manual labour for forty years, and the only release I got was through football. I could earn perhaps five pounds a week playing for Slavia Prague, but even then the Party tried to put me down. I was charged with being a "professional" but I told them when you stop charging people to watch, I'll start playing for nothing. Things are a thousand per cent better now that communism has gone, but it came too late for me.'

Bican's understandable bitterness about the past is a symbol of how ruthless political thought can infect sport. After he and Nejedly stopped playing for Slavia and Sparta respectively, the Party threw its resources behind Dukla Prague, the army team, and that became the core for the national squad. Czechoslovakia returned to World Cup action in 1954, but were beaten by both Uruguay (2–0) and, ironically for Bican, Austria (5–0), and were eliminated. In 1958, they had one good result – a 6–1 thrashing of Argentina – but lost twice to Northern Ireland, first in a group game, then in a play-off to decide which team was to reach the quarter-finals.

In Chile in 1962, an improving Czech side, including a major star in Josef Masopust, reached the final before losing 3–1 to Brazil. However, on their next World Cup excursion, to Mexico in 1970, they lost all three of their group games, despite international sympathy for the 1968 Russian invasion of their country and the overthrowing of Dubcek's liberalizing government. They next qualified in 1982, but again fell in the first round. It was only in 1990 that the Czechs, fired by Tomas Skuhravy's five goals, reached the quarter-finals, where they lost narrowly, 1–0, to the eventual champions, West Germany.

The Czechs, perhaps not unreasonably, always seem to save their best performances for the Germans. Their greatest footballing day came when they beat West Germany in the 1976 European Championship on penalties; and at Euro '96, the newly formed Czech Republic held a 1–0 lead at Wembley in the final, before the Germans came back to equalize and then win with a 'golden goal' in extra time. This looks to me like football as a means of expressing identity and defiance, just as Barcelona continue to represent their region, Catalonia, not Spain. European communism and fascism may no longer be powerful, but the impact that both forms of oppression made on this century will probably linger awhile in football, almost certainly in the form of an increased sense of nationalism; fine as long as it doesn't go too far and trigger the whole cycle all over again.

One player whose whole career took its course under the Soviet communist system is Valentin Ivanov who played in two World Cups for what was then known as the Union of Soviet Socialist Republics (USSR). The red shirts with the CCCP lettering were

Midnight in Moscow, on another leg of the World Cup tour.

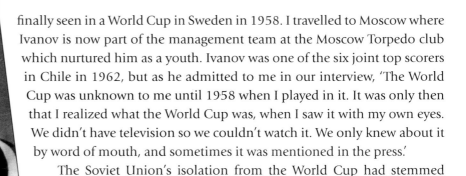

St Basil's cathedral is the backdrop as former Soviet Union striker Valentin Ivanov tells me about Russia's first forays in the World Cup. (*Inset*) Ivanov as he was back in 1962.

finally seen in a World Cup in Sweden in 1958. I travelled to Moscow where Ivanov is now part of the management team at the Moscow Torpedo club which nurtured him as a youth. Ivanov was one of the six joint top scorers in Chile in 1962, but as he admitted to me in our interview, 'The World Cup was unknown to me until 1958 when I played in it. It was only then that I realized what the World Cup was, when I saw it with my own eyes. We didn't have television so we couldn't watch it. We only knew about it by word of mouth, and sometimes it was mentioned in the press.'

The Soviet Union's isolation from the World Cup had stemmed largely from Stalin's foreign policy of enforced separation from the West in the immediate post-war years. There were also well-grounded fears about embarrassing defections from Soviet national teams, although individual clubs such as Moscow Dynamo and Moscow Spartak did travel to western Europe for friendly games in the mid 1950s, as the grip eased slightly after Stalin's death in 1953. Indeed Ivanov was part of the Soviet football team which was sent to the Melbourne Olympics in 1956, a tournament they won with relative ease being *de facto* professionals playing against amateur players. Two other communist countries, Yugoslavia and Bulgaria, finished second and third.

'It was a great honour to go to the Olympics,' Ivanov says, 'not just as a football tournament but as a celebration of all sports. The camaraderie between the different sportsmen was what impressed me; politics didn't come into it. And there's no doubt that winning the Olympic gold medal helped the team when we first went to the World Cup because we had experience of playing abroad. It was exciting and nerve-racking to meet famous footballers in a tournament like that, but we weren't exactly trembling at the knees.'

In Sweden, the USSR team were in the same group as England, Group 4, with whom they drew 2–2 in their first match, Ivanov scoring one of the goals. But after beating Austria 2–0 (another Ivanov goal), the USSR lost 2–0 to Brazil and had to play England again in a play-off to decide who went into the quarter-finals. The Russians duly beat England 1–0, but had to play Sweden two days later and a tired team lost 2–0.

'We were worn out,' Ivanov recalls. 'If we'd had a longer rest we would have been better prepared for Sweden, but I enjoyed the experience, especially scoring two goals. I always loved sticking the ball away, so I was delighted when I scored. We were quite relaxed about our defeat by Sweden because it was our first experience of the World Cup and we looked forward to getting our revenge next time round.'

The USSR went some way towards achieving that by winning the very first European Nations Championship in 1960; and then, after a successful tour of South America, arrived in Chile in 1962 as one of the favourites for the tournament. It was the height of the cold war, with the Cuban missile crisis only a few months away, and Ivanov says that although the team wasn't watched by KGB minders, 'There had to be one person in the party whose job it was to keep an eye on the players to make sure there were no "emergencies". But we didn't have the feeling that we were being prevented from doing anything. We *did* feel some resentment about our country, not just for the lack of freedom but also its economic state compared with the West. It was the difference between heaven and earth, and what we saw abroad made us resent the Soviet system because we didn't have any of it. The players talked about it quite a lot, but nobody ever considered defecting. Lots of clubs invited us to stay in the West, but our generation was more patriotic. Besides, we expected to do very well in Chile, we had a very good team.'

Ivanov scored a goal in the USSR's first game, a 2–0 win over Yugoslavia, and then got two more in the first ten minutes against Colombia. In that match, they led 4–1 before allowing the South Americans to come back to claim a 4–4 draw. Ivanov doesn't recall his goals too clearly – 'I think bitterness made me forget the whole thing.' He scored his fourth goal in a 2 1 win over Uruguay that took the team into the quarter-finals against hosts Chile.

'The team held that goal against me because if it had finished as a draw we wouldn't have played Chile. They were annoyed that we'd have to play the host team with all their fans against us, and probably the referee, too – that had happened to us in Sweden, and sure enough we came unstuck again, losing 2–1. We were all devastated that we hadn't been able to complete the task that we had set ourselves. I was satisfied with my own performances, but I couldn't celebrate because the team hadn't won. Usually we'd get a ticking off from officials if we lost, but this time it passed off quite peacefully. When we lost 5–0 to England in October 1958, the Party took official steps to remove our awards as 'Masters of Sport'. As footballers we lived better than the average worker because of the money and the travels so when we failed, the Party officials criticized us for letting the country down. At Torpedo, we were attached to the Likhachov car factory and there was a Communist Party committee secretary there who would summon us to his office for

> ### GARY'S GOLDEN NUGGETS
> Moscow's assorted football clubs all used to have close associations with various divisions of the Soviet state – CSKA was the army team, Torpedo was linked to a car factory, Lokomotiv was for the railway workers, Dynamo was linked to the electricity trades, but the one you didn't want to beat was Moscow Spartak, which allegedly enjoyed the patronage of the KGB.

Symbols of the communist era still dot the Moscow skyline.

a dressing-down. Sometimes we were hauled before the Moscow city committee and told off there as well. So the whole thing was a bit of a paradox: rewards if you won, punishment and criticism if you failed.'

Despite playing in all the qualifying games and scoring vital goals, Ivanov found himself left out of the USSR squad for the 1966 World Cup in England – 'the coach was told that I was too old, so he got rid of me' – which was a great pity because the team produced its best-ever World Cup performance in reaching the semi-finals where they lost 2–1 to West Germany. Since then, qualification and progress in the tournaments have proved somewhat problematical, with nothing better than quarter-final/second stage places achieved in 1970 (lost 1–0 to Uruguay), 1982 (a 1–0 win over Belgium, a 0–0 draw with Poland) and 1986 (a 4–3 defeat by Belgium). In both 1990, their last tournament as the USSR, and in 1994, their first as Russia, exits in the first stage created the belief that not much will be achieved until the problems of entering the post-communist era have been resolved; notably, Georgia and Ukraine as independent nations no longer supply players to the Russian team, and many of Russia's top players prefer life abroad.

'Everything depends on the players themselves,' Ivanov insists. 'If they realize that they are defending the honour of the country, and if each individual realizes he is defending his own good name as a footballer, then we will achieve something in the future.'

Sadly, that future won't embrace the 1998 World Cup; the Russian team was knocked out in the play-offs by Italy.

GARY'S GOLDEN NUGGETS

Anyone who thinks that the Soviet Union's entry into the 1958 World Cup was a product of President Nikita Khrushchev's desire for better relations with the West, may be only half-right. For I was told in Russia that Khrushchev was actually a very keen footballer as a young man, and even considered a career in the game. So was that a football boot he was banging on the desk at the United Nations in 1960?

One of the players from eastern Europe with whom Ivanov shared the 1962 Golden Boot award was Drazan Jerkovic of Yugoslavia. He has been coaching NK Zagreb of Croatia, but unfortunately he has suffered several minor heart-attacks, one of which occurred on the very morning I was due to interview him at the club. It's a great shame I didn't get to meet him because I'm sure he would have important things to say about the break-up of Yugoslavia and the granting of nationhood to Croatia. Yugoslavia's history has embraced the most recent and violent turmoil in Eastern Europe, but football was once a more powerful unifying force than General Tito or communism. The country had a decent World Cup tradition, having been one of only four European countries to compete in the first World Cup in 1930. They reached the semi-final then, losing 6–1 to Uruguay, but performed only patchily on the other occasions on which they qualified, with the exception of Jerkovic's team in Chile in 1962.

There they reached the semi-finals, after beating Uruguay (3–1), Colombia (5–0) and West Germany (1–0), only to lose 3–1 to their near neighbours, Czechoslovakia. Jerkovic scored four goals in total, and Yugoslavia finished in official fourth place behind Chile.

A fruitless trip to the N.K. Zagreb club in Croatia; unfortunately, Drazan Jerkovic was too ill to be interviewed. (*Inset*) Jerkovic photographed at the 1962 World Cup in Chile.

Left: Jerkovic (No. 9) in action for Yugoslavia during their 1962 semi-final against Czechoslovakia. Jerkovic scored but the Czechs won 3–1.

Valentin Ivanov remembers Jerkovic from the match between their two countries in 1962, which the USSR won 2–0.

'They were clever players, the Yugoslavs, they played with their heads, and Jerkovic was exceptional precisely for this reason. And of course he was intuitive when it came to goalscoring. He never missed an opportunity, he would always pick the spot where the ball might reach him in a scoring position.'

Yugoslavia's best effort since then was in Italia '90 – the last time the united Yugoslavia competed – when they reached the quarter-finals and lost to Argentina in Florence only on penalties. Now Yugoslavia consists of just Serbia and Montenegro, but as they showed by whipping Hungary 12–1 in the European play-offs for 1998, the tradition of good football lives on, and they should be feared in their group, as indeed should Croatia in theirs.

One of the unluckiest of the Eastern Europe Golden Boot winners must be Gregorz Lato of Poland – the very fact that you might be saying 'who?' to the mention of his name underlines the near-invisibility of his achievement, partly because of the communist system which still ruled Poland in 1974, and partly because that year's World Cup was dominated by the big names of Gerd Müller, Franz Beckenbauer and Johan Cruyff. Lato's appearance probably didn't help him either – small, balding, round-shouldered, he looked anything but a dangerous striker on the pitch. One last factor contributing to his relative anonymity may well have been that Poland knocked England out of the qualifiers in that historic match at Wembley in October 1973 when they hung on for a crucial 1–1 draw. In English media terms, Poland therefore became a 'non-team' because of the damage they had done to the nation's morale.

When in Munich...sharing a pint with the 1974 Golden Boot winner, Poland's Gregorz Lato.

Nevertheless, Lato's total of seven goals in a tournament dominated by highly organized defences reflects great credit on the man's abilities, even though he disappeared into relative obscurity afterwards. I caught up with him in Munich, the stage for the 1974 World Cup final, where I invited him to relive his memories. First, I wanted to know what had happened to him after the 1974 World Cup.

'Poland is a democratic country now, a free country. There is a conspicuous difference between when I played as a young man in a communist Poland, and the present day when everyone is free. We did not have the freedom to go abroad, to observe games in other countries, how other players practiced and played. There were exceptional cases but I wasn't one of them. It was my dream to go abroad, but the ruling system did not allow it. You had to be at least thirty years of age before you could move, on the grounds that you were no longer of any use to the state. I finally got my move at thirty, to the Lokeren club in Belgium on a three-year contract. Later, I went to Mexico and then Canada. Now I'm back coaching at my old club, Stal Mielec.'

Lato had originally joined this club at the age of twelve, which underlines one of the few positive elements of the communist sports system. Throughout the network, a great emphasis was put on spotting and developing young talent and allowing the kids to grow up in what might be called a sports club culture, where they were given advice and gained experience by being allowed to work directly with older members, rather than having to go through the English apprentice system, which in any case didn't begin until a kid was aged sixteen. I suppose the main worry about the communist set-up was taking youngsters too early and turning them into state-controlled puppets – think of those teenaged gymnasts like Olga Korbut in the 1970s.

But it certainly didn't appear to have any bad effect on Lato. He was among a group of major playing talents to emerge in Poland in the early 1970s – Lubanski, Deyna, Szarmach and Gadocha to name but four – who combined in a gold-medal-winning team at the 1972 Olympics in Munich. England fatally underestimated this squad in the qualifiers, and it is as well to remember that while the draw at Wembley confirmed Poland's 1974 World Cup qualification, it was their 2–0 win earlier in June that did the real damage to England's cause.

'I think the English thought they would beat us five or six nil at Wembley. They hadn't noticed that we'd earlier drawn 1–1 in a friendly with Holland in Rotterdam. So after we'd qualified, we all began to have faith in our ability. We had a wonderful team and we felt confident, although the experts wrote us off because we had been placed in a group with Italy and Argentina.'

Poland's only prior appearance in a World Cup had been in 1938, when they lasted one, albeit remarkable, game. They lost 6–5 to Brazil after extra time; Ernst

Lato in action against Brazil in the 1974 play-off for third place. He scored in Poland's 1–0 win.

Willimowski scored four goals to match the four from Leonidas. So with no tradition behind them, despite the result over England Poland were clear-cut underdogs – a status they changed in their first game when they beat Argentina 3–2, with Lato scoring two of their goals.

'We'd prepared for just three weeks in Poland, played five friendly games, and then they put us on the plane and said, "Come on, boys, do the best you can, and don't put our country to shame." Our coach, Kazimierz Gorski, was a great man who put his heart into our campaign and created a wonderful atmosphere for the team. This is why we started so well.'

Good fortune was also on Poland's side since, as Lato remembers, the Argentinian defence generously donated his two goals – 'The first came after the keeper and a defender had bumped into each other, letting the ball drop for me in front of an empty net, and the second came when I intercepted the keeper's pass to a defender.'

Poland put seven past the group's whipping boys, Haiti, with Lato getting another two goals. This set up the group's deciding game against Italy, who also beat Haiti but needed a win to stay in the tournament after drawing with Argentina. A ruthless Polish side put them out 2–1, so Poland went into a second-stage group featuring Sweden, Yugoslavia and West Germany.

Lato says that at that stage he 'had no thoughts about becoming top scorer. It only became a possibility when I played in our last match, and I realized that I had six goals to my account, and that the other challengers had five or four.'

Lato's further two goals in the second phase helped them beat Sweden (1–0) and Yugoslavia (2–1), leaving them to play West Germany for a place in the final. The Germans were on home soil, but the Poles had strung together five wins on the trot. The showdown took place in bizarre circumstances, with the rain-soaked pitch in Frankfurt being assaulted with all manner of mops, brushes and mechanical rollers in order to try and make it playable.

'The Germans needed only a draw because of their better goal difference, so the pitch was in their favour because it was easier for them to defend. It was like a game of water-polo. I thought the match should have been postponed really, and played the following day. Gerd Müller got their goal from a defensive mistake after they'd missed a penalty, but the hero of the match was Sepp Maier in the German goal for the saves he made. On a good pitch, I'm sure we'd have won.'

The German defender Paul Breitner more or less agreed with this verdict when he was asked if he feared Holland in the final and replied, 'No, because we've already beaten the best team in the tournament, Poland.'

Despite their narrow defeat, Poland summoned enough spirit to beat Brazil 1–0 for third place, with Lato scoring the vital goal. This brought him up to seven for the tournament, enough to win the Golden Boot outright.

Lato renews his acquaintance with an old rival, the German defender Georg Schwarzenbeck.

'I suppose everybody expected Gerd Müller to win it on German soil, but I had a lot of space to move about in,' Lato says modestly. 'Every team we played treated us with disbelief – "Who are these little Poles? We'll beat them without breaking sweat!" – which allowed me to make it a different story.'

Lato's achievements resulted in no great changes in his life – if anything the Polish authorities were even more reluctant to let him live abroad – but he says, 'We were allowed to tour the world and taste a slightly different lifestyle. But I had to stay behind the Iron Curtain as a club player.'

Lato and Poland qualified for Argentina in 1978. They reached the quarter-final group containing Argentina, Peru and Brazil; they could only beat Peru, but Lato added another two World Cup goals to his collection. By 1982, Lato was approaching the veteran stage, and dropping back into midfield. Poland bravely went all the way to the semi-final where they lost 2–0 to Italy, fired in the main by their new striking sensation, Zbigniew Boniek, who scored four goals on the way. Lato got one more goal, and Poland again won the third-place play-off, beating France 3–2.

Poland, as I know only too well, were at Mexico in 1986 in England's group, and generously allowed me a hat-trick to keep England in the competition, and they were then thumped 4–0 by Brazil in the second round. They haven't qualified since, and England gained some revenge for 1973 by knocking them out in the 1998 qualifiers. So the post-communist era has not been so good in footballing terms, despite the freedom it has brought.

'Nobody sane in mind would want it back,' Lato reflects, 'but we miss the financial support that the system put into sport. We need sponsors and cash investment, and the other problem is that any player of eighteen or nineteen with talent will always want to play abroad. You probably won't see another good Polish team in this millennium.'

Despite his sense of gloom about his country's football, and his own lack of reward – 'the players of my time got only fractions of the money that the Polish FA made out of us' – Lato is hanging in there to do his bit, and may even one day become national coach. His record speaks for itself – an Olympic gold medal, ten World Cup goals, two World Cup third places, and an overall Polish record total of forty-six international goals in 104 appearances. Not bad for a player who people can't remember!

One of the 1994 Golden Boot winners, Russia's Oleg Salenko talks me through his five goals against Cameroon.

The last two Eastern European players on the Golden Boot list are certainly contrasting characters, but apart from sharing the same goals total in the 1994 World Cup they also share careers which straddle both the pre- and post-communist eras in their respective countries. Oleg Salenko scored six goals for Russia in 1994, five of them coming in one match against the Cameroon, a record achievement for the World Cup, while Hristo Stoichkov scored six for Bulgaria on their marvellous run to the semi-final, where they were knocked out by Italy. What they also have in common is that they earn their living abroad. Salenko, having played for Valencia in Spain, now turns out for Besiktas in Turkey, while Stoichkov is in his second spell at Barcelona, having sandwiched a spell in Italy with Parma in between.

Salenko's career mirrors all the turmoil that has affected both the country and its football over the past decade. Born in what was then Leningrad and is now back to St Petersburg, he joined the Ukrainian side Dynamo Kiev as a teenager, but when the Championship of Russia – competed for by clubs from all the former Soviet states – collapsed, he went to Spain. Speaking fluent Spanish, Salenko told me about his career while waiting for a knee operation in a German hospital – we went *everywhere* to get our men!

'I knew that I wanted to play abroad because my level was higher than was generally found in Russia at the time, and I wanted to play good football and, of course, earn good money and live a decent life.'

Despite moving, Salenko was called into the Russian squad for the 1994 World Cup, only to watch it disintegrate into factions. A row about who was the best coach broke out, with one group trying to get Pavel Sadyrin the sack before the tournament, and the other staying loyal.

'The problem was that those players who were living abroad had a different attitude from the home-based players. There was a big difference between them and the players in Russia, both in terms of football and life. Since they didn't come across each other during the year, it was very difficult for the team's pyschology to fit in with that of the players from abroad. It takes time before the two can work together. If any other team had prepared for the World Cup in the same way as us, they wouldn't have got anywhere either. There were practical and financial problems as well as idealogical and political ones. The players were simply used as pawns. You can't live for years and years under one system and then after a few years of a new one expect everything to be fine. Before the change from communism, something like this row would not have happened. There was a line you couldn't cross. If you tried, you'd be out of the team and that's all there would be to it.'

The background to the dispute is that a group of Russia's overseas players, including Andrei Kanchelskis (of Manchester United at the time), Igor Shalimov (Inter Milan) and Igor Kolyvanov (Foggia), went to the Russian Football Federation and accused Sadyrin of incompetence, insisting that he should be replaced by Anatoly Byshovets. Byshovets had coached them when the team was still the Soviet Union and then, for the period of the 1992 European Championship, the Commonwealth of Independent States. The Federation stood by Sadyrin; Kanchelskis, Shalimov, Kolyvanov and Sergei Siriakov promptly refused to go to the World Cup.

There was also a row about bonuses in this troublesome mix. The final squad therefore lacked most of its major overseas stars, but Salenko, and the likes of Sergei Yuran and Dmitri Kuznetsov, who were all playing abroad, stayed loyal. The internal strife left them vulnerable.

'I think it was better that they were not playing in the side,' Salenko says, 'because at least the ones who stayed had the

(*Inset*) The troubled 1994 Russian World Cup coach Pavel Sadyrin.

Left: One of his loyal stars, Dimtri Kuznetsov of CSKA Moscow.

Oleg Salenko in record-breaking action against Cameroon in USA '94.

Below: Victor Ndip of Cameroon finds Salenko ready to meet fire with fire in their World Cup clash.

same view. I think if we'd had a bit of time to get over it, we'd have played a lot better.'

The Russians were hardly given the best of starts, having to play Brazil in their first match, which they lost 2–0, and then the improving Sweden to whom they lost 3–1, with Salenko getting their only goal from the penalty spot. They had little chance of qualifying for the next round by the time they played the Cameroon in their last game. The Africans had drawn with Sweden and lost to Brazil.

'We wanted to win one World Cup game,' Salenko says, 'for the sake of our pride.'

Not even Salenko could have predicted what would happen in the game – a very weird spectacle all round, dogged by rumours of strange betting, and culminating in Russia's 6–1 win and Salenko's five-goal haul. He remembers his goals in great detail, and even plays a tape of them back home if he's feeling low. There's a definite sense of unreality about that game if you look at it now, almost as if the Cameroon were determined to lose it – Salenko's second goal, for example, came from a quickly taken free-kick while the Africans stood around arguing with the referee and not watching the ball. Some of the Cameroon defending would have had Alan Hansen frothing at the mouth.

'People say that they weren't interested,' Salenko admits, 'but before the game they had a single point, and a win over us might have let them stay in the World Cup, so I don't think you can say that they weren't in the game.'

Nevertheless, Salenko's fellow top scorer Stoichkov is not a particularly happy bunny about having to share the award with a man who scored five goals in one match of dubious standing. When I relayed these comments to Salenko, he smiled and shrugged.

'This is pretty normal for Stoichkov. I spoke to him after the World Cup and he said, "I am the best striker!" Well, he can say what he wants because I have my goals and my Golden Boot, and I have my world record. Every time I meet him he says the same thing, trying to put me down. But for me, it's not an important argument.'

No, it's not a fake photo – a smiling Hristo Stoichkov in Barcelona.

Hristo Stoichkov, of course, has the reputation of being the 'Mr Grumpy' of world football. When our interview was arranged, I arrived in Barcelona with some trepidation, worrying that a word out of place might provoke the sort of tantrum that he has often reserved for referees who have disallowed his goals. But the Bulgarian international proved to be a charming host and a thoughtful interviewee. It probably helped that it was a wonderfully warm and sunny Catalan day, and that we were sitting aboard his speedboat moored in Barcelona's smart marina. From personal experience, I can vouch for the city as probably the most pleasant place in the world in which to live and play football. Several years there have plainly begun to mellow the man who was once dubbed 'The Beast of the Balkans' by a rabid tabloid hack.

Stoichkov took me for a ride off Barcelona on his speedboat to tell his World Cup story. Stylish, or what?

For all his success and wealth now, Stoichkov didn't have an easy start in life or indeed in football. He flirted with athletics for a long while before turning to football, and even then, because of his size, he found himself being used as a defender.

'I enjoyed athletics, mostly sprints, but gradually I realized that I was never going to be the best athlete in the world and that I was only ever going to be seen by a couple of thousand people. But with football, with a 100,000 crowd watching you score and chanting your name, it's a little different, which is why I changed. I was a centre-half early on, but when the team wasn't playing well, the coach would say to me, "Go upfield." So it was a pure coincidence, but I enjoyed getting the ball in attacking positions, and as time went on I started to score goals and people began to notice my name.'

At school in Plovdiv, Stoichkov says he 'hated losing' and this competitive streak has stayed with him throughout his career, even threatening to engulf it in his early days with his main club CSKA Sofia. In the 1985 Bulgarian Cup final against Levski Spartak, Stoichkov was heavily involved in a brawl after the match, and was eventually banned for a year.

'I was still relatively unknown, I wasn't an international yet, so the football federation decided to suspend me because of my age, and because I had my military service to do and studies to complete. We were still under communist rule and so it was very difficult to speak out. I know I have a strong personality, but when you're out on the pitch you need this in order to be stronger than the defenders. When I go out and a defender can see that I am stronger than him, and hungrier, then I have the advantage.'

Having served his suspension, Stoichkov made his international debut in 1987 and was voted Footballer of the Year in 1989. But, like most eastern bloc players, he knew that it was unlikely he'd be allowed to live and play abroad, especially as CSKA was officially the 'army team'.

'It was very, very difficult, because communism reigned supreme. I knew really talented players who had won over eighty caps for Bulgaria but who weren't allowed to leave because they had to show that Bulgaria was a good side. But slowly, the political climate began to change and a few players were allowed to move abroad. I consider myself one of the lucky ones to be given permission at just twenty-two years of age. I believe that letting me go then allowed me to develop as a player, and helped me to win my awards and championships overseas, so that now Bulgaria is better known as a small country with a great deal of football talent.'

It was Barcelona's manager Johan Cruyff who first spotted Stoichkov and urged the club to sign him, having decided that a certain G. Lineker was surplus to requirements at the Nou Camp Stadium. Stoichkov insists that he wasn't bought as

A sentimental visit to that little Nou Camp Stadium in Barcelona.

a straight replacement for me – 'I would have loved to play in the same team as you,' he says tactfully – but that's the way it felt. No matter, for Stoichkov himself has experienced the unpredictable side of Cruyff as manager, being substituted when playing at the top of his form, or being told to play in a position he hated.

'I still think he's one of the greatest coaches,' Stoichkov says, 'and he showed me a great deal about the game. He would work with me for hours. His only defect was separating the coach from the player – he was still convinced he was a player, and that was difficult to deal with at times.'

Nevertheless, Stoichkov undoubtedly sharpened his game at Barcelona and this in turn benefited Bulgaria, who qualified for the 1994 World Cup by way of a last-second winner against France in Paris. It was Bulgaria's sixth time at a World Cup finals since their first appearance in 1962, but their previous record had been an appalling one. In the sixteen World Cup games they had played, they hadn't won a single one, drawing six and losing ten. When Nigeria thumped them 3–0 in their opening game of USA '94, that miserable run was extended. You would have been able to get pretty long odds on this team reaching the semi-finals, and beating Germany on the way!

'The very least we wanted to achieve,' Stoichkov recalls, 'was our first victory in a World Cup game, and the squad had been working very hard for several years to change Bulgaria's football history.'

In the next game, Stoichkov's team finally won, easily beating a fragile Greek side 4–0.

'They had a very strong side,' Stoichkov says, talking the opposition up somewhat, 'but in the days before the match the Greek coach had said that his team would beat Bulgaria by at least two goals, so I showed the press cuttings to the other players and our coach, and we were determined that we were going to win.'

Stoichkov didn't say whether this ploy derived from watching bullfights in Barcelona – most teams will see a 'red rag' if they find that their opponents have been bad-mouthing them or shouting the odds – but it certainly worked, with Stoichkov getting two of the goals from the penalty spot. They next played Argentina, a game which had been overtaken by the instant suspension imposed on Diego Maradona after he had failed a drugs test in the previous game.

'I was quite upset when I heard about it, and I tried to speak to Diego to offer him my sympathy. But our job as a team was to think about the game. If we wanted to be in the last eight, we had to win against Argentina, and we were mentally prepared to do it.'

Stoichkov scored his third goal of the tournament in Bulgaria's 2–0 win over a confused and angry Argentina, and then let rip with one of his best against Mexico in the second round, accelerating swiftly down the inside-left channel to smash his shot into the roof of the net on the run from fifteen yards or so. The Mexicans put up stiff resistance, however, coping better in the scorching heat, and after equalizing, they took Bulgaria into extra time and then to penalties, where the steadier nerves of the Bulgarians saw them through by three goals to one.

GARY'S GOLDEN NUGGETS

Like that other maverick footballer, Eric Cantona, Hristo Stoichkov has already begun an alternative career as an actor in films, having starred in the Bulgarian Mafia movie 'Spanish Fly'. He may well do more when his playing days are over. The prospect of Cantona and Stoichkov appearing together cannot therefore be ruled out – how about 'Goodfellas 2'?

Bulgaria's finest hour, as they defeat Germany in the 1994 World Cup quarter-finals. Here Buchwald tries to get the ball off Stoichkov.

Bulgaria's run now looked likely to end as they faced the reigning champions, Germany, in the quarter-finals. But Bulgaria's collection of grizzled pros with playing experience all over Europe proved to be a nasty surprise for the Germans, the defining moment coming when Stoichkov curled a wonderful free-kick in for his fifth goal of the tournament, equalizing an earlier penalty from Lothar Matthaus.

'I was the happiest man in the world when I scored that,' he says with a beam which banishes all notions of grumpiness. 'I felt like a seven-year-old kid again. What made it better was that I'd taken two free-kicks before in the game without much success, very badly in fact. But for this one I was concentrating so hard that when I hit the ball I knew it was a goal. I'd seen how the wall had been set up and where their goalie was, and I was convinced I could score. I think I started celebrating even before it went in!'

When Yordan Letchkov's diving header went in three minutes later, Bulgaria went ballistic. The Germans threw everything into attack, but with Stoichkov coming off for a defender, they couldn't break down the Bulgarian resistance and one of the biggest shocks in years had been achieved.

Bulgaria were probably still celebrating by the time they met Italy in the semi-finals, for within twenty-five minutes Roberto Baggio had bagged two goals.

'We didn't play well at the start of the game,' Stoichkov admits, 'and Baggio is an extremely talented player. Italian football is so disciplined, they defend well and the midfield get behind the ball, that I didn't think we could get back in the game.'

But a penalty, calmly converted by Stoichkov on the stroke of half-time, gave them a glimmer of a chance. Indeed Stoichkov is still more than a little grumpy about a hand-ball by Italian defender Alessandro Costacurta in the second-half which the referee didn't see.

'It was a clear penalty, and we were denied an opportunity to score and maybe go into the final. Anyway, I am convinced that the famous final between Brazil and Italy in 1970 was fated to be played out again twenty-four years later.'

Bulgaria barely tried in the third-place play-off against Sweden, losing 4–0. Nevertheless, Stoichkov had what he cherishes as a great consolation in winning a share of the Golden Boot award.

'It's a great feeling to be the best player in the world, but I owed that to my team-mates. Without them I couldn't have scored the penalties, or the free-kicks or the

Stoichkov strokes home his
penalty against Italy in the
1994 semi-final. Italy
won 2–1.

other goals I scored. And I was happy for two Eastern European players, one from Bulgaria, one from Russia, to share the glory.'

Did he use the word 'happy' then? Well, he wasn't quite, for Stoichkov now thinks there was 'something else going on' in the Russia–Cameroon match which allowed Salenko to score five goals, and feels that the award was somewhat tarnished. It's history now, though.

Stoichkov will be back again in France, Bulgaria having qualified ahead of Russia in their group, and he'll be searching for more World Cup goals to add to his total, especially as Spain are in the same group. He'll be thirty two by the time the tournament kicks off, but any notions that Stoichkov can be written off just yet should be dispelled. Despite a disappointing show in Euro '96, he remains one of the most powerful and charismatic forwards in international football, with a very sharp mind, both on and off the pitch.

So the 1998 World Cup will offer us another measure of just how badly Eastern European football has been affected by the cultural switch from state control and funding to the unpredictable workings of free market forces. With no Russians, no Poles and no Czechs present, the red flag has been replaced by banners of independence, and they will be carried with pride by Yugoslavia, Croatia, Romania and Bulgaria.

Evening shade as Stoichkov and I head for dry land.

1958	1962	1966
Just Fontaine (France) 13 goals	Leonel Sanchez (Chile) 4 goals	Eusebio (Portugal) 9 goals

CHAPTER EIGHT

France, Chile and Portugal

Eighteen down, three to go. Although this trio of Golden Boot winners doesn't fit easily into a single geographic or national category, there is a symmetry to their togetherness here, because they became the top scorers in the three consecutive World Cups from 1958 to 1966. A further link is that two of the players were born in Africa – Just Fontaine in Morocco, Eusebio in Mozambique – and although they didn't represent those countries in the tournaments, their rise to prominence provided several clues to the increasing reach of football as the world game, and to the eventual emergence of formidable African teams. We almost take that challenge for granted now, after the exploits of the Cameroon and Nigeria to name but two, which is a fair indication of the widespread acceptance of African teams. I won't labour any points about racism, but once the likes of Fontaine, Pelé and Eusebio had strutted their stuff at the World Cups of the late 1950s and 1960s, there was certainly less reason to think of football as purely 'a white man's game'.

Chez moi: Just Fontaine's villa in the south of France, named after the 1958 hosts Sweden, complete with football.

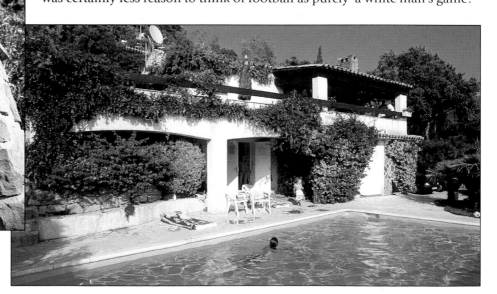

I first met Just Fontaine in Barcelona, where I was watching the European Cup final between Steaua Bucharest and AC Milan in 1989. He elbowed me in the ribs and asked if I was Gary Lineker – well, the ears would have been enough of a clue! – and when I nodded,

Out and about in Marseille, one of the venues for 1998.

he said, 'I scored a few goals in the World Cup, too. I'm Just Fontaine.'

I hadn't even been born at the time of Fontaine's great World Cup success in 1958, but I had heard about his exploits – *thirteen* goals in a single World Cup tournament! Now here he was, modestly describing them as 'a few' – if that's only a few, I'd have loved to have had some of them at any time in my career. It was great to have the chance to talk to Fontaine at greater length than we managed that night at the Nou Camp; and it was no hardship to make my way down to the South of France where Just lives in a spectacular hillside villa, complete with swimming pool and Mediterranean views. The house has two other nice touches – on the gateposts, footballs are mounted instead of the usual stone balls, and the nameplate has a reference to Sweden, the scene of Fontaine's spectacular triumph.

Fontaine was born in Marrakesh in 1933, and played his early football with a Moroccan team, USN Casablanca. By the time he was twenty, the word had got out about this promising young goalscorer, so it wasn't long before a French club signed him – OGC Nice, in 1953. Fontaine repaid their faith by scoring seventeen goals in his first season and helping Nice to the French FA Cup. The Nice team was, like the town itself, a cosmopolitan affair with Hungarian, Spanish and Argentinian players, and although Fontaine fitted in, he began to struggle, as many young players do, the year after his initial success. During the 1955–56 season, Nice won the championship, but Fontaine scored only six goals. Nice's apparent willingness to let him go alerted one of the other top French teams, Stade de Reims, who were looking for a replacement for their outstanding inside-forward Raymond Kopa, who had just been tempted away by the mighty Real Madrid. Fontaine was duly signed for a £12,000 transfer fee, and quickly started to bang in the goals.

The Reims coach was Albert Batteux, and when I caught up with Raymond Kopa, who was to form such a potent partnership with Fontaine in the French national team, he told me about Batteux's abilities to nurture players.

'It was the good fortune of Reims players that they had Batteux as coach because he allowed you to express yourself without restricting your way of playing. In a footballer's career, it's not just talent that counts, but the opportunity to express and develop those qualities that make you different, and Just and I were both fortunate to have Batteux as the mentor in our football lives.'

Fontaine and Kopa missed the chance to play with each other

The other French great of the 1950s, Raymond Kopa.

initially because of their transfers, but when Fontaine eventually joined Kopa in the French team, their contrasting styles seemed to complement each other immediately – 'It was a spontaneous occurrence, an extraordinary meeting of minds,' Kopa says of their intuitive partnership, later dubbed *le tandem terrible*, in which Fontaine played the target man and Kopa the astute provider. Kopa, short in height but very clever on the ball, had led the Reims attack by playing deep, like Hidegkuti of Hungary, while Fontaine was an old-style centre-forward, pushing right up on the defence, always on the alert for a chance, wanting to be played in. It was much the same for me with Peter Beardsley, although we never spoke French to one another!

By the time of the 1958 World Cup, though, Fontaine was not fully established in the national team, having failed to impress in four internationals. According to Kopa, it wasn't expected that he'd lead the attack, 'But the player who was in line for this, René Bliard, got injured, and we were fortunate that Just took his place.'

Fontaine remembers this slightly differently.

'When we travelled to Sweden, the coach took me to one side and told me I was going to play, and that gave me a great confidence boost. In fact, the reason I started scoring goals so quickly was because of this surge of confidence.'

They both agree that the expectations for the French team were pretty low, both from the press and within the team. Fontaine employs a graphic image to sum it up – 'We brought only three sets of shirts, because that's how far we expected to go.'

'I didn't think we'd get too far, either,' Kopa confirms. 'To end up in third place in a World Cup was way beyond my expectations. But right from the start of playing, I knew that things would go pretty well for us.'

In the first game, all France's fears looked like coming true when they found themselves trailing Paraguay 3–2 with forty minutes remaining. A strong rally saw the French score four times in the

time remaining, with Fontaine getting a hat-trick and Kopa getting a goal of his own.

'The Paraguayans were regarded as being as good as the Brazilians at the time,' Kopa recalls, 'so that victory raised our spirits considerably.'

'Getting three goals in my first match was great for my confidence,' says Fontaine, 'but it wasn't an easy game for us despite the final score-line. In the next match, we lost 3–2 to Yugoslavia, and I scored two more goals. I thought we were unlucky because we created lots of opportunities to score goals and didn't take enough of them to get something from the game.'

But with five goals in his first two games, Fontaine could feel ecstatic about his contribution, and about the instant partnership he had struck up with Kopa. The two got a goal apiece as France defeated Scotland 2–1 in their last group match, a victory that sent them through to the quarter-finals, and probably sent the kit manager out to buy some more shirts for the team.

'Scotland was a tough game,' Fontaine says, as if he was letting me in on something I didn't already know. 'They tackled hard, but we were fortunate to get a two-goal lead by half-time, and were able to hold them off in the second half.'

Fontaine's six goals had marked him out as a player to watch. Kopa says, 'Just was always hungry for goals. He was always moving forward and caused such a stir in the opposition's defence that my job was made easier. I was also able to develop my role more, and he was technically gifted enough to allow me to score occasionally!'

'I think I set Kopa up for three of his goals,' Fontaine recalls, 'and he probably made about four out of the thirteen that I eventually scored.'

You might detect a certain edge to the tone here, and indeed there is one because Fontaine's bugbear is being told by everyone that if it wasn't for Kopa he wouldn't have got so many goals. It's not a view that Kopa himself shares, despite the mild provocation.

Take that! Vava scores for Brazil in their 5–2 semi-final win over France in 1958.

'It's true that these remarks irritate Just. But I am privileged to have played with him. My particular style of play needed players around me who were hungry for goals. I had to tie up players, sometimes two or three, even four on occasion, and I was very happy to have a player like Just to give the ball to. I didn't make all his goals, which is why the exaggeration needles him, because there were other good players in our midfield, and anyway, it's the team that counts in football.'

I don't want to get involved in the argument, especially not as a player who knew only too well that it was the contributions of others that helped make me what I became. On the other hand, you do still need someone to stick the ball in the net so I know how Fontaine must feel when fans and critics try to take the credit away from him. No matter, back to the quarter-finals of 1958, where France now beat Northern Ireland 4–0, with another two goals from Fontaine – that's eight in four games! But Nemesis was looming in the shape of the resurgent Brazil, who'd decided to put their faith in two new young players, Garrincha and Pelé. It was France's misfortune that Pelé used that 1958 semi-final to reveal his precocious talent to a world audience. France bothered them for a while, with Fontaine equalizing Vava's early goal, thereby becoming the first player to score against Brazil in the tournament. But as the game wore on, with France determined to stick to their attacking style despite losing defender Jonquet through injury, they simply found themselves out-gunned, as Pelé scored three times.

'He killed us in that game,' says Raymond Kopa. Brazil's eventual 5–2 win put them through to the final, and seemed to have left the French demoralized, and Fontaine stranded on nine goals.

In fact neither was the case, and four days after the disappointment of that defeat, the French and Fontaine took great consolation in thrashing West Germany 6–3 in the third-place play-off match, with Fontaine rattling home another four goals to take his final total to thirteen. He had scored in every game the French had played – not bad for someone who, in most people's eyes, had travelled as a reserve!

'I thought that as we had to stay behind after the defeat by Brazil, I might as well try to score!' Fontaine says with a broad smile.

The goals made Fontaine's name famous across the world, and his career with Reims continued to thrive, especially when Kopa later returned there from Real Madrid. The two great forwards even played against each other in the 1959 European Cup final, when Madrid beat Reims 2–0. Then a badly broken leg affected Fontaine's career quite dramatically; but he had always been a man with a life beyond football – 'My desire in life is not always to kick a football,' he once said – recording songs, occasionally performing in clubs and with a keen business sense. So the tailing off of his career didn't bother him as much as it might a less-rounded individual. He later represented the players' union and was even national coach for a short time, before he returned to the Côte d'Azure to resume what seems to have been a happy and sun-kissed life.

He seemed genuinely moved when I was able to give him his special Golden Boot trophy for being the World Cup's record goalscorer – 'This means more to me

Top: Fontaine (out of picture) scores one of his four goals against West Germany in the third-place play-off match for 1958's World Cup. *(Inset)* Fontaine is chaired off after scoring twice in France's 4–0 quarter-final win against Northern Ireland.

Forty years on, I had the honour to present a Golden Boot trophy to Just Fontaine for his record thirteen goals in the 1958 World Cup.

than any money,' he said, showing the award to his wife. 'In my time, scoring goals at the World Cup wasn't such a big deal. But now if any player beats my total of thirteen goals, he would be a major star!'

Well, he would, Just, but I wouldn't bet on it actually happening!

That 1958 third place was France's best World Cup showing to date, having gone out early in each of the three 1930s World Cups, and again in 1954. But with Kopa ageing and Fontaine retiring in 1961, France couldn't find the resources to qualify in 1962. Their stay in England in 1966 lasted only three matches, and they didn't qualify again until 1978 when, in Argentina, they once again went out in the first round.

A young French midfielder, who was to have a profound effect, revitalizing both the stature and standard of French football over the ensuing twenty years,

A World Cup star and now a World Cup organizer – Michel Platini of France.

made his World Cup debut in Argentina. His name was Michel Platini. Throughout most of the 1980s, either with St Etienne, Juventus or France, Platini was the definitive European playmaker, an astonishingly gifted passer of the ball, who could run and shoot, too.

I went to Paris to have a quick chat with him, while he was putting the finishing touches to the organization of the 1998 World Cup, being Chairman of the French Football Federation's Tournament Committee. In some ways, it would be fitting if France could win this year. Jules Rimet gave us the World Cup, Henri Delaunay the European Championship and Gabriel Hanot, the editor of the French sports magazine *L'Equipe*, dreamt up the European Cup, while Michel Platini was certainly a player who deserved to win the ultimate honour.

He never came closer than that gut-wrenching semi-final against West Germany in Spain in 1982, when the French led the Germans 3–1, deep into extra time, only to see them claw their way back and go on to win the penalty competition. The sheer drama of that match was added to by the actions of the German goalkeeper Harald Schumacher – no relation to Michael, but you might wonder after what he tried to do to Jacques Villeneuve last year! – when he charged from his penalty area to close down Patrick Battiston's run, and then soared through the air to flatten the French player long after the ball had gone.

Platini still goes white with anger when he recalls this incident and the effect it had on the team, not to mention the outcome of the semi-final itself.

'I think we were very unlucky, unlucky in every respect. When Schumacher knocked Battiston senseless, normally you'd have expected him to get a red card. He didn't even get a yellow one. And that changed the game completely – we lost a player and they didn't, and they had a goalkeeper for the penalty shoot-out who should not have been on the pitch. As for the team, we were all devastated because we thought we had lost a friend. We thought Battiston was dead or in a coma. And so we tried to avenge every little injustice on the pitch, and we lost the game. Even now, all the emotions and sentiment of that night make it so big in my life, sixteen years later.'

One of Platini's key opponents that night was Karl-Heinz Rummenigge, whose appearance as substitute also changed the game's narrative in Germany's favour. Rummenigge still deplores Schumacher's foul, but he also remembers talking to Platini after the game.

'I asked Michel why they hadn't simply closed up the game when they were 3–1 ahead, and he told me that they couldn't because they really wanted to "kill" Germany that night, to shake us off their backs, and to show the world that a French team can beat a German team. That was probably their biggest mistake on the night – they had the game won, but wanted more.'

Platini and the French team at least had the chance to show that their form was no fluke when they swept to victory in the European Championship in France in 1984. Platini, with Jean Tigana and Alain Giresse, formed one of the most formidable and talented midfield units of the decade. In the 1986 World Cup in Mexico, France progressed through a wonderful quarter-final with Brazil on penalties, after neither team could break the deadlock of the 1–1 draw set up in normal time.

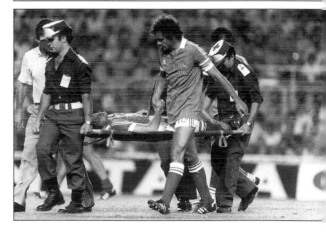

The violent foul on France's Patrick Battiston by West Germany's keeper Harald Schumacher during the 1982 World Cup semi-final in Spain. Platini escorts the stricken Battiston from the field.

'It was a great game for the public to watch, but it wasn't for me, personally,' Platini says with a shrug, before reminding me that he missed one of the penalties in the shoot-out. In the semi-final, fatefully, they met the Germans again, but this time there was less drama, and no revenge, with Andy Brehme and Rudi Völler getting the goals to take West Germany through. France did emulate their predecessors of 1958 by winning the third-place game, 4–2 against Belgium, but since that day in June 1986, they haven't been in a World Cup finals, having missed out in both 1990 and 1994.

So 1998 is a big chance for the French team finally to write their name into the record books of a football competition which their countryman's idea made possible. Their team looks a good one, especially with the likes of Zinedine Zidane and Youri Djorkjaeff, but Euro '96 and Le Tournoi in the summer of 1997 suggested that they might lack a consistent goalscorer – or is there another Fontaine lurking in the squad, ready to rewrite history?

Chile will be taking part in France '98 and will also be seeking to improve on their best finish, third place, in the six appearances they've made in past World Cup finals. The year they were hosts, 1962, was their *annus mirabilis*, and the 1998 draw which groups them with Italy will be of particular piquancy to Leonel Sanchez, one of the six Golden Boot winners in 1962. For apart from his goals, Sanchez was also one of the key figures in the infamous Group 2 game, dubbed the 'Battle of Santiago', between the Chilean and Italian teams, when fouls and fighting during the match carried on after the final whistle.

The spectacular National Stadium in Santiago, Chile, the setting for the 1962 World Cup final.

I took a quick detour over the Andes to Chile during the South American leg of my journey, and met up with Sanchez at the national stadium in Santiago which Chile both graced and disgraced in the same tournament.

GARY LINEKER'S GOLDEN BOOTS

Left: Leonel Sanchez (far right) in legitimate action for Chile v Switzerland. Chile won 3–1.

Below: Sanchez as he is now.

I'd seen some of the black-and-white footage from that 1962 brawl, and was inwardly afraid that I was about to meet the Chilean counterpart of Vinnie Jones, or maybe even a relative of that other Crazy Gang member, *Lawrie* Sanchez. But Leonel is a quietly spoken, silver-haired chap with a wry sense of humour. Of course, the stadium we were sitting in had seen even darker times outside the realms of football; it was used as a holding zone for 'prisoners' during the 1973 military coup against President Allende. We should always keep football in perspective, even the World Cup.

Sanchez currently runs two football schools for five to twelve year olds, and scouts talent for the University of Chile team, whose ground this is and for whom he played throughout his career.

'I'm a sort of icon here,' he says, 'precisely because of that 1962 World Cup, for what we did for Chilean football in finishing third in that tournament. There is still a long way to go before we can ever be world champions, and I'll probably be dead before it happens. Three of the 1962 team have already passed away.'

Sanchez's reflections on mortality may seem a bit premature for a man in his early sixties, but he has lived his life so close to his country's struggle for football success that perhaps it's beginning to weigh him down. He joined the Universidad de Chile club at ten years old, advancing with other talented youngsters so rapidly that they were dubbed 'the blue ballet' because of their elegant way of playing. He became a Chilean international at the age of seventeen in 1955 and was rated one of the best left-wingers in South America, with a penchant for goalscoring.

Chile were awarded the 1962 tournament by FIFA as a way of helping the country rebuild after a traumatic earthquake in 1960.

'It came very quickly,' Sanchez remembers, 'but it wasn't as big as some people think. Lots of things in Chile were improved specially for the World Cup. The poor people got a lot out of it in terms of new housing, and everybody was pretty happy about the tournament coming here. They had reasonable expectations of the team because we'd prepared hard for two years under a coach by the name of Fernando Riera, who'd done a lot work in Europe and then Uruguay. We did a tour of Europe in 1960, losing 6–0 to France among other results, and in 1961 we played sixty-eight matches against assorted club and national sides as part of our build-up.'

Chile were drawn in Group 2, alongside Italy, West Germany and Switzerland, which looked like a classic 'group of death' for the host nation. But in their first game against the Swiss, the young Chilean side won 3–1, with Sanchez becoming an instant hero by scoring two goals.

'Our coach had insisted that we should be relaxed, and we repeated to ourselves "I have to be calm". They told us this because we were very young – I was twenty-four at the time – and because there was a crowd of over 65,000 in the stadium. So when Switzerland scored in the seventh minute and the stadium fell silent, we had talked about this situation already and had prepared for it. We kept playing calmly, stayed confident with the ball and I managed to get our first goal after playing a one–two. Jaime Ramirez put us ahead, and then I scored the third. We started to entertain the crowd then, with them chanting "Ole!" as we passed the ball around. It was a very important victory for us.'

Unfortunately, the next game against Italy turned out to be memorable for all the wrong reasons. The background to what became one of the biggest punch-ups in football history is described by Sanchez.

'There had been a few Italian journalists travelling around Chile, sending back reports which made disparaging remarks about Chilean women. The Chilean community in Italy saw the reports and sent the clippings back to Chile, and though the players didn't get involved in the row, the rest of the country was very upset and hurt by what had been said. So when the Italians came out on the pitch, they were carrying flowers to give out to the women in the crowd as an apology, but the women threw them straight back and started shouting at the Italian players.'

Fired up by the dispute, the Chilean team initially took their revenge in the best form by taking a 2–0 lead in the second half, although the match had teetered on the brink of violence throughout. The Italians were now being goaded by the Chilean players. Sanchez reports that the Italian team was packed with three or four players of Argentinian descent and when the niggling started, they were told by the Chilean players that they'd sold out their country by playing for Italy. And then came the spark which ignited the the firework box.

'We were trying to protect our lead,' Sanchez recalls, 'so as I was two-footed, I was dribbling the ball towards the corner to use up time. The rest of the team were giving me the ball and telling me to keep it, so they have to foul me or concede a corner. Their defender David came in and kicked me, and I fell to the ground, but

as the ball was still trapped between my feet, he kept on kicking at me to try and get it out. So I stood up and clocked him one with my left hand.'

The incident happened in full view of the linesman, and the English referee Ken Aston must have had a reasonable view himself, but he decided to do nothing more than give the players a telling off.

'We had done enough to be sent off,' Sanchez admits, 'but the referee just gave us a warning by way of the linesman who spoke Spanish. About three minutes later, David came flying in at me, feet up, and kicked me again. His foot was almost up to my shoulder. The referee saw it all and sent him off, taking him to the side of the pitch by the arm. I was still on the deck, with the doctor checking me. I didn't have anything major wrong, but you know that in this profession a little bit of acting is required sometimes.'

'It happened like this, Gary.' Sanchez shows me the spot where he decked David with a left hook.

From the footage I've seen of that particular incident, Sanchez was lucky not to be decapitated by David's lunge, so it's pretty doubtful that the referee needed any additional encouragement to send the Italian off. Another, Ferrini, soon followed and at the final whistle, words and gestures were exchanged and a free-for-all broke out and swirled around the field, with some of the team officials joining in the fisticuffs for good measure.

'I think you regret something like that the moment you do it,' Sanchez says, looking a picture of innocence, 'because I could have left my team with one player less. What I did wasn't right, I admit it now and I said the same after the match itself. Both my reaction and his were wrong, and it disappointed our teams, especially mine because we were at home. Ironically, I ended up playing with David at Milan for a while, and we became great friends.'

Surprisingly, Sanchez, who allegedly smacked another Italian player, Maschio, in the face, breaking his nose, wasn't sent off, or suspended, nor were any of his team-mates. But they lost their next game, 2–0 to West Germany, which denied them the chance of topping their group and staying in Santiago, and meant that they now faced the USSR, one of the pre-tournament favourites, in the quarter-final up the coast at Arica.

'It was a tiny stadium, but it was full, with about 17,000 fans in it,' Sanchez remembers. 'They were all in a good mood because we had gone further than people expected.'

When Sanchez blasted in a free-kick from way out on the left, the crowd's mood improved even further.

'It was a set move. I was to hit the ball as hard as I could and the others would look for a rebound. But at the moment I took the kick, the famous Russian goal-keeper, Lev Yashin, moved about six yards off his line, and the shot went whistling into the roof of the net.'

Russia equalized in the second half through Chislenko, but then Sanchez laid on another party piece, dribbling past three Russian defenders and crossing for Elario Rojas to slip the ball past Yashin. Then they just held on for victory and a place in the semi-finals.

'We were disappointed that we had to play Brazil. At that stage, there were two South American teams left and two from Europe; the rules didn't allow for both teams from the same continent to go through. Even without Pelé, Brazil were a strong side, and I think Garrincha was an extraordinary player; they used to give him the ball when they wanted a rest. We had a chance in the first ten minutes with a shot from Contreras which hit the post, but then Garrincha scored twice. We got one back before half-time, and now it was Vava's turn to score two goals. I got another goal for us from a penalty.'

Chile's great adventure ends, as Vava celebrates one of his two goals in Brazil's semi-final victory.

The spot-kick gave Sanchez his fourth goal of the tournament, and by the time the matches had been completed, six players were on the four-goal total. There wasn't actually a Golden Boot in those days, but Sanchez recalls how the top scorer award was later decided by drawing lots at a dinner.

'They put all the names in a bag and a woman pulled one out and it was announced through the microphone that Garrincha would get the trophy, and everybody congratulated him. I felt happy for him because I admired him so much, he was a great player and he deserved it. We all received a beautiful diploma each. I was just proud to be in that company. A top scorer in a World Cup!'

Sanchez played in England in the 1966 World Cup, where Chile faced Italy in their very first match; this time it passed off peacefully with a 2–0 win for the *azzurri*, while Chile managed a single point from a 1–1 draw with North Korea.

Since then, qualification has been limited to two brief appearances, in West Germany in 1974 (two points) and in Spain in 1982 (one point). But with highly rated strikers such as Marcello Salas and Ivan Zamorano, they may well get beyond the first round in France.

Sanchez never got to play against the 1966 World Cup's top scorer, Eusebio, but knew all about him from the Chilean coach who had once worked at Benfica. In fact, news of Eusebio spread around the football world from 1962 onwards, after he had scored two goals in Benfica's 5–3 defeat of Real Madrid in the European Cup final, a match of rabid goalscoring. Eusebio also scored the next year at Wembley, when Benfica lost the final to AC Milan. Instantly nicknamed the 'Black Panther', a name that probably wouldn't get past politically correct watchdogs today, Eusebio did indeed have a big-cat's power and grace to his movements.

He was born in January 1943 in Lorenzo Marques, a coastal town in the Portuguese colony of Mozambique, which finally gained its independence in 1975. He was one of eight children in a family that lost its father when Eusebio was only five years old. As an escape from the drudgery of household chores and other jobs, he played football on wasteland and in the streets around his home. A champion sprinter at school, Eusebio was spotted playing by one of the visiting Sporting Lisbon players as a sixteen year old and was soon registered to his home town club, Sporting Lorenzo Marques. When Sporting returned the next year for a game, they were apparently amazed by the talents of the seventeen-year-old Eusebio, and immediately tabled a bid. Unfortunately, Benfica had also made an offer, which sparked a drawn-out argument over whose property Eusebio was. He was flown to Lisbon – his arrival reportedly marked by a kidnap attempt by agents of one of the competing clubs – and

Eusebio returns to Wembley, the scene of his tearful exit in the 1966 World Cup semi-final.

after a lengthy hearing the Portuguese Football Federation ruled that Benfica should have him. His 'coronation' occurred in June 1961 when Benfica played Brazil's Santos in a friendly – Eusebio was fielded against Pelé. Pelé's team won 6–3, but Eusebio out-scored him by three goals to two!

It's surely no accident that Portugal's first-ever qualification for the World Cup came while Eusebio was in his prime in 1966. They'd been trying since the second World Cup in Italy, but had never made it. For 1966, they finished top of a difficult qualifying group containing Czechoslovakia, Romania and Turkey.

I met up with Eusebio at Wembley Stadium, the scene of much heartbreak for him thanks to Portugal's losing semi-final against England in '66 and Benfica's 4–1 defeat by Manchester United in the 1968 European Cup final. But such are his individual achievements in world football that really no stadium should hold any fears for him. In my experience, it is true to say that wherever he goes he still generates awe and respect from those who know.

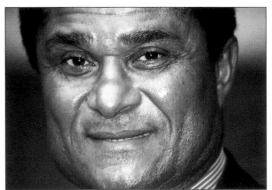

Still a great ambassador for football, Eusebio as he is today.

I asked him about his first memory of a World Cup and he cited the 1958 tournament which he listened to on the radio in Mozambique. Pelé was only just over a year older than Eusebio, so was too young to be an instant role model. Instead, his eyes were on Europe and the likes of Ferenc Puskas and Alfredo di Stefano. Within four years he would be playing against, and beating, these two heroes in that 1962 European Cup final.

'It was a really great match,' Eusebio recalls with that huge smile of his. 'I was very emotional because I was playing in a final against Real Madrid with some of the biggest names in the game. To be on the same pitch as di Stefano, and actually win, gave me a fantastic feeling. At the end of the game, the thing I most wanted was to swap shirts with di Stefano. I wasn't interested in the Cup or the winner's medal. I wanted his shirt, and when I got it, I wept.'

By 1965, Eusebio had made sufficient impact to be voted European Footballer of the Year, and then in 1966 he brought Portugal to England to participate in their first World Cup.

'We had a good team spirit from the start, and this helped us to win the first few matches,' he says.

This is a mild understatement on Eusebio's behalf, given that Portugal found themselves grouped with champions Brazil, Hungary and Bulgaria, and promptly proceeded to rip three goals past each of them. A 3–1 win over Hungary was made to look even better when Hungary took Brazil apart 3–1 at Goodison Park. Portugal were meanwhile easing Bulgaria home, 3–0, with Eusebio getting his first goal of the competition, and then came the crunch match. Brazil, needing a win to stay in the tournament, were Portugal's next victims at a packed Goodison, where the crowds thought they were in heaven, such was the football. But this time, apart from the goals – two from Eusebio, one from Simoes – that sealed the 3–1 win, there was also a ruthless demolition job perpetrated on an already vulnerable Pelé by the Portuguese defence.

'The Brazilians had had some set-backs,' Eusebio pointed out. 'Some of their star players were injured. Pelé was carrying a knee injury, and Garrincha didn't play again after the match against Bulgaria. They brought in some new players, but we played well on the night. The Brazilian journalists said that Morais kicked Pelé. I think he caught him on the ankle, but I think Pelé did a bit of play-acting, a theatrical performance, but I don't think it influenced the result. We deserved to win and Pelé was not a hundred per cent.'

While Eusebio's recollections may be coloured by the inevitable rivalry between Portugal and one of its former colonies, there was no doubt about his goalscoring prowess in the match – a leaping header for the first, and a wonderful volley, his body arched like a bow, for the second.

'I practised a lot. I used to put my whole body behind the ball. I would never shoot with the aim of lifting the ball, I always tried to keep it low. So my way of running and always shooting low with my body over the ball caused it to travel very fast.'

Portugal's next opponents, in the quarter-finals, should have been Italy, but Italy managed to lose to North Korea, and so it was a completely unknown team that the Portuguese faced at Goodison Park on 23 July 1966. Whether the Portuguese were spooked or overconfident, they found themselves 3–0 down after twenty-two minutes, as the North Koreans swarmed through them.

'Our defence was very nervous,' Eusebio recalls, 'and our captain, Mario Coluna, went around trying to keep the players calm on the field, trying to stop us conceding any more goals. But what we also needed was to score before half-time to get back into the match.'

Eusebio obliged, pulling two goals back, one from the penalty spot. Now it was the Koreans turn to get nervous. Eusebio hit another early in the second half to level the scores at 3–3, and won another penalty with a twisting run into the area which the Koreans' could only end with a foul. Eusebio scored again – four goals in the match, seven in the tournament so far. A late goal by José Augusto clinched a momentous 5–3 win for Portugal.

'I remember, after scoring the goals,' Eusebio says mistily of that great day, 'that I took the ball back to the centre spot immediately – celebrations would have lost

Eusebio soars to head home in Portugal's 3–1 win over champions Brazil at Goodison Park in 1966.

Eusebio scores the first of his four goals against North Korea in the dramatic 1966 quarter-final – Portugal won 5–3 after being 3–0 down!

us time. I remember during those moments seeing the Korean coaches fanning themselves because of the heat, or perhaps because we were scoring. It was a fantastic day, and was one of the best games of my life!'

On their World Cup debut, Portugal had now reached the semi-finals. The bad news for them was that they had to face England at Wembley.

'We were not uneasy, because it was England that had to beat Portugal. The pressure wasn't on us to win. So we took to the field in good spirits and just played.'

With Eusebio fully exposed as a threat by now, England deployed Nobby Stiles to try and keep him quiet.

'Nobby was the one who marked the best and most feared players. He had done it before to me when I'd played against Manchester United. I didn't have that much difficulty with him once I got the ball because Nobby didn't have as much pace as me. But he did cut out a lot of passes to me. Nobby played hard, but correctly, and we are still firm friends. But I wasn't happy with my shooting that night, that's the real reason we lost.'

England's 2–1 win had the emotional Eusebio in floods of tears, winning the hearts of the English nation even in the moment of their great triumph.

'At the end of the game, I looked up and said to myself, "My God, what have I done wrong? I never win in this stadium." And I started crying. I didn't cry for having lost the game, because I probably would have cried if we'd won it. It was just an emotional occasion.'

Eusebio's late penalty in the match hoisted his total of goals to eight, and he scored another penalty in Portugal's 2–1 win over Russia in the third-place game.

He was the clear-cut Golden Boot winner, with a third-place medal on his World Cup debut, which seemed a promising start to his international achievements.

'These were the two most wonderful things in my career as a footballer,' Eusebio says sweetly. Sadly, Portugal could never really live up to him, and in fact didn't qualify again until 1986, when they beat…er…England 1–0, but also managed to lose to Poland and Morocco. Since then, nothing.

Eusebio's career represented more than just trophies and awards. He was, and still is, an ambassador for the footballers of Africa, living proof that there is no such thing as a colour-code to football talent.

'African teams have really improved, and there are some great players now. George Weah was World Footballer of the Year, as I was once, too. But I'm not sure about their organization. When they manage to get that right, one of the African teams will definitely win a World Cup. Nigeria are probably the ones with the best

Gordon Banks thwarts Eusebio in England's 2–1 semi-final win at Wembley in 1966.

chance. They're Olympic Champions, beating Brazil and Argentina. It will happen one day.'

Bobby Robson remembers Eusebio as 'the strongest player, the most powerful athlete I ever saw on a football pitch. He is immortal in Portugal, they have statues of him and everything!' Bobby Charlton ranks him 'among the top five best players I ever saw or played with'. This is well-deserved praise for the man who brought so much joy to football, whose goal celebrations were a delight to watch in themselves, and whose sportsmanship shone through even in defeat.

These last three Golden Boot winners, at the end of my journey, emphasize just how random a business scoring goals in the World Cup finals can be. Fontaine was a reserve, Sanchez a winger, and Eusebio a World Cup novice. We may think before the tournament, as most of the players and managers I spoke to do, that Brazil's Ronaldo is a certainty for the top scorer's crown in 1998; but the defences know that he is coming and will prepare themselves in depth. The classic Golden Boot winner is a relative unknown, as I was twelve years ago, a 'sleeper', a newcomer with the daring not to be inhibited by the occasion. Whoever he is in 1998, his life will be changed immeasurably by winning the award. As I've found out on my travels, this wasn't always so, but the modern world of football has put the highest possible prices on the goalscorers because we understand now that whatever else happens in the game, goals mean gold.

URUGUAY
1930

With only four European teams entering this first tournament, and eight from South or North America, the competition had an unbalanced feel to it, reflected by the four pools which were meant to decide the four semi-finalists. Each one had a European team in it to give them a chance, but in the end only Yugoslavia managed to get beyond the first stage, beating Brazil in their group, one of only four victories for the European teams.

The awkward size of the entry – thirteen teams – meant that Pool 1 teams had to play three games rather than two. The favourites for the trophy – Argentina and Uruguay – had met in the 1928 Olympic final, and their superiority over the rest was emphasized by their 6–1 wins in what were supposed to be competitive semi-finals.

Even so, there was no doubt that the public developed an instant taste for the World Cup – an aggregate of 343,500 spectators watched the eighteen matches, of which 90,000 turned up for the final itself. Uruguay took the Jules Rimet trophy in some style, emphasizing the advantage of being the host nation, and therefore adding to the squabbling over who would stage the next World Cup. Some things never change!

MATCH RESULTS:

POOL 1

France 4	**Mexico 1**
Laurent	Carreno
Langiller	
Maschinot 2	

Argentina 1	**France 0**
Monti	

Chile 3	**Mexico 0**
Vidal	
Subiabre 2	

Chile 1	**France 0**
Subiabre	

Argentina 6	**Mexico 3**
Stabile 3	Lopez
Varallo 2	F. Rosas
Zumelzu	M. Rosas

Argentina 3	**Chile 1**
Stabile 2	Subiabre
M. Evaristo	

	P	W	D	L	F	A	Pts
Argentina	3	3	0	0	10	4	6
Chile	3	2	0	1	5	3	4
France	3	1	0	2	4	3	2
Mexico	3	0	0	3	4	13	0

POOL 2

Yugoslavia 2	**Brazil 1**
Tirnanic	Neto
Beck	

Yugoslavia 4	**Bolivia 0**
Beck 2	
Marianovic	
Vujadinovic	

Brazil 4	**Bolivia 0**
Visintainer 2	
Neto 2	

	P	W	D	L	F	A	Pts
Yugoslavia	2	2	0	0	6	1	4
Brazil	2	1	0	1	5	2	2
Bolivia	2	0	0	2	0	8	0

POOL 3

Romania 3	**Peru 1**
Staucin 2	Souza
Barbu	

Uruguay 1	**Peru 0**
Castro	

Uruguay 4	**Romania 0**
Dorado	
Scarone	
Anselmo	
Cea	

	P	W	D	L	F	A	Pts
Uruguay	2	2	0	0	5	0	4
Romania	2	1	0	1	3	5	2
Peru	2	0	0	2	1	4	0

POOL 4

USA 3	**Belgium 0**
McGhee 2	
Patenaude	

USA 3	**Paraguay 0**
Patenaude 2	
Florie	

Paraguay 1	**Belgium 0**
Pena	

	P	W	D	L	F	A	Pts
USA	2	2	0	0	6	0	4
Paraguay	2	1	0	1	3	2	2
Belgium	2	0	0	2	0	4	0

SEMI-FINALS:

Argentina 6	**USA 1**
Monti	Brown
Scopelli	
Stabile 2	
Peucelle 2	

Uruguay 6	**Yugoslavia 1**
Cea 3	Seculic
Anselmo 2	
Iriarte	

FINAL:

Uruguay 4	**Argentina 2**
Dorado	Peucelle
Cea	Stabile
Iriate	
Castro	

Uruguay: Ballesteros, Nasazzi, Mascheroni, Andrade, Fernandez, Gestido, Dorado, Scarone, Castro, Cea, Iriarte

Argentina: Botasso, Della Torre, Paternoster, J. Evaristo, Monti, Suarez, Peucelle, Varallo, Stabile, Ferreira, M. Evaristo

Golden Boot: Guillermo Stabile (Argentina)

The shadow of dictator Benito Mussolini fell darkly across this World Cup, with the Italian team under great pressure to produce a home win. Even the official tournament poster was dated not 1934, but 'Year 12', Mussolini having become Italy's Prime Minister in 1922.

Sixteen teams qualified, although Uruguay, the reigning champions, didn't bother to enter in retaliation for Europe's poor response four years earlier. Italy and Austria were the pre-tournament favourites, with Italy having imported several Argentinian internationals of Italian descent to strengthen their claim. The straightforward knock-out structure did away with the need for groups or pools, and the concepts of extra time and replays were introduced for the first time as a means of settling games. But it was a long way for Brazil and Argentina to come for just one game! Apart from their 7–1 win in the first round, Italy struggled, needing a replay to get past Spain, and then squeezing past Austria with a single goal. Nor was their final performance as convincing as they had hoped, with the tournament's surprise package, the Czechs, taking a lead with twenty minutes left. One of Italy's imported Argentinians scored their vital but apparently flukey equalizer, and Italy went on to score again through Schiavio in extra time to win the trophy for Mussolini. Victory was all that was required in the circumstances.

MATCH RESULTS:

FIRST ROUND:

Italy 7	USA 1
Schiavio 3	Donnelli
Orsi 2	
Meazza	
Ferrari	

Czechoslovakia 2	Romania 1
Puc	Dobai
Nejedly	

Germany 5	Belgium 2
Conen 3	Voorhoof 2
Kovierski 2	

Austria 3	France 2
Sindelar	Nicolas
Schall	Verriest
Bican	
(after extra time; 1–1 at full time)	

Spain 3	Brazil 1
Iraragorri (pen)	Silva
Langara 2	

Switzerland 3	Holland 2
Kielholz 2	Smit
Abegglen	Vente

Sweden 3	Argentina 2
Jonasson 2	Bellis
Kroon	Galateo

Hungary 4	Egypt 2
Teleky	Fawzi 2
Toldi 2	
Vincze	

SECOND ROUND:

Germany 2	Sweden 1
Hohmann 2	Dunker

Austria 2	Hungary 1
Horwarth	Sarosi (pen)
Zischek	

Italy 1	Spain 1
Ferrari	Regueiro
(after extra time; 1–1 at full time)	

Italy 1	Spain 0
Meazza	
(replay)	

Czechoslovakia 3	Switzerland 2
Svoboda	Kielholz
Sobotka	Abegglen
Nejedly	

SEMI-FINALS:

Czechoslovakia 3	Germany 1
Nejedly 3	Noack

Italy 1	Austria 0
Guaita	

THIRD-PLACE PLAY-OFF:

Germany 3	Austria 2
Lehner 2	Horwarth
Conen	Seszta

FINAL:

Italy 2	Czech 1
Orsi	Puc
Schiavio	
(after extra time; 1–1 at full time)	

Italy: Combi, Monzeglio, Allemandi, Ferraris IV, Monti, Bertolini, Guaita, Meazza, Schiavio, Ferrari, Orsi

Czechoslovakia: Planicka, Zenizek, Ctyroky, Kostalek, Cambal, Krcil, Junek, Svoboda, Sobotka, Nejedly, Puc

Golden Boot: Oldrich Nejedly (Czechoslovakia)

FRANCE
1938

The last World Cup before the outbreak of the Second World War, and the tentacles of conflict had already reached football, with Austria having to withdraw after its 'friendly' annexation by Germany three months before the tournament. To add insult to injury, the Germans cherry-picked the best of the Austrian squad for their own team, but the Swiss team refused to honour the Nazi salute and promptly knocked Germany out in the first round. Italy, the champions, had grown in stature since 1934, having won the gold medal at the controversial 1936 Olympics in Berlin, but were nearly caught out by Norway in their first match. They, and a Brazilian team which was gamely coming to terms with travel to Europe, represented the strongest threats, although Hungary showed what talent they were developing by coming right through to the final against Italy. Argentina refused to travel after being turned down as hosts, but FIFA's plans for world expansion also attracted some unusual entries – Cuba (standing in for Mexico) and the Dutch East Indies – among the field of fifteen countries, an awkward number which meant that Sweden were given a bye to the second round in order to guarantee the correct numbers for the quarter-finals. The knock-out formula, with extra time and replays where necessary, was retained from 1934. Oh, and England, offered an invitation to replace the unfortunate Austrians, politely declined. At least there were plenty of goals to savour – eighty-four of them in total!

MATCH RESULTS:

FIRST ROUND:

Switzerland 1	Germany 1
Abegglen	Gauchel

(after extra time; 1–1 at full time)

Switzerland 4	Germany 2
Wallaschek	Hahnemann
Bickel	Loertscher (og)
Abegglen 2	

(replay)

Cuba 3	Romania 3
Tunas	Covaci
Maquina	Baratki
Sosa	Dobai

(after extra time; 2–2 at full time)

Cuba 2	Romania 1
Socorro	Dobai
Maquina	

(replay)

Hungary 6	Dutch East
Kohut	Indies 0
Toldi	
Sarosi 2	
Szengeller 2	

France 3	Belgium 1
Vienante	Isemborghs
Nicolas 2	

Czechoslovakia 3	Holland 0
Kostalek	
Boucek	
Nejedly	

(after extra time; 0–0 at full time)

Brazil 6	Poland 5
Leonidas 4	Willimowski 4
Peracio	Piontek
Romeu	

(after extra time; 4–4 at full time)

Italy 2	Norway 1
Ferrari	Brustad
Piola	

(after extra time; 1–1 at full time)

SECOND ROUND:

Sweden 8	Cuba 0
Andersson	
Jonasson	
Wetterstroem 4	
Nyberg	
Keller	

Hungary 2	Switzerland 0
Szengeller 2	

Italy 3	France 1
Colaussi	Heisserer
Piola 2	

Czechoslovakia 1	Brazil 1
Nejedly (pen)	Leonidas

(after extra time; 1–1 at full time)

Czechoslovakia 1	Brazil 2
Kopecky	Leonidas
	Roberto

(replay)

SEMI-FINALS:

Italy 2	Brazil 1
Colaussi	Romeu
Meazza (pen)	

Hungary 5	Sweden 1
Szengeller 3	Nyberg
Titkos	
Sarosi	

THIRD-PLACE PLAY-OFF:

Brazil 4	Sweden 2
Romeu	Jonasson
Leonidas 2	Nyberg
Peracio	

FINAL:

Italy 4	Hungary 2
Colaussi 2	Titkos
Piola 2	Sarosi

Italy: Olivieri, Foni, Rava, Seratoni, Andreolo, Locatelli, Biavati, Meazza, Piola, Ferrari, Colaussi

Hungary: Szabo, Polgar, Biro, Szalay, Szucs, Lazar, Sas, Vincze, Sarosi, Szengeller, Titkos

Golden Boot: Leonidas da Silva (Brazil)

After being ravaged by war, Europe was in no shape to stage a World Cup, so the competition returned to South America with Brazil. The British teams had finally rejoined FIFA in 1946, and the Home Championship was designated as a qualifying group, with the first two going through. England won, but Scotland apparently decided that being runners-up wasn't good enough for them to travel. A host of other petty politics saw Argentina, France and Turkey withdraw before the competition started, with the result that the entry numbered thirteen, a total which was almost impossible to structure into a meaningful competition. To make matters worse, a pool system had been reintroduced without a knock-out element. Spain and Sweden – but not England – proved to be the biggest European threats, but it was the two major South American teams who dominated. The organizers got out of jail when the last scheduled match turned out to be the tournament decider, although Uruguay's shock win over a free-scoring Brazil was not meant to be in the script for the 200,000 fans inside the Maracana Stadium – a World Cup record attendance.

BRAZIL
1950

IV CAMPEONATO
MUNDIAL DE
FUTEBOL
·TACA JULES RIMET·

JUNHO DE 1950
BRASIL

MATCH RESULTS:

POOL 1:

Brazil 4   **Mexico 0**
Ademir 2
Jair
Baltazar

Yugoslavia 3   **Switzerland 0**
Tomasevic 2
Ognanov

Yugoslavia 4   **Mexico 1**
Bubek   Casarin
Cjaicowski 2
Tomasevic

Brazil 2   **Switzerland 2**
Alfredo   Fatton
Baltazar   Tamini

Brazil 2   **Yugoslavia 0**
Ademir
Zizinho

Switzerland 2   **Mexico 1**
Bader   Velasquez
Fatton

	P	W	D	L	F	A	Pts
Brazil	3	2	1	0	8	2	5
Yugoslavia	3	2	0	1	7	3	4
Switzerland	3	1	1	1	4	6	3
Mexico	3	0	0	3	2	10	0

POOL 2:

Spain 3   **USA 1**
Basora 2   J. Souza
Zarra

England 2   **Chile 0**
Mortensen
Mannion

USA 1   **England 0**
Gaetjens

Spain 2   **Chile 0**
Basora
Zarra

Spain 1   **England 0**
Zarra

Chile 5   **USA 2**
Robledo   Pariani
Cremaschi 3   J. Souza
Prieto

	P	W	D	L	F	A	Pts
Spain	3	3	0	0	6	1	6
England	3	1	0	2	2	2	2
Chile	3	1	0	2	5	6	2
USA	3	1	0	2	4	8	2

POOL 3:

Sweden 3   **Italy 2**
Jeppson 2   Carapellese
Andersson   Mucinelli

Sweden 2   **Paraguay 2**
Sundquist   A. Lopez
Palmer   F. Lopez

Italy 2   **Paraguay 0**
Carapellese
Pandolfini

	P	W	D	L	F	A	Pts
Sweden	2	1	1	0	5	4	3
Italy	2	1	0	1	4	3	2
Paraguay	2	0	1	1	2	4	1

POOL 4:

Uruguay 8   **Bolivia 0**
Schiaffino 4
Miguez 2
Vidal
Ghiggia

	P	W	D	L	F	A	Pts
Uruguay	1	1	0	0	8	0	2
Bolivia	1	0	0	1	0	8	0

FINAL POOL:

Uruguay 2   **Spain 2**
Ghiggia   Basora 2
Varela

Brazil 7   **Sweden 1**
Ademir 4   Andersson (pen)
Chico 2
Maneca

Uruguay 3   **Sweden 2**
Ghiggia   Palmer
Miguez 2   Sundquist

Brazil 6   **Spain 1**
Jair 2   Igoa
Chico 2
Zizinho
Parra (og)

Sweden 3   **Spain 1**
Johansson   Zarra
Mellberg
Palmer

Uruguay 2   **Brazil 1**
Schiaffino   Friaca
Ghiggia

Uruguay: Maspoli, M. Gonzales, Tejera, Gambetta, Varela, Andrade, Ghiggia, Perez, Miguez, Schiaffino, Moran

Brazil: Barbosa, Augusto, Juvenal, Bauer, Danilo, Bigode, Friaca, Zizinho, Ademir, Jair, Chico

	P	W	D	L	F	A	Pts
Uruguay	3	2	1	0	7	5	5
Brazil	3	2	0	1	14	4	4
Sweden	3	1	0	2	6	11	2
Spain	3	0	1	2	4	11	1

Golden Boot: Ademir (Brazil)

SWITZERLAND 1954

As in 1950, the World Cup had a shock for the favourites in the final, with Hungary suffering Brazil's fate of falling at the last hurdle. Sandor Kocsis was top scorer, but lost out on a winner's medal. Shrewd planning by West Germany's coach Herberger certainly played a part, but so too did the tournament's structure, in which the four-team pools produced two games for each country, not three. This allowed Germany to throw their game against Hungary, knowing that they could play-off for a quarter-final place against Turkey, whom they had already beaten. The Germans also exploited the situation whereby the second-placed teams in each pool played each other in the quarter-finals, while the pool winners battled it out amongst themselves. This structure guaranteed one second-placed pool team a place in the final, with West Germany overcoming Austria, while three of the pool winners, Uruguay, England and Brazil were eliminated. Ideally, Hungary should have played the tournament's other best team, Uruguay, in the final, but they played each other in the semi-final instead, producing a memorable game. Not that the final was any less dramatic, with West Germany coming back from a two-goal deficit to win their first World Cup. But this tournament will always be remembered for Hungary's traumatic loss, rather than Germany's victory. But what would have happened if goal difference had decided second place in pool games, as it did for first place? Turkey through, Germany out!

MATCH RESULTS:

POOL 1:

Yugoslavia 1　　**France 0**
Milutinovic

Brazil 5　　**Mexico 0**
Baltazar
Didi
Pinga 2
Julinho

France 3　　**Mexico 0**
Vincent
Cardenas (og)
Kopa (pen)

Yugoslavia 1　　**Brazil 1**
Zebec　　Didi
(after extra time; 1–1 at full time)

	P	W	D	L	F	A	Pts
Brazil	2	1	1	0	6	1	3
Yugoslavia	2	1	1	0	2	1	3
France	2	1	0	1	3	3	2
Mexico	2	0	0	2	2	8	0

POOL 2:

Hungary 9　　**South Korea 0**
Czibor
Kocsis 3
Puskas 2
Lantos
Palotas 2

West Germany 4　　**Turkey 1**
Klodt　　Suat
Morlock
Schaefer
O. Walter

Hungary 8　　**West Germany 3**
Hidegkuti　　Pfaff
Kocsis 4　　Herrmann
Puskas　　Rahn
Toth

Turkey 7　　**South Korea 0**
Burham 3
Erol
Lefter
Suat 2

	P	W	D	L	F	A	Pts
Hungary	2	2	0	0	17	3	4
W. Germany	2	1	0	1	7	9	2
Turkey	2	1	0	1	8	4	2
South Korea	2	0	0	2	0	16	0

PLAY-OFF:

West Germany 7　　**Turkey 2**
Morlock 3　　Mustafa
O. Walter　　Lefter
Schaefer 2
F. Walter

POOL 3:

Austria 1　　**Scotland 0**
Probst

Uruguay 2　　**Czechoslovakia 0**
Miguez
Schiaffino

Austria 5　　**Czechoslovakia 0**
Stojaspal 2
Probst 3

Uruguay 7　　**Scotland 0**
Borges 3
Miguez 2
Abbadie 2

	P	W	D	L	F	A	Pts
Uruguay	2	2	0	0	9	0	4
Austria	2	2	0	0	6	0	4
Czech	2	0	0	2	0	7	0
Scotland	2	0	0	2	0	8	0

POOL 4:

England 4　　**Belgium 4**
Broadis 2　　Anoul 2
Lofthouse 2　　Coppens
　　　　Dickinson (og)
(after extra time; 3–3 at full time)

England 2　　**Switzerland 0**
Mullen
Wilshaw

Switzerland 2　　**Italy 1**
Ballaman　　Boniperti
Hugi

Italy 4　　**Belgium 1**
Pandolfini (pen)　　Anoul
Galli
Frignani
Lorenzi

	P	W	D	L	F	A	Pts
England	2	1	1	0	6	4	3
Italy	2	1	0	1	5	3	2
Switzerland	2	1	0	1	2	3	2
Belgium	2	0	1	1	5	8	1

PLAY-OFF:

Switzerland 4　　**Italy 1**
Hugi 2　　Nesti
Ballaman
Fatton

QUARTER-FINALS:

West Germany 2　　**Yugoslavia 0**
Horvat (og)
Rahn

Hungary 4　　**Brazil 2**
Hidegkuti 2　　D. Santos (pen)
Kocsis　　Julinho
Lantos (pen)

Austria 7	**Switzerland 5**	**Hungary 4**	**Uruguay 2**
A. Koerner 2	Ballaman 2	Czibor	Hohberg 2
Ocwirk	Hugi 2	Hidegkuti	
Wagner 3	Hanappi (og)	Kocsis 2	
Probst		(after extra time; 2–2 at full time)	

Uruguay 4	**England 2**
Borges	Lofthouse
Varela	Finney
Schiaffino	
Ambrois	

SEMI-FINALS:

West Germany 6	**Austria 1**
Schaefer	Probst
Morlock	
F. Walter 2 (2 pens)	
O. Walter 2	

THIRD-PLACE PLAY-OFF:

Austria 3	**Uruguay 1**
Stojaspal (pen)	Hohberg
Cruz (og)	
Ocwirk	

FINAL:

West Germany 3	**Hungary 2**
Morlock	Puskas
Rahn 2	Czibor

West Germany: Turek, Posipal, Kohlmeyer, Eckel, Liebrich, Mai, Rahn, Morlock, O. Walter, F. Walter, Schaefer

Hungary: Groscis, Buzansky, Lantos, Bozsik, Lorant, Zakarias, Czibor, Kocsis, Hidegkuti, Puskas, J. Toth

Golden Boot: Sandor Kocsis (Hungary)

After five World Cup failures, Brazil finally realized their dream, having learnt all the lessons from past mistakes about preparation, team selection and tactics. A European tour to gain experience, an isolated training camp to prepare minds and bodies, and a new 4-2-4 formation to bamboozle opponents combined to produce the winning alchemy with Jules Rimet's trophy the result. Their only regret must have been that they should achieve this in Sweden and not in South America. Only England could stop them scoring, and they quickly rectified that by bringing in Garrincha and, most famously, the seventeen-year-old Pelé who instantly produced six goals in the surge that took them to the final and the winner's rostrum. France, with the stylish Raymond Kopa and the irrepressible top scorer Just Fontaine, took third place in style, while the ageing Swedes surfed a tide of patriotism all the way to the final itself. Wales and Northern Ireland both reached the quarter-finals, offering a world stage to the likes of Ivor Allchurch, John Charles, Danny Blanchflower, Jimmy McIlroy and Peter McParland, a fistful of great British players. England brought Munich survivor Bobby Charlton but didn't play him. Scotland, after a complete blank on their debut in Switzerland in 1954, won their first World Cup point in a draw with Paraguay, while the Soviet Union appeared for the first time but couldn't achieve as much with their football as their tanks had in Hungary in 1956.

MATCH RESULTS:

POOL 1:

West Germany 3	**Argentina 1**
Rahn 2	Corbatta
Schmidt	

Northern Ireland 1	**Czechoslovakia 0**
Cush	

West Germany 2	**Czechoslovakia 2**
Rahn	Dvorak (pen)
Schaefer	Zikan

Argentina 3	**Northern Ireland 1**
Corbatta 2 (1 pen)	McParland
Menendez	

West Germany 2	**Northern Ireland 2**
Rahn	McParland 2
Seeler	

Czechoslovakia 6	**Argentina 1**
Dvorak	Corbatta
Zikan 2	
Feureisl	
Hovorka 2	

	P	W	D	L	F	A	Pts
W. Germany	3	1	2	0	7	5	4
Czech	3	1	1	1	8	4	3
N. Ireland	3	1	1	1	4	5	3
Argentina	3	1	0	2	5	10	2

PLAY-OFF MATCH:

Northern Ireland 2	**Czechoslovakia 1**
McParland 2	Zikan
(after extra time; 1–1 at full time)	

POOL 2:

France 7	**Paraguay 3**
Fontaine 3	Amarilla 2 (1 pen)
Piantoni	Romero
Wisnieski	
Kopa	
Vincent	

Yugoslavia 1	**Scotland 1**
Petakovic	Murray

Yugoslavia 3	**France 2**
Petakovic	Fontaine 2
Veselinovic 2	

Paraguay 3	**Scotland 2**
Aguero	Mudie
Re	Collins
Parodi	

France 2	**Scotland 1**
Kopa	Baird
Fontaine	

Yugoslavia 3   Paraguay 3
Ognjanovic   Parodi
Veselinovic   Aguero
Rajkov   Romero

	P	W	D	L	F	A	Pts
France	3	2	0	1	11	7	4
Yugoslavia	3	1	2	0	7	6	4
Paraguay	3	1	1	1	9	12	3
Scotland	3	0	1	2	4	6	1

POOL 3:

Sweden 3   Mexico 0
Simonsson 2
Liedholm (pen)

Hungary 1   Wales 1
Bozsik   J. Charles

Wales 1   Mexico 1
Allchurch   Belmonte

Sweden 2   Hungary 1
Hamrin 2   Tichy

Sweden 0   Wales 0

Hungary 4   Mexico 0
Tichy 2
Sandor
Bencsics

	P	W	D	L	F	A	Pts
Sweden	3	2	1	0	5	1	5
Hungary	3	1	1	1	6	3	3
Wales	3	0	3	0	2	2	3
Mexico	3	0	1	2	1	8	1

PLAY-OFF MATCH:

Wales 2   Hungary 1
Allchurch   Tichy
Medwin

POOL 4:

England 2   USSR 2
Kevan   Simonian
Finney (pen)   A. Ivanov

Brazil 3   Austria 0
Mazzola 2
N. Santos

England 0   Brazil 0

USSR 2   Austria 0
Ilyin
V. Ivanov

Brazil 2   USSR 0
Vava 2

England 2   Austria 2
Haynes   Koller
Kevan   Koerner

	P	W	D	L	F	A	Pts
Brazil	3	2	1	0	5	0	5
England	3	0	3	0	4	4	3
Russia	3	1	1	1	4	4	3
Austria	3	0	1	2	2	7	1

PLAY-OFF MATCH:

USSR 1   England 0
Ilyin

QUARTER-FINALS:

France 4   Northern
                     Ireland 0
Wisnieski
Fontaine 2
Piantoni

West Germany 1   Yugoslavia 0
Rahn

Sweden 2   USSR 0
Hamrin
Simonsson

Brazil 1   Wales 0
Pelé

SEMI-FINALS:

Brazil 5   France 2
Vava   Fontaine
Didi   Piantoni
Pelé 3

Sweden 3   West Germany 1
Skoglund   Schaefer
Gren
Hamrin

THIRD-PLACE PLAY-OFF:

France 6   West Germany 3
Fontaine 4   Cieslarezyk
Kopa (pen)   Rahn
Douis   Schaefer

FINAL:

Brazil 5   Sweden 2
Vava 2   Liedholm
Pelé 2   Simonsson
Zagalo

Brazil: Gilmar, D. Santos, N. Santos, Zito, Bellini, Orlando, Garrincha, Didi, Vava, Pelé, Zagalo

Sweden: Svensson, Bergmark, Axbom, Boerjesson, Gustavsson, Parling, Hamrin, Gren, Simonsson, Liedholm, Skoglund

Golden Boot: Just Fontaine (France)

CHILE
1962

By now, FIFA had cottoned on to the idea of alternating the World Cup between Europe and South America, but choosing Chile was still a surprise. Argentina had better claims in terms of facilities, but their petulant attitude to previous tournaments counted against them, and a Chilean earthquake swung the sympathy vote. The sixteen-team format was now well and truly established, neatly accommodating four groups of four teams from which eight quarter-finalists could naturally progress. But teams had begun to work the system, knowing exactly how much, or how little, they had to do to go forward, and even being able to plan who they might avoid in the next stage. Holders Brazil and the new European champions, the USSR, were the pre-tournament favourites, while England were overdue for a decent run. Against most expectations the strongest European challenge emerged from the Czechs, despite being well beaten by Mexico in their group match. But they had drawn 0–0 with Brazil, a game in which Pelé was injured and ruled out for the rest of the tournament. For the most part, defences were on top, hence six top goalscorers on a modest tally of four. Hungary and the USSR both looked good in their groups, but both were beaten in the quarter-finals. Brazil ultimately deserved their second World Cup win through the inspirational form, and goals, of Garrincha, ably assisted by Vava. The Chilean supporters saw their team exceed expectations by finishing in third place, but Brazil, even without Pelé, had the goalscoring power when they needed it.

MATCH RESULTS:

GROUP 1:

Uruguay 2	**Colombia 1**
Cubilla	Zaluaga
Sasia	

USSR 2	**Yugoslavia 0**
Ivanov	
Ponedelnik	

Yugoslavia 3	**Uruguay 1**
Skoblar	Cabrera
Galic	
Jerkovic	

USSR 4	**Colombia 4**
Ivanov 2	Aceros
Chislenko	Coll
Ponedelnik	Rada
	Klinger

USSR 2	**Uruguay 1**
Mamikin	Sasia
Ivanov	

Yugoslavia 5	**Colombia 0**
Galic 2	
Jerkovic 2	
Melic	

	P	W	D	L	F	A	Pts
USSR	3	2	1	0	8	5	5
Yugoslavia	3	2	0	1	8	3	4
Uruguay	3	1	0	2	4	6	2
Colombia	3	0	1	2	5	11	1

GROUP 2:

Chile 3	**Switzerland 1**
L. Sanchez 2	Wuthrich
Ramirez	

West Germany 0	**Italy 0**

Chile 2	**Italy 0**
Ramirez	
Toro	

West Germany 2	**Switzerland 1**
Brulls	Schneiter
Seeler	

West Germany 2	**Chile 0**
Szymaniak (pen)	
Seeler	

Italy 3	**Switzerland 0**
Mora	
Bulgarelli 2	

	P	W	D	L	F	A	Pts
W. Germany	3	2	1	0	4	1	5
Chile	3	2	0	1	5	3	4
Italy	3	1	1	1	3	2	3
Switzerland	3	0	0	3	2	8	0

GROUP 3:

Brazil 2	**Mexico 0**
Zagalo	
Pelé	

Czechoslovakia 1	**Spain 0**
Stibranyi	

Brazil 0	**Czechoslovakia 0**

Spain 1	**Mexico 0**
Peiro	

Brazil 2	**Spain 1**
Amarildo 2	Adelardo

Mexico 3	**Czechoslovakia 1**
Diaz	Masek
Del Aguila	
H. Hernandez (pen)	

	P	W	D	L	F	A	Pts
Brazil	3	2	1	0	4	1	5
Czech	3	1	1	1	2	3	3
Mexico	3	1	0	2	3	4	2
Spain	3	1	0	2	2	3	2

GROUP 4:

Argentina 1	**Bulgaria 0**
Facundo	

Hungary 2	**England 1**
Tichy	Flowers (pen)
Albert	

England 3	**Argentina 1**
Flowers (pen)	Sanfilippo
Charlton	
Greaves	

Hungary 6	**Bulgaria 1**
Albert 3	Sokolov
Tichy 2	
Solymosi	

Argentina 0	**Hungary 0**

England 0	**Bulgaria 0**

	P	W	D	L	F	A	Pts
Hungary	3	2	1	0	8	2	5
England	3	1	1	1	4	3	3
Argentina	3	1	1	1	2	3	3
Bulgaria	3	0	1	2	1	7	1

QUARTER-FINALS:

Yugoslavia 1	**West Germany 0**
Radakovic	

Brazil 3	**England 1**
Garrincha 2	Hitchens
Vava	

Chile 2	**USSR 1**
L. Sanchez	Chislenko
Rojas	

Czechoslovakia 1	**Hungary 0**
Scherer	

SEMI-FINALS:

Brazil 4	**Chile 2**
Garrincha 2	Toro
Vava 2	L. Sanchez (pen)

Czechoslovakia 3	**Yugoslavia 1**
Kadraba	Jerkovic
Scherer 2	

THIRD-PLACE PLAY-OFF:

Chile 1	**Yugoslavia 0**
Rojas	

FINAL:

Brazil 3	**Czechoslovakia 1**
Amarildo	Masopust
Zito	
Vava	

Brazil: Gilmar, D. Santos, Mauro, Zozimo, N. Santos, Zito, Didi, Garrincha, Vava, Amarildo, Zagalo

Czechoslovakia: Schroiff, Tichy, Novak, Pluskal, Popluhar, Masopust, Pospichal, Scherer, Kvasniak, Kadraba, Jelinek

Golden Boots: Florian Albert (Hungary), Leonel Sanchez (Chile), Valentin Ivanov (USSR), Vava (Brazil), Garrincha (Brazil), Drazan Jerkovic (Yugoslavia)

ENGLAND

1966

WORLD CUP

JULY 11 to 30
1966
ENGLAND

Football came home at last in 1966, as England finally claimed the crown which some people had always thought of as England's birthright. Not so – it took a single-minded manager, Alf Ramsey, with a clear belief in his team's functional style to produce a hard-fought rather than cavalier victory, although Bobby Charlton provided a few memorable flourishes with his long-range shooting. England used host status to maximum advantage, playing all six of their games at Wembley Stadium and duly turning it into a fortress; the unchanged defence of Gordon Banks in goal, George Cohen, Bobby Moore, Jack Charlton and Ray Wilson conceded only three goals in nine-and-a-half hours of football. Ramsey's masterstroke proved to be the replacement, after the three group matches, of the goalless Jimmy Greaves with West Ham's Geoff Hurst, who promptly scored four goals in his three matches, including a hat-trick against West Germany in the final.

The teams for flair were Hungary and Portugal who ganged up on an ageing Brazil at Goodison Park. Both of them beat the South Americans 3–1 and the reigning champions went home after the first stage. Pelé had little chance to shine before being injured. Portugal, with the goal-power of the brilliant Eusebio, proved to be the stronger stayers, before losing out to England, 2–1, in the semi-final. Their quarter-final against North Korea – the team who had humiliated Italy 1–0 – was a heart-stopper, with Portugal trailing 0–3 before coming back to win 5–3. Eusebio scored four goals. The West German team, under the command of the wily Helmut Schoen, cruised effortlessly into the final, thanks to some inspired football from their young star, Franz Beckenbauer, who was a defender, a midfield player and a goalscorer all in one shirt.

Deployed by Schoen to mark Bobby Charlton in the final, Beckenbauer succeeded only in reducing his own influence on the match, which England seemed to have won at 2–1. But Wolfgang Weber's last-minute equalizer sent the World Cup final into extra time for the first time since 1934 in Italy. Geoff Hurst's controversial second goal was allowed to stand, he completed his hat-trick in the dying minutes of the match, and Bobby Moore lifted the Jules Rimet trophy up to a clear blue sky. It may have been all over for West Germany then, but it's been all over for England since, with 1990's semi-final in Italy being the nearest approach to gold. The tournament was watched by a large world-wide television audience, thanks to improving broadcasting technology – things could only get bigger.

MATCH RESULTS:

GROUP 1:

England 0	Uruguay 0

France 1	Mexico 1
Hausser	Borja

Uruguay 2	France 1
Rocha	De Bourgoing (pen)
Cortes	

England 2	Mexico 0
R. Charlton	
Hunt	

Uruguay 0	Mexico 0

England 2	France 0
Hunt 2	

	P	W	D	L	F	A	Pts
England	3	2	1	0	4	0	5
Uruguay	3	1	2	0	2	1	4
Mexico	3	0	2	1	1	3	2
France	3	0	1	2	2	5	1

GROUP 2:

West Germany 5	Switzerland 0
Held	
Haller 2 (1 pen)	
Beckenbauer 2	

Argentina 2	Spain 1
Artime 2	Pirri

Spain 2	Switzerland 1
Sanchis	Quentin
Amancio	

Argentina 0	West Germany 0

Argentina 2	Switzerland 0
Artime	
Onega	

West Germany 2	Spain 1
Emmerich	Fuste
Seeler	

	P	W	D	L	F	A	Pts
W. Germany	3	2	1	0	7	1	5
Argentina	3	2	1	0	4	1	5
Spain	3	1	0	2	4	5	2
Switzerland	3	0	0	3	1	9	0

GROUP 3:

Brazil 2	Bulgaria 0
Pelé	
Garrincha	

Portugal 3	Hungary 1
Augusto 2	Bene
Torres	

Hungary 3	Brazil 1
Bene	Tostao
Farkas	
Meszoly (pen)	

Portugal 3	Bulgaria 0
Vutzov (og)	
Eusebio	
Torres	

Portugal 3		**Brazil 1**				
Simoes		Rildo				
Eusebio (2)						

USSR 2		**Chile 1**				
Porkujan 2		Marcos				

Hungary 3   **Bulgaria 1**
Davidov (og)   Asparoukhov
Meszoly
Bene

	P	W	D	L	F	A	Pts
Portugal	3	3	0	0	9	2	6
Hungary	3	2	0	1	7	5	4
Brazil	3	1	0	2	4	6	2
Bulgaria	3	0	0	3	1	8	0

GROUP 4:

USSR 3   **North Korea 0**
Malafeev 2
Banichevski

Italy 2   **Chile 0**
Barison
Mazzola

Chile 1   **North Korea 1**
Marcos (pen)   Pak Sung Jin

USSR 1   **Italy 0**
Chislenko

North Korea 1   **Italy 0**
Pak Doo Ik

	P	W	D	L	F	A	Pts
USSR	3	3	0	0	6	1	6
North Korea	3	1	1	1	2	4	3
Italy	3	1	0	2	2	2	2
Chile	3	0	1	2	2	5	1

QUARTER-FINALS:

England 1   **Argentina 0**
Hurst

West Germany 4   **Uruguay 0**
Held
Beckenbauer
Seeler
Haller

Portugal 5   **North Korea 3**
Eusebio 4 (2 pen)   Pak Seung Jin
Augusto   Yang Sung Kook
            Li Dong Woon

USSR 2   **Hungary 1**
Chislenko   Bene
Porkujan

SEMI-FINALS:

West Germany 2   **USSR 1**
Haller   Porkujan
Beckenbauer

England 2   **Portugal 1**
R. Charlton 2   Eusebio (pen)

THIRD-PLACE PLAY-OFF:

Portugal 2   **USSR 1**
Eusebio (pen)   Malafeev
Torres

FINAL:

England 4   **West Germany 2**
Hurst 3   Haller
Peters   Weber
(after extra time; 2–2 at full time)

England: Banks, Cohen, Wilson, Stiles, J. Charlton, Moore, Ball, Hurst, Hunt, R. Charlton, Peters

West Germany: Tilkowski, Hottges, Schulz, Weber, Schnellinger, Haller, Beckenbauer, Overath, Seeler, Held, Emmerich

Golden Boot: Eusebio (Portugal)

There's no doubt about it – this was the best World Cup tournament to date, even allowing for the punishment the players had to endure in performing at altitude, often in blazing afternoon heat as well. Some of the results were certainly distorted by the conditions, and so too was much of the football, but mostly to good effect. The Europeans had no option but to moderate their pace, play keep-ball and plan for openings rather than charge into attack or play hit-and-hope. With substitutes being allowed for the first time, there was more strategy about team selection and line-ups than ever before. A manager could plan for containment, then make a switch of players to transform the play into attack, or vice versa.

It was certainly substitutions which ended England's reign, with Alf Ramsey prematurely taking Bobby Charlton off at 2–0 up against West Germany, and Helmut Schoen bringing on the fresh legs of winger Jürgen Grabowski to torment a wilting English defence. England's 3–2 defeat in Leon, was a dramatic and traumatic exit, but the tournament still held interest after we'd gone, almost exclusively because of the football the Brazil team were playing. England's group game against them was a match of the highest order, full of astonishing moments – like Gordon Banks's save from Pelé – and intense thought and concentration. The manner in which Tostao and Pelé unpicked the England defence for Jairzinho to score the winning goal was just like watching grandmaster chess being played at speed.

Brazil won all of their games, with Jairzinho, nominally a winger, scoring in every one of them, while Pelé finally shook off the memories of his last two injury-dogged World Cups and reminded the world that his dazzling talent was still there. As if that were not enough, Brazil also had Rivelino bending his free-kicks wildly in the thin air, and Gerson orchestrating everything in front of him.

Once England were out, it was left to Italy and West Germany to slug it out in an epic, seven-goal semi-final for the dubious privilege of taking on Brazil. Even Gerd Müller's astonishing goal haul couldn't stop a resurgent Italy getting to the final, where they briefly suggested that Brazil might have a match on their hands, as Boninsegna equalized Pelé's early goal. The second half, though, was filled with the movement and the rhythm of the yellow shirts playing exhibition football in the most important fixture in the world calendar. Brazil's third win meant they could now keep the Jules Rimet trophy, a feat that must have seemed impossible twenty years earlier after their home defeat by Uruguay. Now they were the undisputed masters – we had seen the world's greatest game, as played by the world's best team.

MATCH RESULTS:

GROUP 1:

Mexico 0   USSR 0

Belgium 3   El Salvador 0
Van Moer 2
Lambert (pen)

USSR 4   Belgium 1
Bishovets 2   Lambert
Asatiani
Khmelnitsky

Mexico 4   El Salvador 0
Valdivia 2
Fragoso
Basaguren

USSR 2   El Salvador 0
Bishovets 2

Mexico 1   Belgium 0
Pena (pen)

	P	W	D	L	F	A	Pts
Mexico	3	2	1	0	5	0	5
USSR	3	2	1	0	6	1	5
Belgium	3	1	0	2	4	5	2
El Salvador	3	0	0	3	0	9	0

GROUP 2:

Uruguay 2   Israel 0
Maneiro
Mujica

Italy 1   Sweden 0
Domenghini

Uruguay 0   Italy 0

Sweden 1   Israel 1
Turesson   Spiegler

Sweden 1   Uruguay 0
Grahn

Italy 0   Israel 0

	P	W	D	L	F	A	Pts
Italy	3	1	2	0	1	0	4
Uruguay	3	1	1	1	2	1	3
Sweden	3	1	1	1	2	2	3
Israel	3	0	2	1	1	3	2

GROUP 3:

England 1   Romania 0
Hurst

Brazil 4   Czechoslovakia 1
Rivelino   Petras
Pelé
Jairzinho 2

Romania 2   Czechoslovakia 1
Neagu   Petras
Dumitrache (pen)

Brazil 1   England 0
Jairzinho

Brazil 3   Romania 2
Jairzinho   Dumitrache
Pelé 2   Dembrowski
England 1   Czechoslovakia 0
Clarke (pen)

	P	W	D	L	F	A	Pts
Brazil	3	3	0	0	8	3	6
England	3	2	0	1	2	1	4
Romania	3	1	0	2	4	5	2
Czech	3	0	0	3	2	7	0

GROUP 4:

Peru 3   Bulgaria 2
Chumpitaz   Dermendjiev
Gallardo   Donev
Cubillas

West Germany 2   Morocco 1
Seeler   Houmane
Müller

Peru 3   Morocco 0
Cubillas 2
Challe

West Germany 5   Bulgaria 2
Libuda   Nikodimov
Müller 3 (1 pen)   Kolev
Seeler

West Germany 3   Peru 1
Müller 3   Perico Leon

Bulgaria 1   Morocco 1
Jetchev   Ghazouani

	P	W	D	L	F	A	Pts
W. Germany	3	3	0	0	10	4	6
Peru	3	2	0	1	7	5	4
Bulgaria	3	0	1	2	2	6	1
Morocco	3	0	1	2	2	6	1

QUARTER-FINALS:

West Germany 3   England 2
Beckenbauer   Mullery
Seeler   Peters
Müller
(after extra time; 2–2 at full time)

Brazil 4   Peru 2
Rivelino   Gallardo
Tostao 2   Cubillas
Jairzinho

Italy 4   Mexico 1
Domenghini   Gonzalez
Riva 2
Rivera

Uruguay 1   USSR 0
Esparrago
(after extra time; 0–0 at full time)

SEMI-FINALS:

Italy 4   West Germany 3
Boninsegna   Schnellinger
Burgnich   Müller 2
Riva
Rivera
(after extra time; 1–1 at full time)
Brazil 3   Uruguay 1
Clodoaldo   Cubilla
Jairzinho
Rivelino

THIRD-PLACE PLAY-OFF:

West Germany 1   Uruguay 0
Overath

FINAL:

Brazil 4   Italy 1
Pelé   Boninsegna
Gerson
Jairzinho
Carlos Alberto

Brazil: Felix, Carlos Alberto, Brito, Piazza, Everaldo, Clodoaldo, Gerson, Jairzinho, Tostao, Pelé, Rivelino

Italy: Albertosi, Cera, Burgnich, Bertini (Juliano), Rosato, Facchetti, Domenghini, Mazzola, De Sisti, Boninsegna (Rivera), Riva

Golden Boot: Gerd Müller (West Germany)

Two years after the massacre of Israeli athletes at the Olympic village in Munich, the World Cup edged tentatively into West Germany. The standard-sized entry – sixteen countries – was retained, but a further league structure had been devised for the second stage rather than straight knock-out quarter-finals, with the two winners contesting the final, effectively now the only cup-tie in the competition.

There were some new faces on the field, too – East Germany had qualified, probably determined to spoil the host's party for political reasons, and there were teams from Haiti, Zaire and Australia. Scotland made it for the first time since 1958, and went home proudly unbeaten – not qualified, but unbeaten. Brazil, the champions, had said farewell to Pelé, Gerson and Tostao, and their squad turned out to be thin on talent, but big on muscle. West Germany's form had been franked by a win in the 1972 European Championship, but they had nervous eyes on Rinus Michels' Dutch team, which had been built around the all-conquering Ajax Amsterdam, and was playing the same kind of unpredictable free-form football, orchestrated by their star soloist, Johan Cruyff.

West Germany started cautiously with a 1–0 win over Chile, and then guaranteed their advance with an easy 3–0 win over Australia; but in their last Group 1 game, they lost to their ideological rivals, East Germany, 1–0, a result sufficiently shocking for captain Beckenbauer to begin telling Helmut Schoen the required team changes.

Poland had proved to be the surprise packet of the tournament, reeling off five wins on the trot thanks to goals from Lato and Szarmach; but by the time they faced West Germany in the game to decide the finalist from that group, the hosts were well up on goal difference, and therefore knew they needed only a draw to get through. In the end, the Germans beat the Poles 1–0, on a near-unplayable, saturated pitch, while Holland had hardly broken sweat to win all three games in their group.

So the Dutch had the form, the Germans the strategy. A first-minute penalty for Holland – awarded by England's only presence, referee Jack Taylor – sedated the Dutch and aroused the Germans. By half-time, another penalty and a classic Gerd Müller strike had put the Germans in front where they stayed, collecting their second World Cup, this time on home soil. It wasn't a vintage tournament, and to most neutrals the wrong team had won – but try telling that to the Germans!

FIFA World Cup 1974
Copa Mundial de la FIFA 1974
Coupe du Monde de la FIFA 1974

MATCH RESULTS:

GROUP 1:

West Germany 1 Chile 0
Breitner

East Germany 2 Australia 0
Curran (og)
Streich

West Germany 3 Australia 0
Overath
Cullmann
Müller

East Germany 1 Chile 1
Hoffman Ahumada

East Germany 1 West Germany 0
Sparwasser

Chile 0 Australia 0

	P	W	D	L	F	A	Pts
E. Germany	3	2	1	0	4	1	5
W. Germany	3	2	0	1	4	1	4
Chile	3	0	2	1	1	2	2
Australia	3	0	1	2	0	5	1

GROUP 2:

Brazil 0 Yugoslavia 0

Scotland 2 Zaire 0
Lorimer
Jordan

Brazil 0 Scotland 0

Yugoslavia 9 Zaire 0
Bajevic 3
Dzajic
Surjak
Katalinski
Bogicevic
Oblak
Petkovic

Scotland 1 Yugoslavia 1
Jordan Karasi

Brazil 3 Zaire 0
Jairzinho
Rivelino
Valdomiro

	P	W	D	L	F	A	Pts
Yugoslavia	3	1	2	0	10	1	4
Brazil	3	1	2	0	3	0	4
Scotland	3	1	2	0	3	1	4
Zaire	3	0	0	3	0	14	0

GROUP 3:

Holland 2 Uruguay 0
Rep 2

Sweden 0 Bulgaria 0

Holland 0 Sweden 0

Bulgaria 1 Uruguay 1
Bonev Pavoni

Holland 4 Bulgaria 1
Neeskens 2 (2 pens) Krol (og)
Rep
De Jong

Sweden 3 Uruguay 0
Edstroem 2
Sandberg

continued...

	P	W	D	L	F	A	Pts
Holland	3	2	1	0	6	1	5
Sweden	3	1	2	0	3	0	4
Bulgaria	3	0	2	1	2	5	2
Uruguay	3	0	1	2	1	6	1

GROUP 4:

Italy 3   **Haiti 1**
Rivera   Sanon
Benetti
Anastasi

Poland 3   **Argentina 2**
Lato 2   Heredia
Szarmach   Babington

Argentina 1   **Italy 1**
Houseman   Perfumo (og)

Poland 7   **Haiti 0**
Lato 2
Deyna
Szarmach 3
Gorgon

Argentina 4   **Haiti 1**
Yazalde 2   Sanon
Houseman
Ayala

Poland 2   **Italy 1**
Szarmach   Capello
Deyna

	P	W	D	L	F	A	Pts
Poland	3	3	0	0	12	3	6
Argentina	3	1	1	1	7	5	3
Italy	3	1	1	1	5	4	3
Haiti	3	0	0	3	2	14	0

GROUP A:

Brazil 1   **East Germany 0**
Rivelino

Holland 4   **Argentina 0**
Cruyff 2
Krol
Rep

Holland 2   **East Germany 0**
Neeskens
Rensenbrink

Brazil 2   **Argentina 1**
Rivelino   Brindisi
Jairzinho

Holland 2   **Brazil 0**
Neeskens
Cruyff

Argentina 1   **East Germany 1**
Houseman   Streich

	P	W	D	L	F	A	Pts
Holland	3	3	0	0	8	0	6
Brazil	3	2	0	1	3	3	4
E. Germany	3	0	1	2	1	4	1
Argentina	3	0	1	2	2	7	1

GROUP B:

Poland 1   **Sweden 0**
Lato

West Germany 2   **Yugoslavia 0**
Breitner
Müller

Poland 2   **Yugoslavia 1**
Deyna (pen)   Karasi
Lato

West Germany 4   **Sweden 2**
Overath   Edstroem
Bonhof   Sandberg
Grabowski
Hoeness (pen)

Sweden 2   **Yugoslavia 1**
Edstroem   Surjak
Torstensson

West Germany 1   **Poland 0**
Müller

	P	W	D	L	F	A	Pts
W. Germany	3	3	0	0	7	2	6
Poland	3	2	0	1	3	2	4
Sweden	3	1	0	2	4	6	2
Yugoslavia	3	0	0	3	2	6	0

THIRD-PLACE PLAY-OFF:

Poland 1   **Brazil 0**
Lato

FINAL:

West Germany 2   **Holland 1**
Breitner (pen)   Neeskens (pen)
Müller

West Germany: Maier, Vogts, Schwarzenbeck, Beckenbauer, Breitner, Bonhof, Hoeness, Overath, Grabowski, Müller, Holzenbein

Holland: Jongbloed, Suurbier, Rijsbergen (De Jong), Haan, Krol, Jansen, Van Hanegem, Neeskens, Rep, Cruyff, Rensenbrink (R. Van der Kerkhof)

Golden Boot: Gregorz Lato (Poland)

ARGENTINA 1978

The decision finally to award World Cup host status to Argentina, forty-eight years after they had reached the first final, rebounded on FIFA as the 1976 military coup turned the competition into a propaganda triumph and an effective endorsement for the generals who violently seized power and suppresed dissent. Two years of murders and disappearances brought FIFA to the brink of withdrawing the World Cup from Argentina and giving it to Holland instead, but they bottled the decision after General Videla's assurances that all would go well, which was hardly the point!

Argentina's victory was therefore inevitably tainted, not just by the presence of the military in the VIP boxes, but also by the team's tortuous route to the final. In the first place, their Group 1 defeat by Italy put them into the weaker Group B for the second stage, which led to suspicions that they had thrown away that game. Then in their final Group B game, with Brazil having completed their three matches, Argentina knew exactly what they had to do in order to reach the final – beat Peru by four clear goals and leapfrog Brazil on goal difference. Argentina duly won 6–0, with Peru's goalkeeper providing a particularly feeble performance. Even in the final itself, Argentina were only saved by the width of the goalpost in the last minute when Rensenbrink's close-range effort nearly won the final for Holland. But in extra time, Argentina summoned the nerve and the momentum to win, with Mario Kempes, the man of the tournament, scoring his sixth goal.

The tournament provided contrasting fortunes for some of the big-hitters. West Germany found themselves bounced out after a 3–2 defeat by neighbours Austria, while a non-vintage Brazil overcame a stuttering start to take third place off an Italian side whose revival under coach Enzo Bearzot was to prove a good omen for their 1982 tournament. Ally McLeod's Scotland offered what was to become one of their most memorable World Cup cameos – a 3–1 defeat by Peru, a humiliating 1–1 draw with Iran, and then a thrilling 3–2 victory over Holland, marked by Archie Gemmill's goal of the tournament.

Some spectacular long-range shooting caught the imagination of the viewing audiences, as did the torrent of ticker-tape which preceded every Argentinian match. For all but the Argentine nation and their rulers, however, the tournament proved something of an anti-climax. Holland's 'total football' was beaten in a final for the second-time running, and too many teams contributed too little to the spectacle, with the likes of Spain, Sweden, Mexico and Hungary doing little to justify their qualifications. In contrast, Tunisia, on their World Cup debut, produced two outstanding results, a draw against the Germans and a win over Mexico, which really deserved a place in the second stage. They are back again for 1998, in England's Group G, so we underestimate them at our peril!

MATCH RESULTS:

GROUP 1:

Argentina 2   **Hungary 1**
Luque   Csapo
Alonso

Italy 2   **France 1**
Rossi   Lacombe
Zaccarelli

Argentina 2   **France 1**
Passarella (pen)   Platini
Luque

Italy 3   **Hungary 1**
Rossi   Toth (pen)
Bettega
Benetti

Italy 1   **Argentina 0**
Bettega

France 3   **Hungary 1**
Lopez   Zambori
Berdoll
Rocheteau

	P	W	D	L	F	A	Pts
Italy	3	3	0	0	6	2	6
Argentina	3	2	0	1	4	3	4
France	3	1	0	2	5	5	2
Hungary	3	0	0	3	3	8	0

GROUP 2:

West Germany 0   **Poland 0**

Tunisia 3   **Mexico 1**
Kaabi   Vazquez
Goummiah
Dhouib

Poland 1   **Tunisia 0**
Lato

West Germany 6   **Mexico 0**
D. Müller
H. Müller
Rummenigge 2
Flohe 2

Poland 3   **Mexico 1**
Boniek 2   Rangel
Deyna

West Germany 0   **Tunisia 0**

	P	W	D	L	F	A	Pts
Poland	3	2	1	0	4	1	5
W. Germany	3	1	2	0	6	0	4
Tunisia	3	1	1	1	3	2	3
Mexico	3	0	0	3	2	12	0

GROUP 3:

Austria 2   **Spain 1**
Schachner   Dani
Krankl

Sweden 1   **Brazil 1**
Sjoberg   Reinaldo

Austria 1   **Sweden 0**
Krankl (pen)

Brazil 0   **Spain 0**

Spain 1   **Sweden 0**
Asensi

Brazil 1   **Austria 0**
Roberto

	P	W	D	L	F	A	Pts
Austria	3	2	0	1	3	2	4
Brazil	3	1	2	0	2	1	4
Spain	3	1	1	1	2	2	3
Sweden	3	0	1	2	1	3	1

GROUP 4:

Peru 3   **Scotland 1**
Cueto   Jordan
Cubillas 2

Holland 3   **Iran 0**
Rensenbrink 3
(2 pens)

Scotland 1   **Iran 1**
Eskandarian (og)   Danaiford

Holland 0   **Peru 0**

Peru 4   **Iran 1**
Velasquez   Rowshan
Cubillas 3 (2 pens)

Scotland 3   **Holland 2**
Dalglish   Rensenbrink (pen)
Gemmill 2 (1 pen)   Rep

	P	W	D	L	F	A	Pts
Peru	3	2	1	0	7	2	5
Holland	3	1	1	1	5	3	3
Scotland	3	1	1	1	5	6	3
Iran	3	0	1	2	2	8	1

GROUP A:

West Germany 0   **Italy 0**

Holland 5   **Austria 1**
Brandts   Obermeyer
Rensenbrink (pen)
Rep 2
W. Van der Kerkhof

Italy 1   **Austria 0**
Rossi

West Germany 2   **Holland 2**
Abramczik 2   Haan
   R. Van der Kerkof

continued…

Holland 2 — Italy 1
Brandts — Brandts (og)
Haan

Austria 3 — West Germany 2
Vogts (og) — Rummenigge
Krankl 2 — Holzenbein

	P	W	D	L	F	A	Pts
Holland	3	2	1	0	9	4	5
Italy	3	1	1	1	2	2	3
W. Germany	3	0	2	1	4	5	2
Austria	3	1	0	2	4	8	2

GROUP B:

Argentina 2 — Poland 0
Kempes 2

Brazil 3 — Peru 0
Dirceu 2
Zico (pen)

Argentina 0 — Brazil 0

Poland 1 — Peru 0
Szarmach

Brazil 3 — Poland 1
Nelinho — Lato
Roberto 2

Argentina 6 — Peru 0
Kempes 2
Tarantini
Luque 2
Houseman

	P	W	D	L	F	A	Pts
Argentina	3	2	1	0	8	0	5
Brazil	3	2	1	0	6	1	5
Poland	3	1	0	2	2	5	2
Peru	3	0	0	3	0	10	0

THIRD-PLACE PLAY-OFF:

Brazil 2 — Italy 1
Nelinho — Causio
Dirceu

FINAL:

Argentina 3 — Holland 1
Kempes 2 — Nanninga
Bertoni
(after extra time; 1–1 at full time)

Argentina: Filliol, Olguin, Galvan, Passarella, Tarantini, Ardiles (Larossa), Gallego, Kempes, Bertoni, Luque, Ortiz (Houseman)

Holland: Jongbloed, Krol, Poortvliet, Brandts, Jansen (Suurbier), W. Van der Kerkof, Neeskens, Haan, Rep (Nanninga), Rensenbrink, R. Van der Kerkof

Golden Boot: Mario Kempes (Argentina)

S P A I N
1982

The inevitable expansion of the tournament meant that twenty-four teams would take part, a fifty per cent increase on the usual number. Only the semi-finals and the final itself would remain pure cup-ties. With fifty-two matches in total, it was no surprise that the teams who paced themselves better, finished the stronger. The early 'hares' included England and Brazil who both won all their first-round group matches, before departing in the second stage. Northern Ireland enjoyed themselves with a win over the hosts, Spain, and reached the second stage.

Meanwhile Brazil were so committed to attack that they forgot to defend in their second-stage match against Italy, suicidally going for a win when a mere draw would have been enough to put them through to the semi-finals. The Italians had suffered an appalling start, drawing all of their group games, and only scoring twice – failing to beat the likes of Peru and Cameroon was hardly champion form. West Germany were even more erratic, losing their first game to Algeria and requiring a blatant deal with Austria which let them both go through at the North Africans' expense. France, who'd only beaten Kuwait in England's group, looked unlikely to progress, while Poland were nearly as boring as Italy, despite a 5–1 win over Peru, the only victory in a group of deadly draws.

But in the second stage Poland, with Boniek's goals, and France, inspired by Platini, Tigana and Giresse, blossomed, while West Germany typically ground out results against England and Spain to reach the semi-finals. Italy were a revelation as Rossi's goals and Bearzot's insistence on attack saw them swagger past the South American giants, Argentina and Brazil, and they cruised past Poland in the first semi-final. But France against West Germany became a memorable, traumatic game – four goals were scored in extra time with Germany coming back from 3–1 down; there was Schumacher's horrible, unpunished foul on Battiston; and then we had the first ever penalty shoot-out in a World Cup, which the Germans won 5–4. But their exhausting efforts in that match and an injury-plagued Rummenigge meant they had little to offer once Italy overcame the shock of Cabrini becoming the first player to miss a penalty in a World Cup final. Italy's second-half performance powered them to a 3–1 win. Italy against France, or France against Brazil would have been a dream final, but the emotional charge of Italy's third World Cup win was some compensation for the tournament's duller and uglier moments

MATCH RESULTS:

GROUP 1:

Italy 0	Poland 0

Peru 0	Cameroon 0

Italy 1	Peru 1
Conti	Diaz

Poland 0	Cameroon 0

Poland 5	Peru 1
Smolarek	La Rosa
Lato	
Boniek	
Buncol	
Giolek	

Italy 1	Cameroon 1
Graziani	M'Bida

	P	W	D	L	F	A	Pts
Poland	3	1	2	0	5	1	4
Italy	3	0	3	0	2	2	3
Cameroon	3	0	3	0	1	1	3
Peru	3	0	2	1	2	6	2

GROUP 2:

Algeria 2	West Germany 1
Madjer	Rummenigge
Belloumi	

Austria 1	Chile 0
Schachner	

West Germany 4	Chile 1
Rummenigge 3	Moscoso
Reinders	

Austria 2	Algeria 0
Schachner	
Krankl	

Algeria 3	Chile 2
Assad 2	Neira (pen)
Bensoula	Letelier

West Germany 1	Austria 0
Hrubesch	

	P	W	D	L	F	A	Pts
W. Germany	3	2	0	1	6	3	4
Austria	3	2	0	1	3	1	4
Algeria	3	2	0	1	5	5	4
Chile	3	0	0	3	3	8	0

GROUP 3:

Belgium 1	Argentina 0
Van Den Bergh	

Hungary 10	El Salvador 1
Nyilasi 2	Zapata
Fazekas 2	
Paloskei	
Toth	
Kiss 3	
Szentes	

Argentina 4	Hungary 1
Bertoni	Paloskei
Ardiles	
Maradona 2	

Belgium 1	El Salvador 0
Coeck	

Belgium 1	Hungary 1
Czerniatynski	Varga

Argentina 2	El Salvador 0
Passarella (pen)	
Bertoni	

	P	W	D	L	F	A	Pts
Belgium	3	2	1	0	3	1	5
Argentina	3	2	0	1	6	2	4
Hungary	3	1	1	1	12	6	3
El Salvador	3	0	0	3	1	13	0

GROUP 4:

England 3	France 1
Robson 2	Soler
Mariner	

Czechoslovakia 1	Kuwait 1
Panenka (pen)	Al Dakhed

England 2	Czechoslovakia 0
Francis	
Barmos (og)	

France 4	Kuwait 1
Genghini	Al Buloushi
Platini	
Six	
Bossis	

France 1	Czechoslovakia 1
Six	Panenka (pen)

England 1	Kuwait 0
Francis	

	P	W	D	L	F	A	Pts
England	3	3	0	0	6	1	6
France	3	1	1	1	6	5	3
Czech	3	0	2	1	2	4	2
Kuwait	3	0	1	2	2	6	1

GROUP 5:

Spain 1	Honduras 1
Ufarte (pen)	Zelaya

Northern Ireland 0	Yugoslavia 0

Spain 2	Yugoslavia 1
Juanito (pen)	Gudelj
Saura	

Northern Ireland 1	Honduras 1
Armstrong	Laing

Yugoslavia 1	Honduras 0
Petrovic (pen)	

Northern Ireland 1	Spain 0
Armstrong	

	P	W	D	L	F	A	Pts
N. Ireland	3	1	2	0	2	1	4
Spain	3	1	1	1	3	3	3
Yugoslavia	3	1	1	1	2	2	3
Honduras	3	0	2	1	2	3	2

GROUP 6:

Brazil 2	USSR 1
Socrates	Bal
Eder	

Scotland 5	New Zealand 2
Wark 2	Sumner
Dalglish	Wooddin
Robertson	
Archibald	

Brazil 4	Scotland 1
Zico	Narey
Oscar	
Eder	
Falcao	

USSR 3	New Zealand 0
Gavrilov	
Blokhin	
Baltacha	

Scotland 2	USSR 2
Jordan	Chivadze
Souness	Shengalia

Brazil 4	New Zealand 0
Zico 2	
Falcao	
Serginho	

	P	W	D	L	F	A	Pts
Brazil	3	3	0	0	10	2	6
USSR	3	1	1	1	6	4	3
Scotland	3	1	1	1	8	8	3
New Zealand	3	0	0	3	2	12	0

GROUP A:

Poland 3	Belgium 0
Boniek 3	

USSR 1	Belgium 0
Oganesian	

USSR 0	Poland 0

	P	W	D	L	F	A	Pts
Poland	2	1	1	0	3	0	3
USSR	2	1	1	0	1	0	3
Belgium	2	0	0	2	0	4	0

GROUP B:

West Germany 0	England 0

West Germany 2	Spain 1
Littbarski	Zamora
Fischer	

England 0	Spain 0

	P	W	D	L	F	A	Pts
W. Germany	2	1	1	0	2	1	3
England	2	0	2	0	0	0	2
Spain	2	0	1	1	1	2	1

GROUP C:

Italy 2	Argentina 1
Tardelli	Passarella
Cabrini	

continued…

Brazil 3	Argentina 1
Zico	Diaz
Serginho	
Junior	

Italy 3	Brazil 2
Rossi 3	Socrates
	Falcao

	P	W	D	L	F	A	Pts
Italy	2	2	0	0	5	3	4
Brazil	2	1	0	1	5	4	3
Argentina	2	0	0	2	2	5	0

GROUP D:

France 1	Austria 0
Genghini	

Northern Ireland 2	Austria 2
Hamilton 2	Pezzey
	Hintermaier

France 4	Northern Ireland 1
Giresse 2	Armstrong
Rocheteau 2	

	P	W	D	L	F	A	Pts
France	2	2	0	0	5	1	4
Austria	2	0	1	1	2	3	1
N. Ireland	2	0	1	1	3	6	1

SEMI-FINALS:

Italy 2	Poland 0
Rossi 2	

West Germany 3	France 3
Littbarski	Platini (pen)
Rummenigge	Tresor
Fischer	Giresse

(after extra time; 1–1 at full time)
West Germany won 5–4 on penalties

THIRD-PLACE PLAY-OFF:

Poland 3	France 2
Szarmach	Girard
Majewski	Couriol
Kupcewicz	

FINAL:

Italy 3	West Germany 1
Rossi	Breitner
Tardelli	
Altobelli	

Italy: Zoff, Bergomi, Cabrini, Collovati, Scirea, Gentile, Oriali, Tardelli, Conti, Graziani (Altobelli) (Causio), Rossi

West Germany: Schumacher, Kaltz, K.H. Forster, Stielike, B. Forster, Breitner, Dremmler (Hrubesch), Littbarski, Briegel, Rummenigge (Müller), Fischer

Golden Boot: Paolo Rossi (Italy)

MEXICO
1986

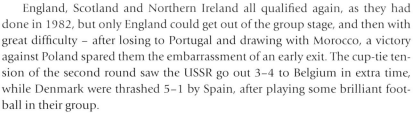

Despite the 'Hand of God' goal against England this was emphatically Diego Maradona's World Cup, as Argentina claimed their second championship in eight years. The tournament had originally been awarded to Colombia, who had to withdraw due to financial difficulties, and so Mexico, who had hosted in 1970, got the nod again despite a spate of earthquakes in 1985. The entry stood at twenty-four teams of which fourteen were from Europe. Three of these – Belgium, France and West Germany – made it to the semi-finals, but there was simply no stopping a Maradona-inspired Argentina.

England, Scotland and Northern Ireland all qualified again, as they had done in 1982, but only England could get out of the group stage, and then with great difficulty – after losing to Portugal and drawing with Morocco, a victory against Poland spared them the embarrassment of an early exit. The cup-tie tension of the second round saw the USSR go out 3–4 to Belgium in extra time, while Denmark were thrashed 5–1 by Spain, after playing some brilliant football in their group.

The quarter-finals became even more tense, with three of the games having to be settled by penalties after extra time had failed to produce a winner. Only England's match against Argentina produced a clean result, though that word hardly applies to Maradona's gross example of cheating which edged the tie Argentina's way. Brazil fell to France in a pulsating game, while West Germany couldn't score against hosts Mexico, and had to see them off in the shoot-out. France, the reigning European champions seemed to be the major challengers to Argentina, having knocked out holders Italy in the second round, and Brazil in the quarters; but they proceeded to lose limply to a non-vintage German team in the semi-final, thereby repeating some of their torment from 1982. Meanwhile, Maradona made short work of the solid but dour Belgians in the other semi-final, leaving a potentially classic final between Europe and South America in the Aztec Stadium. The 3–2 scoreline may look impressive, but Argentina were 2–0 up and coasting before the Germans snatched two late goals. Even then Maradona had the last word, slotting a pass through to Burruchaga for the winning goal. England's consolation for their controversial quarter-final defeat came with the Golden Boot award for one G. Lineker.

MATCH RESULTS:

GROUP A:

Bulgaria 1   **Italy 1**
Sirakov   Altobelli

Argentina 3   **South Korea 1**
Valdano 2   Park Chang Sun
Ruggeri

Italy 1   **Argentina 1**
Altobelli (pen)   Maradona

Bulgaria 1   **South Korea 1**
Getov   Kim Jong Boo

Argentina 2   **Bulgaria 0**
Valdano
Burruchaga

Italy 3   **South Korea 2**
Altobelli 3   Choi Soon-Hoo
             Huh Jung-Moo

	P	W	D	L	F	A	Pts
Argentina	3	2	1	0	6	2	5
Italy	3	1	2	0	5	4	4
Bulgaria	3	0	2	1	2	4	2
South Korea	3	0	1	2	4	7	1

GROUP B:

Mexico 2   **Belgium 1**
Quirarte   Van Den Bergh
Sanchez

Paraguay 1   **Iraq 0**
Romero

Mexico 1   **Paraguay 1**
Flores   Romero

Belgium 2   **Iraq 1**
Scifo   Rahdi
Claesen (pen)

Paraguay 2   **Belgium 2**
Cabanas 2   Vercauteren
           Veyt

Mexico 1   **Iraq 0**
Quirarte

	P	W	D	L	F	A	Pts
Mexico	3	2	1	0	4	2	5
Paraguay	3	1	2	0	4	3	4
Belgium	3	1	1	1	5	5	3
Iraq	3	0	0	3	1	4	0

GROUP C:

USSR 6   **Hungary 0**
Yakovenko
Aleinikov
Belanov (pen)
Yaremchuck 2
Rodionov

France 1   **Canada 0**
Papin

USSR 1   **France 1**
Rats   Fernandez

Hungary 2   **Canada 0**
Esterhazy
Detari

France 3   **Hungary 0**
Stopyra
Tigana
Rocheteau

USSR 2   **Canada 0**
Blokhin
Zavarov

	P	W	D	L	F	A	Pts
USSR	3	2	1	0	9	1	5
France	3	2	1	0	5	1	5
Hungary	3	1	0	2	2	9	2
Canada	3	0	0	3	0	5	0

GROUP D:

Brazil 1   **Spain 0**
Socrates

Northern Ireland 1   **Algeria 1**
Whiteside   Zidane

Spain 2   **Northern Ireland 1**
Butragueno   Clarke
Salinas

Brazil 1   **Algeria 0**
Careca

Spain 3   **Algeria 0**
Caldere 2
Olaya

Brazil 3   **Northern Ireland 0**
Careca 2
Josimar

	P	W	D	L	F	A	Pts
Brazil	3	3	0	0	5	0	6
Spain	3	2	0	1	5	2	4
N. Ireland	3	0	1	2	2	6	1
Algeria	3	0	1	2	1	5	1

GROUP E:

West Germany 1   **Uruguay 1**
Allofs   Alzamendi

Denmark 1   **Scotland 0**
Elkjaer

Denmark 6   **Uruguay 1**
Elkjaer 3   Francescoli
Lerby
M. Laudrup
J. Olsen

West Germany 2   **Scotland 1**
Voller   Strachan
Allofs

Scotland 0   **Uruguay 0**

Denmark 2   **West Germany 0**
J. Olsen
Eriksen

	P	W	D	L	F	A	Pts
Denmark	3	3	0	0	9	1	6
W. Germany	3	1	1	1	3	4	3
Uruguay	3	0	2	1	2	7	2
Scotland	3	0	1	2	1	3	1

GROUP F:

Morocco 0   **Poland 0**

Portugal 1   **England 0**
Carlos Manuel

England 0   **Morocco 0**

Poland 1   **Portugal 0**
Smolarek

England 3   **Poland 0**
Lineker 3

Morocco 3   **Portugal 1**
Khairi 2   Diamantino
K. Merry

	P	W	D	L	F	A	Pts
Morocco	3	1	2	0	3	1	4
England	3	1	1	1	3	1	3
Poland	3	1	1	1	1	3	3
Portugal	3	1	0	2	2	4	2

SECOND ROUND:

Mexico 2   **Bulgaria 0**
Negrete
Servin

Belgium 4   **USSR 3**
Scifo   Balanov 3 (1 pen)
Ceulemans
De Mol
Claesen
(after extra time; 2–2 at full time)

Brazil 4   **Poland 0**
Socrates (pen)
Josimar
Edinho
Careca (pen)

Argentina 1   **Uruguay 0**
Pasculli

France 2   **Italy 0**
Platini
Stopyra

West Germany 1   **Morocco 0**
Matthaus

England 3   **Paraguay 0**
Lineker 2
Beardsley

Denmark 1   **Spain 5**
J. Olsen (pen)   Butragueno 4 (1 pen)
            Goicoechea (pen)

QUARTER-FINALS:

France 1   **Brazil 1**
Platini   Careca
(after extra time; 1–1 at full time)
France won 4–3 on penalties

continued...

West Germany 0 Mexico 0
(after extra time)
West Germany won 4–1 on penalties

Argentina 2 **England 1**
Maradona 2 Lineker

Spain 1 **Belgium 1**
Senor Ceulemans
(after extra time; 1–1 at full time)
Belgium won 5–4 on penalties

SEMI-FINALS:

Argentina 2 **Belgium 0**
Maradona 2

West Germany 2 **France 0**
Brehme
Völler

THIRD-PLACE PLAY-OFF:

France 4 **Belgium 2**
Ferrari Ceulemans
Papin Claesen
Genghini
Amoros (pen)

FINAL:

Argentina 3 **West Germany 2**
Brown Rummenigge
Valdano Völler
Burruchaga

Argentina: Pumpido, Ruggeri, Brown, Cuciuffo, Giusti, Enrique, Batista, Burruchaga (Trobbiani), Olaricoechea, Valdono, Maradona

West Germany: Schumacher, Brehme, Jakobs, K.H. Forster, Berthold, Matthaus, Magath (Hoeness), Eder, Briegel, Rummenigge, Allofs (Völler)

Golden Boot: Gary Lineker (England)

ITALY
1990
ITALIA 90

A huge investment in stadium design and building by the Italian authorities provided a dramatic setting for this World Cup, a prolonged celebration of the style and depth of Italian football culture. Everything went pretty much to plan until the *azzurri* were street-hustled out of the semi-final by the most anti-romantic team in the tournament, Argentina.

Italy's progress before then had become a carnival once the virtually unknown Toto Schillaci had started the scoring spree which would bring him the Golden Boot trophy. But the Germans were ominously powerful in the group stage with Matthaus in midfield and Jürgen Klinsmann and Rudi Völler up front. Their encounter with Holland in the second round was a blood and thunder affair, which saw the Germans through to the quarter-final. Brazil were the main absentees, having been ambushed by Caniggia's breakaway goal for Argentina. England blossomed after a turgid Group F of few goals and even less quality football. Jack Charlton's Ireland team and the Cameroon also battled their way through to the last eight.

The four quarter-finals were tense affairs – Argentina squeezed out a talented Yugoslavia team on penalties in Florence, while Schillaci ended Ireland's run with a single goal. West Germany, for once, were laboured in beating the Czechs, while England needed two penalties to come from behind against the Cameroon in Naples.

Argentina, marshalled by an increasingly desperate Maradona, plunged a stiletto into Italy's heart by beating them on penalties in the semi-final, and it needed the same cruel process to send the Germans past the English. Italy and England provided a gracious third-place game. But the next night, Argentina framed the high culture of the Three Tenors with a dismal final, with two Argentinian players dismissed, was aptly won by the Germans with a dubious, but nonetheless welcome penalty, which spared the world extra time.

MATCH RESULTS:

GROUP A:

Italy 1 **Austria 0**
Schillaci

Czechoslovakia 5 **USA 1**
Skuhravy 2 Caligiuri
Bilek (pen)
Hasak
Luhovy

Italy 1 **USA 0**
Giannini

Czechoslovakia 1 **Austria 0**
Bilek (pen)

Italy 2 **Czechoslovakia 0**
Schillaci
Baggio

Austria 2 **USA 1**
Ogris Murray
Rodax

	P	W	D	L	F	A	Pts
Italy	3	3	0	0	4	0	6
Czech	3	2	0	1	6	3	4
Austria	3	1	0	2	2	3	2
USA	3	0	0	3	2	8	0

GROUP B:

Cameroon 1 **Argentina 0**
F. Biyick

Romania 2 **USSR 0**
Lacatus 2 (1 pen)

Argentina 2 **USSR 0**
Troglio
Burruchaga

Cameroon 2 **Romania 1**
Milla 2 Balint

Argentina 1 **Romania 1**
Monzon Balint

USSR 4　　　　　Cameroon 0
Protasov
Zygmantovich
Zavarov
Dobrovolsky

	P	W	D	L	F	A	Pts
Cameroon	3	2	0	1	3	5	4
Romania	3	1	1	1	4	3	3
Argentina	3	1	1	1	3	2	3
USSR	3	1	0	2	4	4	2

GROUP C:

Brazil 2　　　　**Sweden 1**
Careca 2　　　　　Brolin

Costa Rica 1　　**Scotland 0**
Cayasso

Brazil 1　　　　**Costa Rica 0**
Muller

Scotland 2　　　**Sweden 1**
McCall　　　　　　Stromberg
Johnston (pen)

Brazil 1　　　　**Scotland 0**
Muller

Costa Rica 2　　**Sweden 1**
Flores　　　　　　Ekstrom
Medford

	P	W	D	L	F	A	Pts
Brazil	3	3	0	0	4	1	6
Costa Rica	3	2	0	1	3	2	4
Scotland	3	1	0	2	2	3	2
Sweden	3	0	0	3	3	6	0

GROUP D:

Colombia 2　　　**United Arab**
　　　　　　　　　　Emirates 0
Redin
Valderrama

West Germany 4　**Yugoslavia 1**
Matthaus 2　　　　Jozic
Klinsmann
Völler

Yugoslavia 1　　**Colombia 0**
Jozic

West Germany 5　**UAE 1**
Völler 2　　　　　Mubarek
Klinsmann
Matthaus
Bein

West Germany 1　**Colombia 1**
Littbarski　　　　Rincon

Yugoslavia 4　　**UAE 1**
Susic　　　　　　Jumaa
Pancev 2
Prosinecki

	P	W	D	L	F	A	Pts
W. Germany	3	2	1	0	10	3	5
Yugoslavia	3	2	0	1	6	5	4
Colombia	3	1	1	1	3	2	3
UAE	3	0	0	3	2	11	0

GROUP E:

Belgium 2　　　**South Korea 0**
Degryse
De Wolf

Uruguay 0　　　**Spain 0**

Belgium 3　　　**Uruguay 1**
Clijsters　　　　Bengoechea
Scifo
Ceulemans

Spain 3　　　　**South Korea 1**
Gonzalez 3　　　Kwan

Spain 2　　　　**Belgium 1**
Michel (pen)　　Vervoort
Gorriz

Uruguay 1　　　**South Korea 0**
Fonseca

	P	W	D	L	F	A	Pts
Spain	3	2	1	0	5	2	5
Belgium	3	2	0	1	6	3	4
Uruguay	3	1	1	1	2	3	3
South Korea	3	0	0	3	1	6	0

GROUP F:

England 1　　　**Ireland 1**
Lineker　　　　　Sheedy

Holland 1　　　**Egypt 1**
Kieft　　　　　　Abdel-Ghani (pen)

England 0　　　**Holland 0**

Egypt 0　　　　**Ireland 0**

England 1　　　**Egypt 0**
M. Wright

Holland 1　　　**Ireland 1**
Gullit　　　　　Quinn

	P	W	D	L	F	A	Pts
England	3	1	2	0	2	1	4
Ireland	3	0	3	0	2	2	3
Holland	3	0	3	0	2	2	3
Egypt	3	0	2	1	1	2	2

SECOND ROUND:

Cameroon 2　　**Colombia 1**
Milla 2　　　　　Redin

Czechoslovakia 4　**Costa Rica 1**
Skuhravy 3　　　Gonzalez
Kubik

Argentina 1　　**Brazil 0**
Caniggia

West Germany 2　**Holland 1**
Klinsmann　　　Koeman (pen)
Brehme

Ireland 0　　　**Romania 0**
(after extra time)
Ireland won 5–4 on penalties

Italy 2　　　　**Uruguay 0**
Schillaci
Serena

Yugoslavia 2　　**Spain 1**
Stojkovic 2　　　Salinas
(after extra time; 1–1 at full time)

England 1　　　**Belgium 0**
Platt
(after extra time; 0–0 at full time)

QUARTER-FINALS:

Argentina 0　　**Yugoslavia 0**
(after extra time)
Argentina won 3–2 on penalties

Italy 1　　　　**Ireland 0**
Schillaci

West Germany 1　**Czechoslovakia 0**
Matthaus (pen)

England 3　　　**Cameroon 2**
Platt　　　　　　Kunde (pen)
Lineker 2 (2 pens)　Ekeke
(after extra time; 2–2 at full time)

SEMI-FINALS:

Italy 1　　　　**Argentina 1**
Schillaci　　　　Caniggia
(after extra time; 1–1 at full time)
Argentina won 4–3 on penalties

West Germany 1　**England 1**
Brehme　　　　　Lineker
(after extra time; 1–1 at full time)
West Germany won 4–3 on penalties

THIRD-PLACE PLAY-OFF:

Italy 2　　　　**England 1**
Baggio　　　　　Platt
Schillaci (pen)

FINAL:

West Germany 1　**Argentina 0**
Brehme (pen)

West Germany: Illgner, Berthold
(Reuter), Kohler, Augenthaler,
Buchwald, Brehme, Littbarski,
Matthaus, Hassler, Völler, Klinsmann

Argentina: Goycoechea, Ruggeri
(Monzon), Simon, Serrizuela, Lorenzo,
Basualdo, Troglio, Burruchaga
(Calderon), Sensini, Dezotti, Maradona

Golden Boot: Salvatore Schillaci
(Italy)

1994

It was inevitable that commercial interests would one day lead to the staging of the World Cup in America, but it was still a gamble of huge proportions for FIFA to award host status to a country where the first attempts at establishing a football league in the 1970s had petered out, and which still had no formal club structure. There was, at least, a decent network of stadia, even if some of them, such as the plastic-roofed and plastic-pitched Silverdome, needed real turf to be laid. Also, the ethnic groupings which dominated certain areas of America allowed the organizers to place some national teams in areas where they might attract local support, and attendances were better than expected.

The upgrading of wins in the first-round group matches to three points from two, was clearly another move to interest the domestic audience in America, which doesn't really accept the concept of the draw, or tie. Only eight of the thirty-six matches ended level, so it must have worked, although it wasn't any easier sorting out the qualifiers, apart from Brazil, Germany and Romania, who finished clear in their groups. There was a four-way tie in Group E, with all teams on four points and the same goal-difference – Norway got the boot for fewer goals.

In Group D, Nigeria and Bulgaria proved the surprise teams, after Argentina had been left reeling by Maradona's positive dope test. The hosts scraped into the second phase, courtesy of a 2–1 win over Colombia, a match that was to have fatal implications for Andres Escobar, scorer of an own goal, who was shot dead on his return to Colombia.

The most dramatic second-round matches were Italy's comeback to win in extra time against Nigeria and Romania's victory over Argentina. The last eight were made up by Germany, Holland, Brazil, Sweden, Spain and Bulgaria – Europe 7, South America 1. But when the one is Brazil...their 3–2 defeat of Holland was probably the best of the quarter-finals, although Bulgaria's win over holders Germany was the biggest shock. Italy needed goals from both Baggios to get past a stylish Spain, while Sweden had to go to the very limit of the penalty shoot-out – 5–4 – to beat Romania. Thereafter, both semi-finals and the final itself were on the dull side, and the heat and exhaustion inevitably delivered the first penalty shoot-out in a World Cup final, after Brazil and Italy had somehow managed not to score. Baresi, Massaro and Roberto Baggio were Italy's duds, the latter having done most to get Italy to the final. Only Brazil's achievement of winning the World Cup for the fourth time made the day in any way historic. But the blatant anti-climax did at least move official thinking in favour of the golden goal – the first score in extra time – as a means of preventing the shoot-out becoming a regular finale.

Now thirty-two teams will compete in France – the World Cup just keeps on growing!

MATCH RESULTS:

GROUP A:

Switzerland 1   **USA 1**
Bregy   Wynalda

Romania 3   **Colombia 1**
Raducioiu 2   Valencia
Hagi

USA 2   **Colombia 1**
Escobar (og)   Valencia
Stewart

Switzerland 4   **Romania 1**
Sutter   Hagi
Chapuisat
Knup
Bregy

Romania 1   **USA 0**
Petrescu

Colombia 2   **Switzerland 0**
Gaviria
Lozano

	P	W	D	L	F	A	Pts
Romania	3	2	0	1	5	5	6
Switzerland	3	1	1	1	5	4	4
USA	3	1	1	1	3	3	4
Colombia	3	1	0	2	4	5	3

GROUP B:

Cameroon 2   **Sweden 2**
Embe   Ljung
Omam-Biyik   Dahlin

Brazil 2   **Russia 0**
Romario
Rai (pen)

Brazil 3   **Cameroon 0**
Romario
Marcio Santos
Bebeto

Sweden 3   **Russia 1**
Brolin (pen)   Salenko (pen)
Dahlin 2

Russia 6   **Cameroon 1**
Salenko 5 (1 pen)   Milla
Radchenko

Brazil 1   **Sweden 1**
Romario   K. Andersson

	P	W	D	L	F	A	Pts
Brazil	3	2	1	0	6	1	7
Sweden	3	1	2	0	6	4	5
Russia	3	1	0	2	7	6	3
Cameroon	3	0	1	2	3	11	1

GROUP C:

Germany 1   **Bolivia 0**
Klinsmann

Spain 2   **South Korea 2**
Salinas   Hong Myung-Bo
Goicoechea   Seo Jung-Won

Germany 1   **Spain 1**
Klinsmann   Goicoechea

South Korea 0   **Bolivia 0**

Bolivia 1   **Spain 3**
Sanchez   Guardiola (pen)
      Caminero 2

Germany 3   **South Korea 2**
Klinsmann 2   Hwang Sun-Hong
Riedle   Hong Myung-Bo

	P	W	D	L	F	A	Pts
Germany	3	2	1	0	5	3	7
Spain	3	1	2	0	6	4	5
South Korea	3	0	2	1	4	5	2
Bolivia	3	0	1	2	1	4	1

GROUP D:

Argentina 4   **Greece 0**
Batistuta 3
Maradona

Nigeria 3   **Bulgaria 0**
Yekini
Amokachi
Amunike

Argentina 2   **Nigeria 1**
Caniggia 2   Siasia

Bulgaria 4   **Greece 0**
Stoichkov 2
(2 pens)
Lechkov
Sirakov

Nigeria 2   **Greece 0**
George
Amokachi

Bulgaria 2   **Argentina 0**
Stoichkov
Sirakov

	P	W	D	L	F	A	Pts
Nigeria	3	2	0	1	6	2	6
Bulgaria	3	2	0	1	6	3	6
Argentina	3	2	0	1	6	3	6
Greece	3	0	0	3	0	10	0

GROUP E:

Ireland 1   **Italy 0**
Houghton

Norway 1   **Mexico 0**
Rekdal

Italy 1   **Norway 0**
D. Baggio

Mexico 2   **Ireland 1**
Luis Garcia 2   Aldridge

Ireland 0   **Norway 0**

Italy 1   **Mexico 1**
Massaro   Bernal

	P	W	D	L	F	A	Pts
Mexico	3	1	1	1	3	3	4
Ireland	3	1	1	1	2	2	4
Italy	3	1	1	1	2	2	4
Norway	3	1	1	1	1	1	4

GROUP F:

Belgium 1   **Morocco 0**
Degryse

Holland 2   **Saudi Arabia 1**
Jonk   Amin
Taument

Belgium 1   **Holland 0**
Albert

Saudi Arabia 2   **Morocco 1**
Al Jaber (pen)   Chaouchi
Amin

Holland 2   **Morocco 1**
Bergkamp   Nader
Roy

Saudi Arabia 1   **Belgium 0**
Owairan

	P	W	D	L	F	A	Pts
Holland	3	2	0	1	4	3	6
Saudi Arabia	3	2	0	1	4	3	6
Belgium	3	2	0	1	2	1	6
Morocco	3	0	0	3	2	5	0

SECOND ROUND:

Germany 3   **Belgium 2**
Völler 2   Grun
Klinsmann   Albert

Spain 3   **Switzerland 0**
Hierro
Luis Enrique
Beguiristain

Sweden 3   **Saudi Arabia 1**
Dahlin   Al Ghesheyan
K. Andersson

Romania 3   **Argentina 2**
Dumitrescu 2   Batistuta (pen)
Hagi   Balbo

Holland 2   **Ireland 0**
Bergkamp
Jonk

Brazil 1   **USA 0**
Bebeto

Italy 2   **Nigeria 1**
R. Baggio 2 (1 pen)   Amunike
(after extra time; 1–1 at full time)

Bulgaria 1   **Mexico 1**
Stoichkov   Garcia Aspe (pen)
(after extra time; 1–1 at full time)
Bulgaria won 3–1 on penalties

QUARTER-FINALS:

Italy 2   **Spain 1**
D. Baggio   Caminero
R. Baggio

Brazil 3   **Holland 2**
Romario   Bergkamp
Bebeto   Winter
Branco

Bulgaria 2   **Germany 1**
Stoichkov   Matthaus (pen)
Lechkov

Sweden 2   **Romania 2**
Brolin   Raducioiu 2
K. Andersson
(after extra time, 1–1 at full time)
Sweden won 5–4 on penalties

SEMI-FINALS:

Brazil 1   **Sweden 0**
Romario

Italy 2   **Bulgaria 1**
R. Baggio 2   Stoichkov (pen)

THIRD-PLACE PLAY-OFF:

Sweden 4   **Bulgaria 0**
Brolin
Mild
Larsson
K. Andersson

FINAL:

Brazil 0   **Italy 0**
(after extra time)
Brazil won 3–2 on penalties

Brazil: Taffarel, Jorginho (Cafu), Aldair, Marcio Santos, Branco, Mazzinho (Viola), Dunga, Mauro Silva, Zinho, Romario, Bebeto

Italy: Pagliuca, Mussi (Apolloni), Maldini, Baresi, Benarrivo, Berti, Albertini, D. Baggio (Evani), Donadoni, R. Baggio, Massaro

Golden Boot: Hristo Stoichkov (Bulgaria), Oleg Salenko (Russia)

INDEX

Entries in **bold** refer to photographs.

GARY LINEKER'S GOLDEN BOOTS

Photograph acknowledgements

AllSport: 9(br), 11, 32, 63(bl, br), 102(mr), 103, 140.
AllSport Historical Collection: 63(bl, br), 112
AllSport/Hulton Deutsch: 96(t), 97(b).
AllSport/MSI: 99(mr).
Central Press Photos Ltd/AllSport: 86(b).
Colorsport: 13(mr), 15, 20, 28, 31, 34(m), 35(tr), 36, 39, 40, 41, 42, 65(tr), 78(ml), 79(tl), 81(t), 101(tl), 105 (tr), 106, 109(t), 135, 136(t), 153.
Colorsport/Olympia: 77(b), 78(br), 105(tl), 136(b).
Empics: 144, 145(t).
Hulton Deutsch: 24(t), 109(m, b).
Hulton Deutsch/Keystone: 19, 26.
Hulton Getty: 71(m), 94, 123.
Nemzeti Sport Archives: 121(m).
Popperfoto: 4, 6(t), 8(b), 9(t), 17(bl), 24(ml), 58(t), 59, 61, 68, 72, 73, 74(ml), 76, 86(ml), 88(tr, b), 89, 90, 95, 99(t), 102(t, ml, b), 116, 118, 155(t), 158.
Press Association/Topham: 93, 96(ml), 161, 163.
Presse Sport: 149(t), 151(m).
Sporting Pictures (UK) Ltd: 34(tl), 35(mr), 64, 82, 98.
Topham Picturepoint: 60, 62, 85, 97(t), 130(m), 133(m, b), 150, 151(t), 157(t), 162.
Ullstein: 69(tr).
The Worldmark Production Company: iii, iv, 2, 3(tl), 3(br), 7(m), 10, 13(t), 17 (mr), 18, 21, 23(b), 30, 37, 38(bl), 43, 44, 45, 46, 47, 49(tr), 52, 53, 54, 55, 57, 58(bl), 63(tr), 65(mr), 66, 67, 70, 74(t), 77(mr), 79(mr), 80, 81(mr), 83, 87, 88(tl), 91, 92 100, 101(tr), 110, 111, 113, 114, 119, 120, 121(b), 122, 126, 127, 128, 129, 130(t), 132, 133(t), 134, 137, 138, 139, 141, 142, 145(b), 146, 147, 148, 149(m), 152, 154, 155(m), 157(m), 159, 160.
Fédération Internationale des Football Associations: 164, 165, 166, 167, 168, 169, 170, 172, 173, 175, 176, 178, 180, 182, 184.
Other sources: 3(tr), 6(bl), 7(tr), 8(t), 23(t), 38(ml), 49(tl), 50, 51, 69(b), 71(tr), 71(b), 108, 125.